Airways Abroad

SMITHSONIAN HISTORY OF AVIATION SERIES

On December 17, 1903, on a windy beach in North Carolina, aviation became a reality. The development of aviation over the course of little more than three-quarters of a century stands as an awe-inspiring accomplishment in both a civilian and a military context. The airplane has brought whole continents closer together; at the same time it has been a lethal instrument of war.

This series of books is intended to contribute to the overall understanding of the history of aviation—its science and technology as well as the social, cultural, and political environment in which it developed and matured. Some publications help fill the many gaps that still exist in the literature of flight; others add new information and interpretation to current knowledge. While the series appeals to a broad audience of general readers and specialists in the field, its hallmark is strong scholarly content.

The series is international in scope and includes works in three major categories:

SMITHSONIAN STUDIES IN AVIATION HISTORY: *works that provide new and original knowledge.*

CLASSICS OF AVIATION HISTORY: *carefully selected out-of-print works that are considered essential scholarship.*

CONTRIBUTIONS TO AVIATION HISTORY: *previously unpublished documents, reports, symposia, and other materials.*

Airways Abroad

The Story of

American

World

Air Routes

Henry Ladd Smith

Smithsonian Institution Press
Washington, D.C.

Reprinted 1991 in the Smithsonian History of
Aviation Series, Classics of Aviation History,
with new Editor's Introduction,
© 1991 by Smithsonian Institution

Printed in the United States of America
96   95   94   93   92   91
5   4   3   2   1

∞ The paper used in this publication meets the
requirements of the American National Standard
for Permanence of Paper for Printed Library
Materials Z39.48-1984.

This book is part of the Smithsonian History of
Aviation Series. Published in the United States by
the Smithsonian Institution Press, this series of
books is distributed in the United Kingdom,
Europe, the Middle East, and
Africa by Airlife Publishing Ltd.

Library of Congress Cataloging-in-Publication Data

Smith, Henry Ladd, 1906-
    Airways abroad : the story of American world
air routes / Henry Ladd Smith.
        p.   cm. — (Smithsonian history of aviation
series. Classics of aviation history)
    Reprint, with new pref. Originally published:
Madison: University of Wisconsin Press, 1950.
    Includes bibliographical references and index.
    ISBN 1-56098-053-2
    1. Aeronautics, Commercial—United States—
History.   I. Title.   II. Series.
TL521.S52   1991
387.7'2'0973—dc20   90-21379

TABLE OF CONTENTS

EDITOR'S INTRODUCTION

EVERY DAY, travelers step aboard commercial jetliners bound for destinations everywhere on the globe. With seemingly little preparation—purchasing a ticket, packing a suitcase, taking a taxi to the airport—a person can travel just about anywhere anytime. The ordinary traveler, overtaken by thoughts of meeting schedules, making connections, and getting luggage at the other end of the trip, takes little note of the welter of arrangements that allow airplanes to fly over international airspace. To the air line passenger, how this happens is somehow "magical," just like plugging in a television set and having a picture appear.

Aside from the elaborate infrastructure of people and services that permit air line passengers to travel freely, much of what determines who can fly where and when is controlled by the ICAO, the International Civil Aviation Organization, based in Montreal. Although ICAO is an important international body with ties to the United Nations, little is known about it. The chronicle of how ICAO came into being and of the delicate negotiations that preceded its advent is contained in Henry Ladd Smith's *Airways Abroad: The Story of American World Air Routes,* a book published forty years ago, and herewith reprinted in the Smithsonian History of Aviation Series.

Smith takes the readers from the prewar period in which there was only one American carrier flying internationally, Pan American Airways, through World War II, when much of the deliberation over international air routes took place, to the postwar period.

This interval, Smith says, "ended a decade of aviation progress such as the world had never seen before, nor would likely see again." The results were truly miraculous. The agreements hammered out through these ten or so years form the basis for international air travel as we know it today.

Airways Abroad focuses on the competition between the United States and Great Britain in establishing international routes in the postwar period. Both countries foresaw that commercial aviation would be an important tool of international statesmanship and economic power and both acted quickly to be in the forefront of the emerging enterprise.

In this regard, *Airways Abroad* serves as the perfect companion to Smith's previous and equally important book *Airways: The History of Commercial Aviation in the United States*, published in 1942 and now reprinted in the Smithsonian History of Aviation Series. *Airways* describes the evolution of air transportation in the United States from the early days of the air mail, aviation's first truly commercial venture, to the dawn of World War II. If *Airways* is the story of the era of air line pioneering, then *Airways Abroad* is, in Smith's own words, the "history of an important transport system, a system that has progressed rapidly through the phases of rugged individualism and government support to international cooperation."

In an exciting and rigorous way, *Airways Abroad* elucidates the events and players in the game, little known except to historians and a few knowledgeable laymen. The International Civil Aviation Conference, held in Chicago in November 1944, for example, was a milestone on the road to consensus on global air routes and the first attempt to iron out the differences that existed between the United States and Great Britain on international air policy.

Although it was a contentious meeting, this conference owes much to Adolf A. Berle, a brilliant New Deal lawyer, handpicked by Franklin Delano Roosevelt to be the United States representative in the negotiations. Better known as a member of FDR's academic Brain Trust, Berle, Smith says, "did much of the diplomatic spade work needed to begin the cultivation of our civil aviation policy" and "produced more results in the short time he was in control of aviation than anyone in office before or since."

Another milestone was the Bermuda Conference held in the opening months of 1946. This meeting ended a quarrelsome period of negotiation between the British and the Americans, for now, Smith writes, the "two great air powers had made an amicable adjustment of their differences." Smith calls the Bermuda Agreement "one of the most important aviation documents in the history of international air transportation."

Finally, Smith analyzes the creation of the Provisional International Civil Aviation Organization (PICAO), its successor the International Civil Aviation Organization (ICAO), which became the permanent world body responsible for regulating international air commerce, and the International Air Transport Association (IATA), an organization designed to set rates and the frequency of flights. Both the ICAO and the IATA exist today, nearly a half century after their creation.

In addition to providing an exhilarating account of important events, *Airways Abroad* is thoroughly researched and well documented. Each chapter includes footnotes, endnotes, references, and a highly readable essay on sources (personal interviews, State Department and Civil Aviation Board documents, congressional hearings, British Air Ministry publications, proceedings of the House of Lords and the House of Commons, diaries, and periodical articles). There is also an excellent index and a useful chronology of the major events in the history of international air commerce. The scholar who comes to this wealth of information for the first time will find it an invaluable reference.

All in all, *Airways Abroad* is a delight, a story full of insight and drama that will excite professional historians and laymen alike.

Dominick A. Pisano
Series Editor

AUTHOR'S PREFACE TO
ORIGINAL EDITION

T HIS is the story of how one great
American enterprise developed from humble beginnings into
a business of international significance. It is the history of an
important transport system, a system that progressed rapidly
through the phases of rugged individualism and government
support to international cooperation. Because international air
commerce was one of the first postwar problems to be solved,
it is of particular significance, not only to transportation, but
to those who need encouragement in solving problems of
world peace.

Like the Bretton Woods and Dumbarton Oaks conferences,
the aviation agreements near the end of the war were prelim-
inaries to the plan for future world order. Unlike the food and
monetary conferences, the aviation meetings were expected to
produce not merely a statement of principles, but an actual
working agreement for immediate use. Civil aviation thus became the first postwar experiment in world cooperation to be
carried through to a conclusion. It was more than that. It presented in capsule form most of the issues that had to be settled
around the peace table. It gave us a case history of how nations
of the world could learn to work together with a considerable
degree of harmony.

It is encouraging for the future of world air commerce that
the Western nations were able to develop international air
routes even before the war had ended. It is encouraging because for previous decades most nations had erected invisible

walls along their borders to keep out alien merchant airmen. It was not easy to level these barriers. Each government had to give up cherished privileges. Statesmen had to develop philosophies of world-mindedness utterly at variance with prewar concepts. All had to submerge jealousies for the common good. Air transportation was thus a kind of catalyst for the many issues that had to be faced when the war was won. Solution of the aviation problems did not prove that success at the peace table was to be assured. But failure to have found peace in the air at this time would have indicated that the nations could never achieve peace on earth.

Two great powers led the scramble for the air routes that many coveted as the greatest prize of the war. These two powers were Great Britain and the United States. Both had to adjust to each other as rivals in the postwar world — even as they had had to adjust to each other as allies in the struggle to survive during the war. Spokesmen of each nation had peculiar ideas of the proper methods for developing world air routes. These ideas were based upon fundamentally different economic factors — factors that often appeared to deny any chance of agreement between the two nations. Both nations sought to lure other nations into their respective camps. Sometimes this trade rivalry threatened to burst into open hostility. Neither nation could risk that at a time when the Western bloc was in danger of being split. It was imperative that the United States and Great Britain work out their differences in the air. How they did it is described in these pages.

But before the United States and Great Britain could settle their differences they had first to decide what was expected of international air transportation. In both countries there were powerful groups, some selfish and some sincere, seeking to impose various aviation philosophies on diplomats. . . . Therefore, to understand the difficulty in working out the international problem, it is necessary to review the aviation backgrounds of the rivals. National and international aspirations in the air were determined to a large degree by past experiences.

It is difficult to write a story of this type. Many of the events chronicled are so recent that one cannot see them in proper perspective. Even today there is wide divergence of opinion regarding our aviation policy. Many respectable authorities will not agree with the conclusions reached in this book. It is the purpose of the author to present all the arguments so as to give all critics a fair hearing. Even this is sometimes beyond the limitations of the most objective writer. Some of the most significant decisions were made behind closed doors. Reports of those meetings may very well reflect the prejudices of the informer. All that an author can do is to set down the facts as he knows them. If some of the details are missing, at least the broad outline is presented as clearly and as honestly as human nature permits.

Research for this book was made possible by a fellowship of the John Simon Guggenheim Memorial Foundation. This opportunity is taken to express gratitude to those who read over all or parts of the first draft, including: Adolf A. Berle, Jr., former assistant secretary of state and leader of the United States delegation at the International Civil Aviation Conference at Chicago in 1944; Stokeley Morgan, president of Air Carrier Supply Corporation, formerly in charge of aviation matters for the Department of State, an important figure at the Chicago and Bermuda conferences and an erstwhile executive of Pan American Airways; Lloyd Welch Pogue, Washington attorney and former chairman of the Civil Aeronautics Board during the most critical days of international negotiation; John Parker Van Zandt, of American Aviation publications, formerly of the Brookings Institution, an observer of the Chicago Conference and long a student of aviation problems; E. Balluder, a vice-president of Pan American World Airways; David L. Behncke and John M. Dickerman of the Air Line Pilots Association; and Oliver James Lissitzyn, author of "International Air Transport and National Policy." Readers should not infer that all the above approved of the manscript. Indeed, Messrs. Balluder and Lissitzyn were severe judges of the entire thesis. Nevertheless, all the readers rendered valuable advice for the innumerable revisions of the text.

Edward E. Slattery, Jr., chief of Public Information, CAB, made research and interviews profitable and pleasant during the summer of 1946. Arthur G. Renstrom, Aeronautics Section, Library of Congress Annex, showed a continuing and friendly interest in the progress of the manuscript and was always ready to track down eluusive material. Miss Agnes Gautreaux, assistant librarian, Civil Aeronautics Administration, supplied bibliographical data and frequent advice. Miss Ruth Davis and Mrs. Litta B. Bascom, Document Section, University Library at Madison, Wisconsin, put up with endless annoyance in checking references.

To many others, whose names are not listed, the writer hereby expresses gratitude for help received.

H. L. S.

Airways Abroad

FROM FLIGHTS TO FLEETS

ON JULY 8, 1939, the Pan American Airways flying boat, *Yankee Clipper*, Captain Arthur E. La-Porte commanding, lifted from the swept channel at Port Washington, Long Island, and set course on the first leg of a Great Circle arc for Southampton, England. On board were 17 passengers, a crew of 12, and 615 pounds of mail — a small load for this largest of commercial air carriers, but indicative of the traffic that soon was to flow over the trans-Atlantic airways. Turned by the most powerful engines ever installed on a merchant aircraft, the four propellers generated a mighty blast. But the turbulence of the slip stream was mild in comparison with the international disturbances involved in the flight.

For the inauguration of the complete trans-Atlantic air service presented new problems to our statesmen and to our air line pioneers. Until 1939 Pan American Airways had been our only international air line.* Originally a Caribbean and South American operation, Pan Am had later extended its empire across the Pacific. Pan American Airways was, in short, a model of private enterprise. Efficiently operated and wisely managed, it had overcome all opposition and had defeated all serious rivals. It was a credit to the American business ideal. The Atlantic air route could not, therefore, frighten Pan American

*The round-the-world division is known as Pan American World Airways, but the corporate name remained Pan American Airways. The names will be used where appropriate throughout the book.

Airways executives as an operational problem. But there were other hazards in developing this route that even Pan American genius could not overcome.

Pan American Airways had spread through Latin America because there was need of an air-transportation system. In the Pacific area the company had constructed an air track without any threat of restriction or rivalry. But these conditions did not apply on the Atlantic route. For the first time the U.S. international air line had to penetrate an area already well supplied with modern transportation systems, such as steamships, railroads, and busses. Other air lines offered opposition such as Pan American had never faced before. European operators were just as eager as the American airmen to develop world routes. They were not only jealous of foreign rivals who might try to secure even temporary advantages, but they were, for the most. part, closely associated with their governments, so that they were in a position to block the granting of European landing rights to the aggressive Americans. Their price for such concessions was equal consideration in the Western Hemisphere.

In Latin America, where such exchanges of privilege were seldom demanded, Pan American representatives had conducted private negotiations — between the company and the various governments — aided by a friendly U.S. State Department. These unilateral agreements were entirely out of order in the Atlantic area. The only authority that could grant landing concessions in this country was the U.S. government. Thus, Pan American was prevented from making its favorite type of agreement and could only operate over the Atlantic when the governments of the United States and Europe had granted concessions to each other.

After 1939 it was the diplomat, rather than the air-line promoter, who determined the pattern of U.S. air-route expansion. Before that date, only technical and economic factors had needed to be considered in exploiting new areas. After 1939 politics and national policy set the course. Thus this year marked the beginning of a new era in commercial aviation.

In discussing present-day aviation policies, however, it would be foolish to ignore what happened to U.S. international aviation before 1939. For, to this day, there are proponents of our earlier policy who maintain that the United States "got off the beam" when the U.S. Government reversed itself on the matter of competition and regulation of U.S. international air lines.

The history of these early years is largely the history of Pan American Airways. Pan Am had endured the trials of the pioneer and had succeeded in surviving countless rivals. This may explain why the company fought so stubbornly against government restriction in later years. Pan Am had fought hard for what it had won, and it was determined to hold on to what it had wrested.

The story of Pan American Airways has been told so often and so well that it would be superfluous to recount it in detail here. The following pages merely describe episodes in the company's history which have some bearing on the U.S. pattern of international air transportation.

Pan American Airways was the creature of Juan Terry Trippe, who was only twenty-eight when he organized the air line in 1927. By the time he was thirty, Trippe had become a legend. Like Colonel Charles A. Lindbergh, he combined a record of achievement with a charming diffidence that made him irresistible to those who write for public consumption. Volumes have been written about this colorful character. In all the mass of material it is sometimes difficult to distinguish fact from fiction. We know that he was born into a wealthy family; that he was educated at fashionable boys' schools and traveled through Hill and Yale; that he contracted the aviation fever while flying for the Navy in World War I; and that he developed an air-line system such as the world had never seen before. Those are the facts. But the evidence is not as reliable regarding his ability to see out of the back of his head or to appear simultaneously in three widely separated places. On the other hand, who could refute such assertions? Those who pointed to Trippe as a superman, appearing out of the air to perform miracles, spoke convincingly. Time and again he was given sole credit for the amazing victories of his invincible air line. Such credit was unfair both to Trippe and to his associates. A man's greatness can be measured by the caliber of his subordinates, and much of Pan American's success must be attributed to the brilliance of lesser known executives. Just as Napoleon had his Marshals Ney and Murat, so Trippe had his Priester, Cooper, Leuteritz, Bixby, Rihl, and a dozen other able lieutenants who have won triumphs in many company battles. The genius of Juan Trippe was in having such a staff around him, but the consensus appears to be that Pan American Airways would not have pushed to the top so rapidly had it not been for the dynamic generalship of its key promoter.

It was just after World War I that Juan Trippe tried to make a business of flying. Those were bleak days for commercial aviation. There were no lighted airways or radio ranges in 1920. There were few laws and regulations for stabilizing the industry. Business leaders looked on all aviation ventures with amusement and contempt. The result was that the potential air-transportation market was reduced to a virtual cipher.

During these aeronautical dark ages enthusiasm in commercial aviation was kept alive by a little band of adventurers known as "gypsy flyers" or "barnstormers." They flitted about the country in patched up Jennies, Canucks, and Standards selling rides to thrill seekers. Operating out of cow pastures, with ancient equipment held together with baling wire, these aeronautical hoboes were a threat to a gullible public, but they did keep alive an interest in the future of aviation. Some of these poor dreamers had plans more ambitious than the mere "hopping" done by curious yokels. Some made pathetic attempts to establish a secure business at an established air field. "Fixed-base operators," they were called. Occasionally such a promoter would dignify his operation with the title of air line, although actually he was merely offering taxi services to nearby points.

One of these young wishful thinkers was Juan Trippe. Against the sound advice of his parents he bought half a dozen surplus Navy planes. With these he started Long Island Airways in 1923. Despite its impressive title, LIA was primarily a charter service for wealthy commuters. Trippe was president, sales manager, and often grease monkey for his flimsy company. He acquired a wealth of experience in this venture but very little cash. Customers were nervous and scarce, traffic was seasonal, and costs were high. In 1925 Long Island Airways and the Navy planes disintegrated together.

The school of experience had taught Trippe, as it had countless other promoters, that there was no profit in transporting passengers by plane. The belief remained, just the same, that the airplane was here to stay, and Trippe, again like many others, decided to try once more. This time, however, Uncle Sam, rather than the public, was to be the customer.

Under the Kelly Bill, which became the Air Mail Act of 1925, the Post Office Department turned over the transportation of air mail to private operators. Mail payments were to serve as a subsidy until air lines had safely passed the pioneering stage. As a result of this law, commercial aviation received the kind of nourishment it needed. Indeed, many of the early air-mail contractors actually made a profitable business out of their contracts with the Government. And when businessmen discovered the possibilities of the new enterprise and found that there was blood in the beast, they began to hunt in packs for likely-looking air lines.

Trippe rounded up some of his wealthy friends, some of whom he had known as members of the Yale Flying Club. He persuaded them to invest in a Boston syndicate that was ready to bid on the New York-to-Boston air-mail route. They were successful bidders and the new air line was a creditable operation, according to the standards of that day. Trippe and his cronies found the older members of the syndicate to be a little stuffy, however, and the Yale contingent decided to cultivate its own patch in the field of aviation.

By 1927 domestic air lines were twining all over the United States, thanks to the Kelly Bill. No one appeared to have much interest in overseas and foreign routes, however. Operations of this type were believed to be too costly. And as yet the Government had made no provisions for subsidy, as it had in the domestic field. It was possible to obtain some mail payments, but the return apparently did not justify the risks. Trippe, ever one to leave the door ajar when opportunity was knocking, saw that the time was ripe to start an international service before others beat him to it. Under the pending Foreign Air Mail Act, national, or "flag line" air lines to other countries were promised benefits even more attractive than those supplied under the domestic air-mail law. And just to make it easier on promoters seeking financial backing, the "great awakening" in commercial aviation occurred in 1927.

The sound that caused the great awakening was the acclaim given to a modest young airman named Charles A. Lindbergh. Lindbergh's famous solo flight from New York to Paris has been vastly overrated as a contribution to aviation. The flight proved nothing about aircraft. Ocean flights had been predicted and planned for years. The ocean itself had first been flown years before by the U.S. Navy's NC-4 flying boat, and thirty-odd persons had since been transported by air across the Atlantic. But Lindbergh's flight provided the stimulus that was needed just at the time to lure businessmen and brash young promoters into the aviation game. Coupled with the passage of the air-mail acts and the findings of the President's aircraft committee recommending revival of aircraft manufacture, the flight of the *Spirit of St. Louis* started off a boom in civil aviation. Suddenly there was a scramble for aviation stocks. For a brief period capital was more than sufficient to start promising aviation companies. At this opportune moment Trippe and his partners started their air line.

What they wanted was the Key West–Havana route. Even in the reckless days of the Lindbergh era the operation of this overseas route was looked upon as a daring venture. A hardy promoter, Inglis M. Uppercu, one of the great figures in early aviation, had developed this airway in the early twenties. His Aeromarine West Indies Airways established a fine record of reliability. It had carried more passengers than any other air operation in the United States. With enough mail pay from the U.S. Government, Uppercu might have survived. The seasonal slack in traffic and inefficient equipment (converted Navy patrol flying boats — safe, but expensive to operate) were handicaps Uppercu could not overcome. The amazing thing is that he did as well as the records show. At any rate, a fatal crash (the only one in four years of operation) and mounting deficits brought an end to this first serious attempt at international air transportation. The Aeromarine failure was one reason for the slowness of other promoters in taking over the Havana route. They reasoned that if the efficient Mr. Uppercu could not make a go of the operation, no one could.

Mr. Trippe and his colleagues were not to be discouraged by this example. They believed that the admirable Mr. Uppercu had never understood the function of air transportation and that he certainly did not see the possibilities in that particular route. There was no justification for an air route for either mail or passengers between Key West and Havana. Key West was almost inaccessible for outgoing traffic. It was easier for passengers and mail to be loaded at Miami, from which fast steamers provided good service across the ninety miles of straits. Even in the busy season an air route could not lure sufficient traffic to make the investment pay, but to make matters worse there were long seasons of traffic stagnation that brought efficient utilization of equipment down to the zero mark.

Trippe and his friends were looking far beyond Havana, and the picture they painted was quite different. In the year 1927 the pot of gold sought by Mr. Trippe and his associates was, as it is today, far beyond the most distant terminus of the air line. Trippe's reach has always exceeded his grasp. He had only a casual interest in the Key West–Havana route. South America was his pot of gold. Trippe had the vision to see that Havana was one of two gateways to that continent. The other gate was Cristobal, in the Canal Zone, and he wanted that, too. With exclusive flying rights in and out of these two points, the air to the south was his, as the record will show.

And why did he choose South America as the happy hunting ground for the smart air-line operator? Because South America — indeed, all Latin America — was made to order for air transportation. Land routes connecting the regions were poorly developed, partly because of the terrain and partly because of insufficient capitalization. There is always need of transportation pioneers in an undeveloped area. In some parts of South America the airplane alone could meet this need. There were points in Latin America where the plane was not only the safest, but the most efficient means of transportation. Sometimes it was the *only* means of penetrating an area. Latin-American governments were therefore willing to grant favorable franchises to daring promoters who wished to start up air lines in that region.

Trippe was an American pioneer in Latin-American aviation, but he was not the first to develop air transportation on the southern continent. French and German air lines were well established by the time the U.S. flag began to be seen beyond the Caribbean. One of the most interesting of these early promoters was Doktor Peter Paul von Bauer, a World War I Austrian warbird. In 1919 Dr. von Bauer organized some of his old war buddies into a company called Sociedad Colombo–Alemana de Transportes Aéreos, better known as SCADTA. Incorporated under the laws of Colombia, SCADTA was one of the world's first scheduled air lines.

Dr. von Bauer had visions of a great air transportation system linking the two western continents. In 1925 and again in 1926 he came to the United States to ask for landing rights. The U.S. Government, on the advice of military and naval authorities, refused. This was embarrassing, because the Government saw the need of such a system, yet it had no American countersuggestion for Dr. von Bauer's plan. The main objection appeared to be the potential danger of allowing a foreign air line to operate so close to the Panama Canal.

The U.S. Government was therefore eager to help any qualified American promoter who had his eyes on Latin America. In 1927 there were three candidates for this role. One was Florida Airways, organized by two war pilots, Captain Edward V. Rickenbacker and Major Reed Chambers.* Their financial

*Rickenbacker, a former automobile racer and wartime ace, later was

angel was Richard F. Hoyt of Hayden, Stone and Company, the investment house that sponsored so many early air-line ventures. Another applicant for the short route to Havana was a company known as Pan American, Incorporated. It had been organized by Captain J. K. Montgomery and Grant Mason. Captain Montgomery, a former war pilot, was looking for a chance to prove the possibilities of aircraft. Mason had seen the merit of Dr. von Bauer's program and had even gone so far as to win a mail contract from the Cuban Government for the company he now represented. Pan American, Incorporated, was backed by Richard and K. M. Bevier and by Lewis Pierson of the Irving Trust Company, New York.

The third contender for the route was called The Aviation Corporation of the Americas. It was organized by Trippe and his associates. At first the company was willing to listen to co-operation in the venture. Florida Airways, Pan American, and Aviation Corporation were to take equal shares in the new route and were to put up equal capital. Pan American could raise only 20 per cent of its share, but insisted that its Cuban mail contract was worth the difference, since apparently it could block any other bidder for Cuban mail pay. The company did not take into consideration the generalship of Trippe or the venality of the Machado government in Cuba. Trippe and his friend, John Hambleton, made a flying trip to Havana. When they returned they brought with them an exclusive concession for landing rights. This, of course, made Mason's mail contract of little value, and the Pan American group sold out, not without cries of anguish and threats of reprisal. Later Mr. Trippe was to tangle again with some of the more bitter members of the old Pan American company. The Aviation Corporation of the Americas renamed its acquired company Pan American Airways. It became the operating agency for Trippe and his group.

In the meantime, Florida Airways had also struck severe head winds. Its assets had included the first of the Stout all-metal

responsible for building Eastern Air Lines into one of the great U.S. transportation systems.

transports that later became standard equipment on many successful air lines. Florida Airways planes were the forerunners of the Ford-Stout tri-motors, still flying twenty years later in some parts of the world. The original Stouts were powered with a single Liberty engine, and they were so good that Florida Airways used them as a bargaining point in its negotiations with the Trippe group. In one way or another the company lost all its equipment. With little to bargain away, Florida Airways also sold out to the Aviation Corporation of the Americas. The negotiations were apparently amicable, however, for some of Florida's key men later appeared in the new air-line roster.

The myth has been fostered that Trippe was something of a wizard in the way he swallowed up competitors, expanded his routes, and negotiated for mail contracts. Admittedly, no one ever got back too much change from Mr. Trippe. Those who underestimated his shrewdness usually were singed. But the truth is, legerdemain had less to do with his success than his help from the U.S. Government. Mail payments spelled success for Pan American Airways in the early days, and it is worth while to analyze some of Trippe's methods in obtaining mail contracts.

In the first place, Trippe had the right kind of friends. They were wealthy, generous, and enthusiastic about flying. They were willing to back him with plenty of cash, and they did not demand an immediate return on their investments. With this kind of backing, Trippe was welcome in the important offices in Washington. The Postmaster General, was ready and willing to aid such a promoter. He wanted solid organizations to complete with foreign air lines on overseas routes. Not only was he willing to give a company like Pan American fat mail contracts; he was able to do even more. He could see that the new flag line was protected from rivals. With lucrative mail cargoes and a virtual monopoly of foreign routes, it is difficult to see how Pan American Airways could have been anything except a great enterprise. But how did Trippe win this favored spot?

The air-mail laws stipulated that contracts between the U.S.

Post Office and private operators were to be awarded only after competitive bidding. There were ways of avoiding such competition, however. Postmaster General Harry S. New was determined to make Pan American Airways our "chosen instrument" on the proposed foreign routes. There were then excellent arguments for the chosen instrument, or monopoly. The Postmaster General was more interested in building up a great international air system than he was in finding the cheapest way to transport air mail. The Post Office Department has always taken responsibility for helping to develop new transportation systems, and air-mail subsidy was one method of applying such aid.

Competition for air-mail contracts was all right for the domestic operators (although even in this sphere competition was subject to the postmaster's modifications). Government regulation could compensate for flaws in the domestic pattern. In the international sphere Government regulation might be ineffective beyond the U.S. border, although it still could be used as a big stick by a clever postmaster. Certainly competition beyond our borders would be dangerous, it was reasoned. The U.S. company would be grappling with foreign operators supported by their respective governments. The Americans would need every cent of post-office subsidy, if they were to wage a successful battle against such rivals. Scattering mail payments among a score of competitors, each the winner by a low bid, would spell only slow starvation for these operators and could result only in the eventual disintegration of the international air-transportation system, post-office officials held.

This philosophy is clearly brought out in the words of Walter Folger Brown, who succeeded Mr. New as postmaster in 1928. To an air-line operator who complained about Pan American Airways' favored position, Brown stated the post-office policy in unmistakable terms. He wrote:

. . . I have stated frankly to the air-mail operators that in the present state of the industry, it did not seem the part of wisdom to invade each others' territory with competitive services and that I did not believe the money paid for postal service should be used to set up services to injure competitors. In the pursuance of this policy I suggested the abandonment by Pan American Co., of the domestic field in the United

States, and as a result of that suggestion you are now negotiating with the Pan American Co., for the taking over of their Atlantic City service. . . . Consistently with the policy outlined, it would seem improper for any of our domestic air-mail operators to use mail pay to invade the peculiar field of the Pan American Co.[1]

It was with this encouragement from the Post Office Department that Pan American Airways won the Key West–Havana air-mail route in July, 1927. According to the contract, operations were to begin not later than October 19, 1927. Negotiations had dragged on slowly, however, and Pan American was not ready on that date. Captain J. E. Whitbeck, the company's Key West manager, was in a fine frenzy as the sun rose on the nineteenth. The mail had arrived by domestic carrier on schedule, but the poor manager had no planes available for the hop to Cuba. The new Fokker tri-motors, which had been selected as standard equipment, had not been delivered as promised. Trippe and other key executives were in Washington trying to win an extension of time, but unless they wired soon or sent planes to the rescue, Pan American was in danger of forfeiting its franchise.*

The help arrived — literally out of the blue. Cy Caldwell, a colorful pilot who later became a famous aviation columnist, landed at Key West in a squatty, Fairchild floatplane. He was on his way to Haiti, but had stopped to refuel. Captain Whitbeck, his beard streaming in the wind, rushed down the ramp to greet the visitor. Would Pilot Caldwell stop at Havana with the sack of outbound mail? Unaware that he was about to step into the pages of aviation history, Caldwell agreed. He took off well within the dead line, carrying the mail on his lap.†

From this inauspicious beginning Pan American expanded

---

*Probably there was no such risk. Pan American later failed to meet contract deadlines and no complications arose. But this was the first operation and Captain Whitbeck's fears may therefore have been justified.

†Regular mail service was not started until October 28, after the new Fokkers had been delivered. Ed Musick, the famous ocean flyer who later pioneered the Pacific air track, has always been credited with starting the regular Havana service. The logbook of Fokker NC-53 for that day lists Hugh Wells as captain, however, with Musick riding as "assistant pilot."

rapidly. In many ways this expansion paralleled the history of previous transportation systems. It requires a certain amount of ruthlessness to establish a great company. The history of the American railroads furnishes plenty of examples. Commodore Vanderbilt, one of the great barons of the Steam Age, scuttled many a rival in his day. The wars of the Goulds, Hills, and Harrimans are notorious for their ferocity. In lesser degree the same pattern was repeated in the air.

Postmaster General Brown was empowered by the McNary-Watres amendment to pay up to $1.25 a mile for the transportation of air mail within the United States. Various qualifications and the competition of rival operators kept the average mail payment far below this rate. In 1933 mail payments to domestic operators averaged only 54 cents a mile. But on the international routes the story was different. Under the Foreign Air Mail Act of 1928, as amended, the Government could pay up to $2 a mile for air-mail transportation. Pan American Airways got all the foreign contracts, and all at the maximum rate (with one exception, which was soon corrected). Trippe was awarded maximum payments because he had his own way of winning contracts and losing rivals.

The domestic operators had to bid low on contracts because contracts amounted to route franchises. If three companies operated in the same general area, the one which won the contract stayed in business. The others disappeared. Every operator knew that a line could not be operated without mail, so they outdid themselves to win bids. The Postmaster had his own method of weeding out an incompetent bidder, but he could use this competition as a club to enforce his wishes.

The Pan American policy was just the opposite. Trippe sent representatives to foreign countries long before there was any talk of mail service to those shores. His men worked quietly until they had secured exclusive concessions from foreign governments. Later, when the U.S. Postmaster called for bids on routes to these countries, rivals found that Pan American agents had sewed up all the landing rights. Since no other operator could fly planes to the points designated by the post-office advertisement for bids, Pan American could demand the maximum rate authorized in the air-mail act. There was nothing about these tactics that most go-getting American businessmen could criticize, except that it did look as though the U.S. Government were working closely with the private company. Surely the Post Office Department knew what Mr. Trippe was up to in foreign lands. The fact is, Trippe's tactics fitted in perfectly with post-office department plans.

Occasionally a Pan American rival was brash enough to fight back. When the Postmaster decided to extend air-mail service from Havana across the Caribbean, a promoter by the name of Harrington Emerson tried to put in a bid for the route. Emerson was told by the post-office officials that it was useless for him to apply for a contract because he could not provide the required service within the specified six months. Emerson objected to the timing of the advertisement for bids, which made it impossible for an operator to survey the route in time to turn in a bid. These objections were dismissed as immaterial and the contract was awarded to Pan American Airways. Six months later Pan American was still struggling to begin service in the specified time. It never did meet the deadline, but the company was not seriously penalized for the clause that had disqualified Emerson.

Another company, West Indian Aerial Express, was actually operating a route that Pan American Airways was allowed to snatch away when the foreign contracts were let. West Indian operators asked only for mail payments over the segment of the route that they had been flying. It might even have been agreeable had the entire route been handed over to Pan American Airways with the stipulation that the short segment be sublet to West Indian. The West Indian operators believed that to be only fair, since they had already invested $92,000 in the enterprise. Moreover, the law granted certain privileges, or priorities, to companies that had pioneered routes. This "pioneer equity" was what West Indian counted on in its negotiations with the Post Office Department. The Postmaster answered these objections by awarding the coveted contract to

Pan American Airways. Four days later West Indian sold out to its successful rival.

This type of "deal" made many enemies for the Pan American group, but it is only fair to point out the other side of the argument. After the award of the West Indian route to Pan American, the successful bidder could have picked up the broken pieces of the rival for a song. It could even have ignored the cries of the unsuccessful bidder. For without a mail contract the West Indian line was worth nothing at all. In ordinary private negotiations the stockholders of West Indian would have had to take their losses without a whimper. But the Postmaster General saw to it that West Indian stockholders were repaid a substantial amount. An order to turn over a route to a successful bidder was also frequently an order for the winner to give a fair price for the assets of the loser. That was within the power of the Postmaster General at that time. Many critics to this day do not realize that it was used other than ruthlessly. They have charged him with having been "in cahoots" with Pan American Airways. If this had been so, Pan American would not have been forced to buy up worthless competitors. The Postmaster merely favored Pan American because it fulfilled his requirements for a flag-line system.

Other potential competitors of Pan American Airways were eradicated as they sprang up. On the Mexican route, essential as the approach to the Cristobal gateway, a whole batch of experienced operators was eliminated at one stroke when Pan American acquired control of Compañía Mexicana de Aviación (CMA), the only air line authorized by the Mexican Government to carry mail in that country.

Pan American's toughest early rival was a company called New York, Rio and Buenos Aires Air Lines, Incorporated—usually known as NYRBA. "Near Beer," as the pilots nicknamed the line, was almost the real thing. It was organized in 1929 with plenty of capital, a great amount of nerve, and the finest long-range aircraft then available. Two of its officers had a special reason for fighting Trippe. They were Richard

Bevier, board chairman, and J. K. Montgomery, vice-president, who had never forgotten the way they had been treated during the negotiations for the Key West–Havana route.

Financial angel of NYRBA was James Rand of Remington-Rand, but the spark plug of the apparatus was actually Captain Ralph O'Neill. Captain O'Neill had visited South America a few years before with Jimmy Doolittle, the famous flyer and World War II hero. As salesmen for Boeing aircraft, the airmen had seen the possibilities of South American air lines. Captain O'Neill returned to the United States to find backers for his proposed company. He went to Pan American Airways, but executives there ironically showed no interest at that time. The captain then went to Major Reuben Fleet, who had helped establish the early air-mail routes in the United States. Major Fleet was still interested in air routes as an outlet for his aircraft factory at Buffalo. It was he who sold James Rand the idea of starting a South American air-line system. Lewis Pierson got in on the plan because his Irving Trust Company of New York specialized in South American investments. Pierson believed that an air line would stimulate commerce, to the benefit of his banking associates. It was through Pierson that his son-in-law, Richard Bevier, was brought into the new air-line company to joust again with his old rival, Juan Trippe.

Trippe has spoken patronizingly of the "Near Beer" enterprise, but the record of the company was impressive. It had won air-mail contracts from half a dozen Latin-American governments. It had developed a reasonably efficient service in a very short time along an airway that presented many problems. It had better planes than had Pan American Airways—Consolidated Commodores, forerunners of the famous Catalina flying boats of World War II.

The feud between NYRBA and Pan American began when the Havana route was extended to the north coast of South America. A little later, when Pan Am began to stretch down the east coast of South America into NYRBA's area, the rivalry flared into violence. This was the case at the "Battle of Lake Montenegro," where NYRBA employees armed with monkey wrenches drove off the crew of a Pan American plane on a survey flight. It was clear from the very beginning, however, that NYRBA was fighting a losing battle.

The reason NYRBA had no chance was that it could not obtain a U.S. mail contract. Captain O'Neill had been able to wangle foreign contracts, it is true, but they were inadequate for the support of such a transportation system. And with the arrival of Pan Am on the east coast, even these contracts were threatened. Competition between rival American air lines made it possible for foreign governments to pry more service at less cost out of struggling NYRBA. Argentina, for example, began to insist that mail from that country reach the United States in seven days, as stipulated in the contract. NYRBA had been completing such flights in eight or nine days. There was no complaint until Pan American representatives appeared in Buenos Aires. Then the Argentine postal authorities began to apply the screws to the contract carrier.

To meet his obligations Captain O'Neill had to resort to desperate measures. He brought down a Consolidated Speedster, then one of the fastest commercial planes on the market. He also hired a famous air-mail pilot, Howard Stark, to fly this craft. A day before the final closing of the northbound mail sacks, Captain O'Neill dispatched a Commodore flying boat with the week's accumulation of mail. On the following day Pilot Stark chased after the scheduled plane in the much faster Speedster carrying the late mail bags. The objective was to transfer the last minute mail to the regular plane at Florianopolis or Porto Alegre, but the orders to the Commodore's skipper were to keep on schedule. If the Speedster were delayed for any reason, it might have to continue its pursuit right up the South American coast. Sometimes Pilot Stark did not overtake his quarry until the Commodore came down to refuel at Recife or Natal. That was expensive operation.

By the summer of 1930 the great depression in the United States had sapped the enthusiasm of NYRBA's backers. The air line began to send up distress signals. Had it won a U.S. mail contract, it might have weathered the storm, but Postmaster General Brown refused to heed the cries for help. Then the banks began to dig in for the long struggle. They began calling their loans. One by one the NYRBA promoters picked up their hats and departed quietly. Only James Rand stood fast. For a time he financed the air line out of his own pocket, hoping, apparently, to stave off utter collapse until negotiations could be completed for the sale of the faltering company.

Such a sale was difficult because it was painfully evident that Pan American Airways could be the only buyer. Postmaster General Brown had convinced the promoters that no air-mail contract would be handed out until the merger was effected. That is exactly what happened. On August 19, 1930, the sale of NYRBA to Pan American was announced. On the day after the merger, the Post Office Department advertised for bids on the east-coast mail route. Since Pan American's only possible competitor had just been eliminated, the bid submitted was for the maximum rate, and Pan American Airways won it without delay.

That appeared to be rough treatment for the plucky promoters of the first intercontinental trunk air-line system. Strangely, however, Captain O'Neill and his associates were happy at the way matters had turned out. Pan American Airways could have taken over NYRBA without any consideration whatsoever. Instead, NYRBA stockholders received about fifty cents on the dollar, which in that year of panic was about as much as any investor could expect. NYRBA backers had only Postmaster Brown to thank for the gratuity — if the words of an NYRBA official are any evidence.

"How did you persuade Pan American to buy us out in these hard times?" W. S. Grooch, NYRBA's chief pilot, asked Captain O'Neill.

"They didn't have to put up cash," answered the captain, "just transferred a block of stock to us. We'd never have managed it, though, if the postmaster general hadn't stuck by us. He knows we pioneered that line and took all the hard knocks."

"So what?" asked Mr. Grooch.

"He hands out the mail contracts," replied the captain. "All he did was let it be known that he approved the merger." [2]

The NYRBA incident shows how Pan American Airways could dispose of even the more powerful rival. It also explains some of the air-transportation philosophy of the Postmaster General.

Mr. Brown had no personal reason for favoring Pan American Airways. He did desire a single company for world air commerce because he believed that was the only way this country could afford to compete successfully with nationally owned foreign air lines. Mail payments, as the Postmaster understood them, were only a means to an end. After the international air network had been nourished by the Post Office into maturity, such payments might be reduced gradually. Eventually the air lines would not only cease to be subsidized but might actually be cultivated as revenue producers. That was in the future, however. Until our flag line was well established it would need all the help the Government could give it. Allowing small competitors to weaken Pan American would only prolong the day when air transportation could support itself on world routes, Brown believed. There were, of course, dangers in a private monopoly supported by the Government, but the Postmaster General believed these dangers could be minimized by the power given him by law for the regulation of air commerce. Regulation would offer the public protection — the protection it usually enjoyed under the competitive system.

According to his interpretation of the air-mail laws, Postmaster General Brown was well within his rights in denying contracts to such companies as West Indian Aerial Express and NYRBA. It is true that the air-mail laws had originally provided for competitive bidding on new routes, but not long after the passage of the first act there was a definite trend away from competition. The powers of negotiation given to the Postmaster General were an indication of this change. He had the right, under law, to determine who was the "responsible" bidder, and to award contracts to such operators, even though they charged more for their services. Revision of the domestic air-mail laws gave the postmaster the right to exchange "route certificates" for the original air-mail contracts. Lawmakers soon realized that it was unfair for a low bidder to take a route away from a pioneer who had established needed transportation under adverse circumstances. And so they granted certificates recognizing these "pioneer equities," giving the operator what amounted to a ten-year franchise. Such certificates were not authorized for foreign routes, but ten-year contracts might be negotiated, which amounted to about the same thing.[3]

But if mail routes were to be the exclusive property of particular air lines for such a long period, the Postmaster did not care to risk handing out certificates and long contracts to shaky operators or to companies that did not fit his pattern for a great air-line system.

Congress had also given the Postmaster the power to *extend* or to *consolidate* routes when, *in his opinion,* such negotiations *promoted the public interest.*[4] Thus, by merely designating a more distant terminus, the Postmaster could allocate miles of airway that would otherwise have had to be put up for bids. That was how Pan American won much of its Caribbean empire. There was nothing illegal, or even unethical, in this procedure, for the Postmaster maintained all along that he was only following the mandate of Congress.

Sometimes competition could be warded off by the powers of consolidation granted to the Postmaster. For example, Pan American Airways' first route to Havana was won after bidding on a mail contract. This contract was to have expired in June, 1933. In the meantime Pan American had been awarded Foreign Air Mail Route Number Five (FAM-5) across the Caribbean from Havana to the mainland of South America. Long before the expiration date of the Key West–Havana contract Pan American representatives in Washington asked that the original route be merged with FAM-5. The Postmaster agreed. He had the right to do this under the consolidation clause of the air-mail law. To the outsider, however, this type of negotiation appeared to be highly unethical. For the merger of the old route with the new FAM-5 prevented anyone else from bidding on the original route when the contract expired. Furthermore, the consolidation meant more than revenue to the air line. Pan American Airways had to control the strategic Havana gateway, for otherwise a competitor could threaten its South American operations.

The Postmaster General's action would have been inconsistent with national policy at the time had he given companies such as NYRBA mail contracts. By an amendment to the Foreign Air Mail Act, he was authorized to pay up to $2 a mile for the transportation of mail *from,* as well as *to,* foreign countries. The Post Office was then to collect payments for *incoming* mail from the respective Latin-American governments, thus reimbursing the U.S. Post Office Department for part of the air-mail expenditures. Pan American Airways fitted into this plan. Protected from competition, it won almost all its routes at the maximum rate of $2 a mile for both north and southbound mail. Foreign governments along the route were then asked to repay the U.S. postal authorities a prorated share of the postal revenue, based on the $2 figure. Foreign government officials might have complained about this system, especially if competitors had offered to carry northbound mail at much lower rates, but they needed the complete, two-way service, and as no other air line from the United States except Pan American reached them, they had to meet the terms.

This pattern was spoiled by such companies as NYRBA. Carrying the northbound mail at a fraction of the rate provided in our air-mail laws, NYRBA made it impossible for the U.S. Post Office to collect $2 a mile from the various governments for incoming mail. As a result, air-line competition, even though it brought lower rates for incoming mail transportation, was actually more expensive than the single operation carrying mail at the maximum rate. The only way the Post Office could break even on expenses under the competitive system was by lowering payments on outgoing mail. In that case, however, the carrier would not have earned enough profit to overcome foreign rivals, and a strong, aggressive air-line system was the main purpose of the Postmaster General.

That was why Brown was so enthusiastic about making **Pan American Airways** the chosen instrument of the Post Office Department. Nor was his the only Government agency advocating this policy. The State Department approved. Diplomats found it much easier to bargain when a unified transportation system was an implement of our Government. At first the Secretary of State did balk a little at performing chores for a private company. Asked to settle a dispute between Pan American Airways and a rival known as Pickwick Latin American Airways, Secretary of State Stimson wrote back to the Postmaster General and stated coldly that his department was not interested in the quarrels of private operators. Brown soon, convinced Stimson that Pan American was certainly more than a private company — it was, in fact, an arm of the Government. Said Brown: "I think when we started . . . conversations with the State Department they were not aware that we had a contract . . . with Pan American for this service. . . . They thought they were asked to choose between two companies on the same footing, but when they finally reached the conclusion the Government itself had an interest in Pan American, then I think they exerted themselves in every proper way." [5]

By the time Pan American had been pushed across the Caribbean, the State Department had discovered how valuable the air line could be as an unofficial agent of the Government. For years Pan American employees sent back valuable information obtainable in no other way. It was through our chosen instrument that our statesmen learned much about Axis activity in Latin America. It kept tabs on subversive operations within our entire defense periphery. In return, the State Department used its good offices to smooth the way for the private carrier. When Honduras staged a revolt in protest against concessions granted to Pan American Airways, our minister applied cool hands to fevered brows. In Chile, Argentina, and later, in countries beyond the Western Hemisphere, the State Department also came to the rescue whenever the air line sent up a flare.

Enemies of Pan American Airways tried to use this so-called

partnership with the government as an argument for the breaking up of the air line. In 1934 all the air lines of the United States were brought to book, following the investigation of air-mail and ocean-mail contracts. As a result of certain disclosures at that time, mail contracts of all the *domestic* carriers were canceled. Of all aviation companies, Pan American Airways alone escaped this punishment, despite charges that it was more to be blamed than any other company. Brown's successor, James A. Farley, knew all about Pan American's favored position in the Republican administration. The New Dealers would have liked very much to penalize Trippe and his company for some of the negotiations that had been made in the early days of Pan American's growth. The fact is, Farley did not dare cancel Pan American's mail contracts. He told Senator Hugo Black, chairman of the air-mail investigating subcommittee: "The cancellation of these contracts would not be in the public interest, as such action would probably disrupt American service to the Latin American countries and might result in great harm to our trade relations." [6]

Pan American Airways was just too big to be treated as ruthlessly as were the domestic carriers. Military and naval experts were fearful that Axis-controlled air lines would dominate Latin-American skies if the U.S. flag line were to be hauled on to the carpet in Washington. The State Department was well aware what a blow a rebuke to our only international air line would mean to the carrying out of the Good Neighbor Policy, at that time one of the favorite projects of the New Deal. The Navy began to worry about the maintenance of air bases around the Canal, if Pan American Airways were to be forced out of the area by lack of Government support. But of all the agencies in Washington, the Department of Commerce was most concerned over the threat to our pioneer flag line. Faster communications had done much to orient Latin Americans to American trade leadership, and the department was alarmed at the possibility of losing this prestige. Trade between the continents was, after all, the soundest basis for Good Neighborliness.

Before World War I the U.S. share of South American trade was only about 16 per cent of the European commerce with that area. At that time Great Britain alone had more than twice as much trade with South America as had the United States. When the war cut off much of the business intercourse between the Old World and South America, the United States quickly took advantage of the situation. And so many allied ships were sunk by the Germans that Europeans could not regain their lost business when peace came. During the war the United States became the leading trader with South America. By 1926 this country was doing 26 per cent of the international business with South America.

The airplane was Europe's bid for its former share of South American commerce. Italy, France, Great Britain, Germany, and Portugal all had plans for great air-transportation systems serving Latin America. Italy, France, and Germany were already well established on the South American air lanes by the time Pan American muscled into the area. Foreign operations were all under government supervision. All received large subsidies. And they all offered far more than mere transportation. They were powerful agencies for foreign communication, propaganda, trade stimulation, ideological advertising, and even intimidation.

Pan American Airways was our defense against these foreign influences. As such, it was not above criticism. It was sometimes greedy. Often it was arrogant in its negotiations. Hondurans and Chileans, for example, so resented the highhandedness of Pan American Airways that the State Department had to be called in, as pointed out on page 24. Occasionally the company made some regrettable mistakes, such as quarrelling with other American businessmen in South America. (The feud with W. R. Grace and Company will serve as an example.) But on the whole, Pan American Airways succeeded very well in its extracurricular activities as a salesman of the American Way. Indeed, by 1934, when the air-mail scandals made the newspaper headlines, Pan American Airways was the fair-haired boy of aviation. To have injured the company at this time would certainly have aroused strong public indignation.

As a result, Pan American Airways emerged from the cancellation fiasco virtually unblemished. For face-saving purposes the Post Office administered a mild slap on the wrist by *recommending* that mail payments be reduced 25 per cent. A revision of schedules and mail routes later cut revenue by about 10 per cent, but all business suffered at least that much during the depression retrenchment, so this could scarcely be called a rebuke.

The attempt to pluck a few tail feathers out of the Pan American goose had no effect whatsoever on the expansion of the company. Pan American stretched out for more trade routes to gobble up before it had even swallowed the last bite. Long before the air line had consolidated its Caribbean acquisitions it had begun to work its way down both coasts of South America. Engineers were still struggling to establish bases through the West Indies at the very moment that Trippe was planning work for them thousands of miles to the south. Sometimes the areas selected for development appeared to have no relationship with each other. In every case, however, they eventually fitted like the pieces of a puzzle.

In this march on South America Pan American found itself poaching on the preserve of W. R. Grace and Company. For years Grace had enjoyed a trading monopoly on the west coast of South America. Grace was more than a company; it was an institution, or U.S. satrapy. It was a bank, a steamship company, an importer, and an exporter. Had events not moved so rapidly, Grace might have found a way to keep an interloper like Pan American out of its melon patch. After all, when the Grace interests spoke up, they were listened to with respect by South American governments. Characteristically, Mr. Trippe and his minions established a beachhead before Grace and Company was aware of the danger.

Pan American established a fifth column by quietly buying up a small Peruvian airway started in 1926 by an American crop-duster. The little company had prospered and, indeed, had considerable influence with the Peruvian government. It

had succeeded in keeping foreign rivals out, and it later convinced the authorities that Pan American Airways was worthy
of encouragement. It is very possible that the Peruvians welcomed a possible rival of W. R. Grace and Company. Pan
American was the only U.S. air line that could buck the transportation dominance of the famous Grace "Santa" fleet. Since
the air line controlled the essential Canal Zone bottleneck, no
other air line from South America could reach the United
States directly.

Grace and Company could still make plenty of trouble, however. It had enough power to make things uncomfortable for
a rival. Although it was prevented from starting an air line
of its own to the United States because of the Canal Zone port-
cullis, it had the facilities at hand to operate a rival coastal airway. The Santa fleet provided a ready-made weather-service
system. Grace agencies in South America and the United
States were experts at traffic promotion, and they could supply
conveniences for travelers, such as hotels, that would certainly
appeal to tourists. Apparently the two rivals recognized each
other's power for they decided to compromise.

Each took a 50 per cent interest in the Peruvian line and in
a Chilean aviation company existing only on paper. The reorganized company was to be known as Pan American–Grace
Airways, or Panagra. As a small child, Panagra grew up in a
broken home. Both parents fought for custody of the offspring,
but since each had exactly equal rights and privileges under
the law neither could win control. Panagra grew up to be an
important air line but its full development was always ham-
pered by the family squabbling. When the parents did become
reconciled, Panagra had lost its chance to become an exclusive
trunk line operating directly to the United States.

But with the establishment of Panagra, Trippe had achieved
a great air-transportation system in South America. He now
had access to both coasts. There remained only one serious
obstacle. That was his lack of a connecting link between the
United States–Canal Zone segment and the west coast line
operated by Panagra. The missing link could be supplied only

upon approval of the government of Colombia, and the most persuasive Pan American Airways spellbinders had not yet been able to warm the cold hearts of the Colombians.

Colombians had been extremely suspicious of gringo tricks since the day Theodore Roosevelt had helped the northern provinces become the Republic of Panama. Teddy had been accused of favoring the Panamanian revolt from Colombia in order to negotiate for the Isthmian Canal on terms more favorable to the United States. Subsequent attempts to mollify the Colombians by a kind of indemnity had only lessened their respect for a great nation that offered hush money for such an outrage to Colombian pride. American popularity was never high in the little republic, but special dislike was reserved for the Pan American Airways people. It was a popular, naturalized Colombian, Dr. Peter Paul von Bauer, who had been denied the U.S. landing rights that SCADTA would have had to have to become a great trunk air line. Colombians saw their air line turned down in favor of the very company that now sought favors from Colombia. It was no wonder, then, that Pan American had trouble linking its U.S. and South American divisional routes across the Colombian air spaces.

The blockade was broken by means of a very curious agreement. After long negotiations Dr. von Bauer sold SCADTA to Pan American Airways. He probably realized that with Colombia surrounded by the Pan American system, there was no purpose in clinging longer to the dream of an international Colombian air system. But in reaching this conclusion, the wily Austrian had found a way to make Pan American pay for, some of its privileges. Colombian law stipulated that only, citizens of that country could own *or operate* air lines. Dr. von Bauer was a naturalized citizen and was entitled under the law to own and operate an air line. All that Pan American could do was to buy non-voting stock in SCADTA. Under this arrangement actual control of SCADTA still remained with Dr. von Bauer and his associates. Later, this agreement was to cause Pan American officials much embarrassment, but at that time the U.S. air line appeared to have made about the best bargain possible under the circumstances. The influential SCADTA group had thus been taken care of; now our diplomats had to make peace with the Colombian government.

This was accomplished by the Kellogg-Olaya pact, signed in 1929. It is the oldest bilateral aviation agreement in state department files. It provided for equal concessions in the respective countries to the air lines of both nations. Colombian pride was thus appeased by granting them the same rights they were granting us, but because it would have been economically unsound for them to compete with Pan American Airways, no one expected the Colombians to take advantage of the terms. It was primarily a face-saving device — or that is what it was believed to be at the time.*

By the end of 1930 Pan American's future in Latin America was assured. It had the right of way for a trunk route down each coast to Buenos Aires. Central America and the West Indies were criss-crossed with airways. Still, Trippe was not satisfied. He looked upon the Caribbean as only a laboratory for more ambitious experiments. Long before he had completed all the South American negotiations he had started a program that amazed even his stalwart lieutenants. He proposed that Pan American Airways conquer the vast Pacific Ocean air spaces.

Apparently Trippe had hoped to develop the Atlantic air track first, for only a year after organizing Pan American Air-

*There is an interesting side-light to this story. The Kellogg-Olaya pact was drawn up in great haste one afternoon in Washington. The SCADTA negotiations had just been completed and the deadline for the first mail flight to Colombia was drawing near. It was necessary to obtain an agreement at once. Actual authors of the document were Francis White of the State Department and Juan Trippe. Neither had any idea of what should be included in a bilateral pact, and so, when the draft was completed, they found that they had opened up the entire U.S. coast, including the Atlantic, Pacific, and Gulf ports of entry. This meant that a Colombian air line could operate to any of these points. Since Colombian civil air power was not expected to be much of a threat, the terms of the pact were seemingly of little importance. After World War II, however, when world routes were under discussion, Colombia found itself with one of the finest air documents of any nation in the world. Then the Kellogg-Olaya pact boomeranged, much to the discomfiture of the State Department. Source of this information is a former state department official who prefers not to have his name mentioned.

ways he had discussed the matter of landing rights with British officials. Political obstacles were too great, however, and rather than delay expansion, Trippe turned to the wider ocean.

He began his attack by taking over two small Alaskan air lines. Alaska was on the Great Circle route to Asia and the aquisition of routes in that area might help to stall off any rival with the same big ideas. Next objective was the establishment of a bridgehead on the Asiatic mainland. This was a much more difficult problem, but as usual, it was accomplished before other potential operators were aware of the ambitions.

China was the logical place for a trans-Pacific terminus. It was a country very much in need of an air-transportation system. Highways and railroads were inadequate and the airplane offered a cheap, quick means of both communication and transportation. General Chiang Kai-shek, who was striving to unify his country for the inevitable war with Japan, was the first to admit that air transportation was the answer to his immediate problem. Unfortunately for him, China had not advanced far enough technologically to develop air lines of its own. It had to have the help of experienced foreign operators. The Chinese probably would have been willing to grant special concessions to European and American aviation companies, but peculiar circumstances made it necessary to deny such transit rights. The Generalissimo had to adopt the "closed-sky" policy for China because, if he had granted rights to any outsider, he would also have had to grant rights to Japan. China was at that time not strong enough to have resisted Japanese pressure, and Chiang Kai-shek knew only too well what any kind of Japanese exploitation would lead to. It would merely become another step in the progress toward a Greater East Asia, for which the Japanese were working.

That was why Trippe had difficulty in finding an Asiatic base for his proposed Pacific air track. Despite this discouragement, he went right ahead with his plans. If he could not win exclusive rights, the next best thing was to merge with a company that could exact concessions. Trippe and his associates bought into an air line controlled by the Chinese government. This was China National Aviation Corporation (CNAC), or the Middle Kingdom Space Machine Family, as it was known to the natives. CNAC had been operated for a time by an American aircraft company that had run into financial difficulties at home when the aviation bubble burst in 1929. The Pan American interests took over this share in CNAC. Under the terms arranged by one of the company's able vice-presidents, Harold M. Bixby, China retained financial control of the air line, but the Americans were to have full charge of operations. Actual chief executive of CNAC under the reorganization was William L. Bond. He had come to China as a trouble shooter for the original operator of the line. When Pan American assumed responsibilities for the operation of CNAC, Bond remained as general manager. Under his leadership China National began to thrive, in spite of the unsettled conditions of the country, which were bad enough to have ruined most air lines in a matter of weeks.

The point is that CNAC could now provide the Pacific airway with a splendid connecting service, if only Trippe and his staff could find some way of establishing a common air base. For even though Pan American and China National were now partners in a sense, the Americans were still denied landing rights under the closed-sky policy of the country. The only way for Pan American to obtain a base on the continent was to win such a right from governments beyond control of the Chinese.

There was Hong Kong, for example, which could have provided the ideal gateway. This was a British stronghold, but the teeming port had been designated as a terminus for the expanding Imperial Airways system—Britain's bid for civil air supremacy—and the British had no intention of granting concessions to an American company that was obviously just as ambitious. The strange thing about this opposition to Pan American Airways was that the Kuomintang government, supposedly a partner of the Americans in Chinese aviation, actually was more responsible for keeping Pan American out of Hong Kong than were the British. The Chinese argued logically, but utterly unrealistically, that Hong Kong belonged to China, not to Great Britain. They maintained that sovereignty over the city remained with the Chinese government, despite the liberal concessions that had been wrested under duress by the British. To have asked the British to give landing rights to the Americans would therefore have been the equivalent of admitting British sovereignty over the city. This the Kuomintang could not do, even for its partner in aviation.

There was one other possible gateway. This was the sleepy Portuguese port of Macao, across the bay from Hong Kong. It was within easy reach of the proposed Pan American co-terminal at Manila, and it was accessible to both the Chinese and American air lines. Long before Trippe announced his intention of bridging the Pacific he had foreseen trouble in Hong Kong. Characteristically, he had prepared for such an emergency. Pan American agents completed negotiations for the use of Macao as a base for Pan American operations. These commercial diplomats worked so quietly that they had won concessions from the Portuguese before the British realized what was going on. As it turned out, Macao never did become the greater terminus in Asia. For the British, fearful that Hong Kong would be cheated of a potentially rich trade, eventually granted similar concessions. Macao went on drowsing away without benefit of American high-pressure business methods, but it had served its purpose well.

With Macao and Hong Kong tied up, Pan American Airways had a monopoly in the Pacific area. No one else had access to Asia. The next step was to blaze the trail. By 1935 Trippe was ready to order the all-out attack. He has called that year the end of the preliminary period of Pan American development. All the Latin-American tussling had been only the warm-up.

Elaborate preparations for the Pacific expansion had been made by Trippe and his generals. They had tested ocean aircraft in the Caribbean laboratory until they knew exactly what they needed. By 1935 Pan American had the finest long-range planes in the world. They were the superb Sikorsky S-42's, soon to be surpassed by even greater craft, but at that time holders of world's records for speed, range, and pay load. The S-42's were used in the Pacific flight surveys, but by the time the air line was ready to begin regular service to the Orient the bigger Martin M-130 Clippers were coming off the production line.

While crews were being trained for the Pacific operations, Pan American engineers were preparing a string of bases across the widest ocean. At this point the U.S. Government had a special interest in the airway. Military and naval experts knew we needed an outer ring of Pacific defenses, but there was no way of obtaining them on an official level without offending the Japanese. The Japanese were being treated with kid gloves in those days, and so the Government had to advance warily. There could be no objection, however, if a private company, such as Pan American Airways, prepared bases for its own use—bases that in wartime might be very useful.

State department officials did all they could to straighten out diplomatic snarls, such as the question of the right of Americans to land on certain disputed islands. But the most effective Government agency was the U.S. Navy. The Navy was interested in developing Midway, Wake, and Guam islands as outer bastions. The Navy therefore rendered every possible assistance in helping Pan American Airways set up elaborate establishments on these islands.

With such help the Pacific air track was developed in record time. Bases sprang up almost overnight. It all happened so quickly that it looked easy. That was because the work was done by men who knew their business, and who had met every emergency on other pioneer routes.

The wonder of the feat was disclosed to the public on November 22, 1935, when Pan American Airways began regular mail service across the Pacific. It was a day of triumph for Juan Trippe. From all over the country important officials had gathered at the Alameda base to pay homage. Postmaster General Farley had made a special air trip from Washington in order to preside at the launching ceremony. A crowd of spectators lined the bay as the crew climbed aboard the Martin flying boat, *China Clipper*. Thousands of other proud Americans caught the spirit of the scene as the radio announcer painted a word picture of the take-off:

ANNOUNCER: The "China Clipper," a beautiful sight resting on the quiet waters of Pan American's enclosed base here, is turned toward the opening in the breakwater. By radio, now, Mr. Trippe will get the report from the Clipper and from the far-flung airways bases across the vast Pacific. . . . Here is Mr. Trippe now, speaking to the Clipper.

MR. TRIPPE: "China Clipper," are you ready? Over.

PILOT MUSICK: Captain Musick. Standing by for orders, sir. Over.

MR. TRIPPE: Stand by, Captain Musick, for station reports.

CODE SIGNALS: (KNBF, Honolulu). Standing by for orders. Over. (Repeat from KNBH, Midway; KNBI, Wake; KNBG, Guam; and KZBQ, Manila).

MR. TRIPPE: Stand by all stations. Postmaster General Farley, I have the honor to report, sir, that the trans-Pacific airway is ready to inaugurate air mail service . . . from the mainland across the Pacific to the Philippines by way of Hawaii, Midway, Wake, and Guam islands.

MR. FARLEY: Mr. Trippe, it is an honor and a privilege for me as postmaster general of the United States of America to order hereby the inauguration of the first scheduled service on Foreign Air Mail Route Number 14 at 3:28 P.M. Pacific Standard Time, on this day, which will forever mark a new chapter in the glorious history of our nation.

MR. TRIPPE: Captain Musick . . . You have your sailing orders. Cast off, and depart for Manila in accordance therewith. Over.

(Sound of engines increasing to crescendo. The Clipper moves out into the bay. As the plane passes the breakwater a band breaks into the National Anthem.)

PILOT MUSICK: Pan American Airways' "China Clipper" airborne 3:46. Departing for Manila. Out.*

So effective had been the training in the Caribbean and South Atlantic areas that the Clipper landed at Honolulu only one minute behind schedule. Sixty hours after the take-off KXBQ reported the arrival of Captain Musick and crew at Manila after a flight "without incident." If ever the company

*This report appears in the files of the Air Transport Division, Civil Aeronautics Board. Another version of the radio transcript appears in Josephson's *Empire of the Air,* pp. 123-125.

has to defend itself before the public, it could do no better than to recall its conquest of the Pacific. Unfortunately, there is space here for only a few of the high lights. All the courage and toil were repaid a thousand fold after the Japanese attack on Pearl Harbor. Without the experience gained in five and a half years of Pacific operations, the United States might have lost the war in the Pacific. Air supply saved us until we could gather our might for the deathblow. Pan American Airways taught us what air transportation could do. It was only fitting that Juan Trippe and Pilot Musick should receive the two highest aviation awards that civilians can win—the Collier and Harmon trophies, respectively—for their contributions to air commerce in the Pacific. Even Trippe's numerous enemies could not begrudge him the honor. In the case of Pilot Musick, the award was the climax to a career. He died only a short time after in the mysterious crash of a Clipper.

For Trippe, however, the Pacific adventure was only an episode. More spectacular undertakings were already planned before the Alameda take-off. But from that time on, Pan American's difficulties were not the type that could be overcome by courage and professional skill. Aided by the U.S. Government, Pan American had had things its own way up to the victory over the Pacific. Shortly after that the company found itself enmeshed in a new national aviation policy that was to cause it far more trouble than the establishment of pioneer routes.

REFERENCES

1. *Air Mail and Ocean Mail Contracts,* Hearings, Special Committee on Investigation of the Air Mail and Ocean Mail Contracts, U.S. Senate, 73d Congress, 2d Session, p. 2459. (See especially the testimony of Walter Folger Brown, pp. 2349 ff.) These hearings will hereafter be called Black Committee Hearings.
2. William Stephen Grooch, *Winged Highway* (New York, 1933), 109.
3. *U.S. Statutes at Large,* 45:248.

4. *Air Mail Contracts* (72d Congress, 1st Session, Senate Document No. 70, 1932).
5. *Air Mail and Ocean Mail Contracts.* (Black Committee Hearings), pp. 2465 ff.
6. *Ibid.,* 718-719.

A NOTE ON SOURCES

For the story of Trippe, see Matthew Josephson, *Empire of the Air,* New York, 1944. The best source of information on the air-mail cancellation period is the voluminous testimony before the Black Committee (Senator Hugo Black, chairman), cited under *Air Mail and Ocean Mail Contracts,* Hearings, Special Committee on Investigation of the Air Mail and Ocean Mail Contracts, United States Senate, Seventy-third Congress, Second Session, 1933. Of special interest in this investigation is the testimony of Walter Folger Brown (pp. 2349 ff.), and the "Letter from the Postmaster General to the Chairman of the Special Committee on Investigation of the Air Mail and Ocean Mail Contracts." The story of NYRBA is told in W. S. Grooch's *Winged Highway,* New York, 1933, and in H. W. Lanier's *The Far Horizon,* New York, 1933. A discussion of Pan American Airways as a business enterprise appears in two articles published in *Fortune* magazine: "Colossus of the Caribbean," April, 1931; and "Pan American Airways," April, 1936. The history of the China National Aviation Corporation (CNAC) is described by Theodore H. White in "China's Last Life Line," *Fortune,* May, 1943. For a summary of Pan American's pioneering, see the speech entitled "Ocean Air Transport," delivered by Trippe before the Royal Aeronautical Society at London, June 17, 1941, as reprinted in *CAB Docket No.* 855, Exhibit PA-2, Vol. 7, original series. The *Annual Reports* of the Postmaster General give valuable statistics on international air transportation. Of particular interest is the 1940 report. More on this subject can be found in the *Annual Report of the Civil Aeronautics Board, 1941* and the Pan American Airways' *Annual Reports, 1939–47.* Information for this chapter was also obtained from interviews with Samuel F. Pryor and E. Balluder, vice-presidents of Pan American Airways; Stokeley Morgan, formerly with Pan American Airways and the State Department, later president of the Air Carrier Supply Corporation, Washington, D. C.; and Walter Folger Brown, Postmaster General in the Hoover administration.

AMEX GETS IN MR. TRIPPE'S AIR

ALL the energies of the Pan American Airways planners were now directed toward building an Atlantic route to Europe. In many respects this presented a more difficult task than the spanning of the Pacific. Conquering the Pacific was primarily a problem of distance, something the Pan American experts could solve with ease after the South American experiments. These same experts were powerless in overcoming opposition resulting from a changing U.S. aviation policy, however, and for a time the company appeared to be getting the worst of it.

Trippe had been planning a trans-Atlantic air service since 1928. In that year he met with representatives of Imperial Airways of Great Britain and with the promoters of France's Compagnie Générale Aeropostale for the purpose of working out an agreement for division of the ocean routes. Pan Am wanted Bermuda as a refueling base on the long over-water hop, but the British withheld landing rights until they could bargain for similar privileges in the United States. Pan American Airways had no right to bargain away U.S. landing rights. That was a problem for statesmen to settle. Furthermore, the British were in no hurry to press their demands because they were not yet ready to fly the ocean, but they would not yield to American requests until the negotiations had been completed.

Pan American might have by-passed the British island by flying via the Azores. But the French had secured an exclusive franchise for the use of the Portuguese islands, and they, too, insisted on sharing privileges with the U.S. Possibly Aeropostale would have reached an agreement with the Americans, but just at that moment the French company was ruined by a financial scandal and had to forfeit the Azores rights. The Portuguese Government listened sympathetically to the requests of Pan American representatives, but here again Great Britain stepped in to block American moves. Great Britain has been a big brother to Portugal since Napoleonic times, and the relationship was used to discourage the ambitions of the American promoters.

Thwarted in their efforts to reach Europe by the southern route, Pan American planners decided to try a route followed by the pioneer ocean flyers. This was the Great Circle arc by way of Greenland and Iceland. In many ways it was the most logical solution to the problem. Water hops were shorter, and that meant lighter fuel loads and more pay load. The diplomatic difficulties were also more easily overcome. Main objection to the northern route was the unsuitability of landing facilities for flying boats, at that time the only available equipment for such long-range operations. As a last resort, Pan American survey crews made studies of this airway. When all the data of "the weather kitchen" were correlated, it was discovered that conditions were far less hazardous than had been supposed. Indeed, Pan American was all ready to start preliminary operations along this route when it ran into another kind of trouble.

To fly the northern route, Pan American Airways had to cross Newfoundland, at that time enjoying dominion status. Alan Winslow, a World War I pilot, had won concessions from the Newfoundland Government after long negotiations, but in 1933 there was a political upheaval in the country caused by economic pressure, and the government requested intercession by Great Britain. As a result, Newfoundland became a crown colony, under the control of the British Government. This gave the British power to block the Americans once again by canceling the earlier concessions.

To tell of all the frustrations experienced by the men of Pan

American Airways during this period would take many chapters of this book. It is sufficient to say that Mr. Trippe and his staff kept slugging away, until eventually, by dogged determination, they won out. Pan American Airways and Imperial Airways reached an understanding after long negotiations culminating in official documents signed by their respective governments. The terms of the agreement gave the American company exclusive landing rights in Great Britain for fifteen years. Imperial was to enjoy similar privileges in this country. In June, 1937, the two air lines began a joint operation between Bermuda and Baltimore. Purpose of this service was to give pilots training in ocean flying before they took over the European route. As soon as the crews were ready for the test, Pan American tried to schedule full service between the two nations, but again the British caused delay. They would not allow the Americans to serve the British Isles until the British air line could start full operations to the United States. To let the Americans fly the ocean alone would have been damaging to British prestige. Unfortunately, the British were running into operational troubles.

Failure of the British to perfect planes capable of flying the Atlantic with sufficient pay load to justify the service made Imperial Airways the target for abuse and ridicule. American equipment made the British aeronautical engineers appear to be backward. But the British may not have been as far behind after all. The strong head winds of the westbound crossing made it more difficult to fly from Europe to America. Sometimes it took a third longer to fly west than it had taken to cross eastbound. That meant heavier fuel tanks, smaller pay loads, and more hazardous flying. The famous Boeing Clippers, the finest flying boats built up till that time, also had trouble on westbound crossings. For a long time the westbound Pan American planes were routed homeward by way of Africa and South America. That was a long way around to avoid head winds, but it was the only way to carry back heavy cargoes when the war imposed strains upon the ocean carriers. The British did not have planes that were the equal of the Boeings, but they did try some interesting devices for making westbound flights possible, and the experiments were a credit to British ingenuity.

The original "Empire Class" flying boats developed by Britain's Short Brothers for Imperial Airways were excellent craft for the short water hauls on the India and Africa runs, but they were inadequate for the long ocean hops. New, "C-Class" aircraft were developed, but even they could not fly the Atlantic economically. They had to be so overloaded with fuel in order to carry any cargo at all that take-offs were extremely hazardous.

Once in the air, however, overload is not very dangerous. The problem was to get the heavy craft safely launched from the water. With this in mind, the British tried an interesting experiment. They reinforced two C-Class flying boats, *Cabot* and *Caribou,* so that these planes could take off from Southampton Water with a gross weight of 46,000 pounds (5,500 pounds over the standard models). *Cabot* or *Caribou* then climbed to about 6,000 feet, until the pilot found a quiet parcel of air. A Handley Page Harrow then pulled overhead and let down a hose. If all went well, 7,000 pounds of fuel could be transferred in mid-air. That was the margin needed to get a profitable pay load safely across the Atlantic. It was slow, dangerous, and expensive as an operation, however, and so the British tried something even more novel.

This was the composite plane developed by Major R. H. Mayo. It consisted of two units—a reinforced flying boat and a smaller seaplane. The smaller craft was overloaded with fuel far beyond its ability to take off from the water. It was then placed on top of the larger plane. The planes took off pickaback, and since the launching aircraft had been lightened of its fuel load, the combined horsepower of the two planes was sufficient for a safe take-off. Zooming into the air like two dragonflies, the upper element was separated at a safe altitude. The Mayo device achieved what engineers had long desired—high performance with high wing-loading. Main problem was to separate the planes in mid-air without collision. Each plane was fitted with a set of instruments registering the lift of the upper plane. Release mechanism was operated by a push button in each plane, and both buttons had to be pressed while the upper element was actually lifting before the release could be effected. It was a clever device, but even at the time it looked crude. *Mercury,* the upper element of the Mayo Composite did complete the first commercial British flight across the Atlantic in 1938, but the British were forced to admit that the Mayo system was not the answer to their problems. One can be a little more sympathetic to the British, knowing their difficulties, however.

All this was irrelevant to Mr. Trippe's problems. He was impatient to begin ocean flying at once. With the delivery of the first Boeing trans-Atlantic flying boat he was in a position to force the hand of the British. The new planes had such enormous range that they could have flown beyond the British Isles to a terminus on the continent, if Imperial Airways continued to obstruct the proposed operation. Pan American Airways therefore went ahead with the Atlantic survey flights and applied for a route certificate from the Civil Aeronautics Authority. On May 18, 1939, the government agency granted the request, and the President signed the document on the following day. On May 20, Captain Arthur E. LaPorte took off on the first scheduled commercial flight for Europe. Circling the cheering crowd at the nearby World's Fair, he set his course for the first leg of the journey. That was the inauguration of trans-Atlantic mail service. Passenger service was not started until July 8, the date that can be celebrated as the beginning of air transportation between the New World and the Old.

It is apparent from even this brief summary of Pan American history that the company had set aside much of its reserve capital for pioneering purposes. Equipment alone cost as much as many domestic operators were allocating for total operation expenses. The Martin flying boats, for example, cost about $417,000 each, as compared with $80,000 for the standard transports used on the U.S. air lines. Improved models of the Boeing boats cost as much as $700,000, and the company had ordered twelve. Yet these were only the tangible costs. Construction of bases, weather stations, and maintenance depots was an even greater drain on financial resources. The same could be said of the diplomatic missions, survey expeditions, and research. When, after all this trouble and expense, routes were finally opened up, they were not capable of producing nearly enough revenue to balance the costs. J. Carrol Cone, manager of the Atlantic division of Pan American, once testified that his company lost $20,000 a month on the Bermuda run.[1] Although in this particular case the U.S. Government made good the losses, the statement indicates the risks involved.

Despite these expansion costs, Pan American Airways made money out of air transportation. This was a feat most foreign operators could not comprehend. Pan American lost about $300,000 the first year of its existence. That was because mail payments on the short Key West–Havana route were not sufficient to balance the costs of new routes across the Caribbean. The next year the company reports showed a cumulative deficit of about $650,000. Then Pan American began to reap the benefits of its pioneering when revenue from the longer routes began to roll in. At this point the income curve turned up sharply. There was a profit in 1931—not much, only about $100,000, but enough to make Trippe the wonder boy of aviation. In any other business such a return on an investment of about $17,500,000 would have been hooted, but to the air-transportation industry any profit at all was a miracle. In the midst of a terrible depression that had wrecked many an old, conservative industry, the operator of one of the riskiest businesses in the world had made his company an outstanding example of the success story that Americans so love to tell.[2]

After 1931 Pan American began to show impressive earnings. By 1932 it was in the black by $700,000, and in 1934, when the air-mail contract cancellations brought the domestic carriers to the verge of bankruptcy, Pan American showed a net profit of $1,100,000. Such profit, earned in spite of unbelievable expansion costs, aroused the suspicions of certain critics. Other operators had said all along that Pan American showed profits only because it charged exorbitant rates for its Latin-American services. The air-mail revenues on thousands of miles of contract routes came out of taxpayers' pocketbooks, it was said, and these critics declared it was unfair for the air line to use taxpayers' money for the pioneering of ocean routes. They argued that Pan American Airways' revenue from South American routes gave it a virtual monopoly as the U.S. international carrier because no other air line could afford the expensive preparation underwritten by the mail contracts paid by the U.S. Government.

On the theory that there must be fire where there is smoke, the Civil Aeronautics Authority ordered an investigation of the Latin-American rates paid to Pan American. Some of the findings appeared in the annual report of the Postmaster General for 1940. Pan American Airways, and its affiliate, Panagra, had received $47,202,000 in mail payments since 1929, said the report. All other U.S. operators combined had been paid only $59,852,000 for air-mail transportation during this same period, although the domestic carriers had flown more than eight times as many passenger miles as our international flag line. Since air mail was admittedly a subsidy for the development of passenger traffic, the figures stirred up a controversy in aviation circles.

One thing is certain—whatever price the U.S. taxpayer paid for international air routes by means of air-mail subsidy, every cent invested brought us returns that cannot even be estimated in trade, defense security, and prestige. No other country in the world could boast of an air line the equal of our Pan American Airways. The only question was whether the U.S. Government might not have gotten more for its money. It is difficult to answer that question because cost and profit figures of domestic and international operators are not comparable. There is no measuring stick for the early operations of Pan American. Certainly the air-mail payments of the two air transportation systems cannot be used as a criterion of efficiency. Equipment, traffic, and ground facilities are different on the domestic and international routes. Expansion problems are peculiar to the respective systems. One item will show this. Pan American had to provide its own navigational aids and landing fields along thousands of miles of airways through thinly populated areas. The same services were made available at no direct cost to the operator on the domestic routes. It was partly for this reason that the post office was willing to pay much higher mail rates on its international routes. It was merely a means of compensating for fixed costs. So air-mail revenue did not necessarily indicate the financial status of the contract air-mail operators.

There was a way of measuring the merits of the domestic and international systems, however. As pointed out by Samuel Gates, public counsel for the Civil Aeronautics Board when the Latin-American rate case was being investigated in 1942, there should have been some relationship between costs and revenue.* Gates, who was acting as a kind of tribune for the people before the Board, was willing to assume that costs for international service could be as much as four times greater than costs for domestic operations, although he believed that was giving Pan American the benefit of a big doubt. But if that were true, Pan American should have been paid only four times as much as the domestic operator in mail revenue. Instead, declared Gates, Pan American received six times as much subsidy as the domestic carriers.† He estimated that the return on average capital invested by Pan American Airways in Latin-American operations had been as much as 31 per cent.[3]

Defenders of the Pan American policy denied that they took advantage of Government mail payments. They argued that the later experiences of the domestic operators in postwar international air transportation had silenced many an early critic of Pan American Airways. These defenders admitted that Latin-American rates were indeed high, but that no personal gain had come from the revenue. Instead, most of the Latin-

*The Civil Aeronautics Authority was reorganized during this period to include the independent Civil Aeronautics Board, which is roughly the policy-making agency, and the Civil Aeronautics Administration, or administrative body under the Department of Commerce. Together they constitute the "Authority," but reference is seldom made to it.

†The word "subsidy" is always an irritant to air-line operators. Government payment to private carriers for carrying mail is not in itself a "subsidy."

American profits were turned back into the development of other routes, for which the Government would have had to furnish payments anyway. It was argued that the average earnings of Pan American stockholders was only about 2½ per cent on original capital.[4]

The fact remains that Pan American could afford to pioneer the Pacific and Atlantic areas because of the backlog of profitable Latin-American mail routes. Other companies, with no such payments to absorb development costs, could not hope to survive the lean years of pioneering. Under such a system, it was charged, no other air line could ever compete with Pan American on world routes. Was it not time for this monopoly to be broken, they asked? Many government officials believed that the answer was "yes." They agreed that Pan American's coddling days should be ended. The consensus in Washington by 1938 was that regulated competition would be good for international air commerce.

All during the depression no other rival had seriously challenged Pan American's dominance as a U.S. flag line. All other competitors had been absorbed, bought off, or shouted down. Then a scrappy little champion of competition appeared in the guise of American Export Airlines, Incorporated, which was often called "Amex" in the various aviation hearings and negotiations.

Amex was the subsidiary of a steamship company sailing to Mediterranean ports under the flag of the American Export Lines. The shipping company had developed a profitable freight trade and had exclusive U.S. mail contracts in the area, but when its directors considered the possibilities for starting a passenger service, they found that they would have to compete with such crack ocean packets as the super ships *Rex* and *Conte di Savoia*. These vessels were operated by the Italian

---

In that sense, modern air lines in most cases are not subsidized. Subsidy exists only when payments are disproportionately greater than the service would warrant. Subsidy has come to mean a kind of artificial feeding for young or sickly systems. Air mail thus becomes a subsidy when the government pays out more for aid than it takes in from postal revenue (stamps, etc.).

government, which was only mildly interested in any profit they might return. The airplane offered a cheap and effective means of answering the foreign threat, and in 1937 American Export directors authorized a study of possible air routes to Southern Europe. The report was so encouraging that Amex was authorized late in the same year.

The men who took over the organization of the new air line had already shown their business skill. They had taken over a decrepit steamship fleet that soon was earning millions of dollars annually. To be sure, not all this financial progress could be attributed to the management. The Merchant Marine Act of 1936, which was America's answer to the threat of foreign-subsidized shipping lines, pumped healthy profits into the emaciated U.S. steamship companies. War pressures also brought business. But the fact remains that good management made American Export into one of the most successful shipping enterprises, for, a year after the marine law was passed, the line was leading all others as a revenue producer.

One of the directors responsible for this prosperity was John E. Slater. He had been called in to help William H. Coverdale prescribe for the sick steamship company. After the Export line recovered, Slater remained to manage the aviation subsidiary. He was aided by James M. Eaton, formerly an executive of Ludington Lines and Pan American Airways.* These were the two men who were to lead a successful rebellion against Pan American domination of international air commerce.

First of all Amex had to win permission from the U.S. Maritime Commission to set itself up as a subsidiary of the steamship line. The commission had the same relation to the shipping industry as had the Civil Aeronautics Board to air transportation. When the application for an air-line subsidiary of American Export was presented to the commission, Rear Admiral Emory S. Land, chairman, granted the request. Later, the admiral

---

*Ludington was noted in its day as one of the few air lines to show a profit without air-mail payments. It carried passengers between New York, Philadelphia, and Washington. The company tried to get a mail contract

appeared to have changed his ideas as to the relationship of air lines and steamship companies, but in 1937 the only restriction he imposed on Amex was that it be kept operationally and financially separate from its steamship company parent.[5]

The next step involved an elaborate financial program, subject to much scrutiny later on. By the end of 1938 Amex had spent about $200,000 on flight surveys made in Consolidated Catalinas piloted by airmen loaned by the U.S. Navy. An excellent weather service was organized, with the help of broadcasts from vessels of the parent company spaced at convenient intervals across the ocean. The system was so good that in October, 1938, during one of the survey flights to the Azores, Dr. James H. Kimball of the U.S. Weather Bureau declared: "No transatlantic flight has ever enjoyed the benefits of such a complete weather report at so many points along the entire Atlantic route. The report was superior in all its features and particularly adapted to peacetime use."[6]

By 1939 Amex had completed six ocean-survey flights and had gambled about $700,000 on the purchase of equipment. It had a staff of pilots, aerologists, and technicians. Now it was ready to spend an additional $1,700,000 to begin regular ocean service, but first it had to have assurance that the Government would help it. Without mail payments, Amex could not continue, but before it could get the post office to award a contract, it had to convince the Civil Aeronautics Authority that a route certificate was justifiable, as stipulated in the Civil Aeronautics Act of 1938. Here it ran into difficulties.

Application for a second Atlantic route certificate was somewhat embarrassing at this time. Heretofore the chosen instrument had been the U.S. aviation policy as far as international operation was concerned. Certification of a second carrier brought up the very important issue of whether or not this country would continue its traditional plan for international routes or whether competition would best serve the needs of

later on, and when it was turned down by the Postmaster General, it was absorbed in the usual way by the air line that fitted into the post-office plan — in this case the operation now known as Eastern Air Lines.

the nation. As might have been expected, Pan American Airways officials exerted every possible pressure to convince the U.S. authorities that the old system had proved itself and thus should be continued.

Pan American spokesmen at the various hearings declared that a second carrier across the Atlantic was only an extravagance. Trippe himself appeared in Washington to argue that the solution to the problem was the authorization of more frequent flights for Pan American Airways, then restricted in its schedule by the terms of the original negotiations. Each additional trip would reduce the cost per trip, he said, because fixed costs were about the same regardless of the number of flights. Lower costs would make it possible to lower mail payments, Mr. Trippe insisted. And with the breath of competition hot on his neck, he was willing to go one step beyond that. He declared that he would even go so far as to carry mail without any subsidy whatever—that is, for the actual cost of service.

The assistant postmaster general in charge of air mail admitted that on the basis of 100 per cent performance it would cost the Post Office Department about $1,388,400 more annually to maintain a second carrier than to increase Pan American's flight frequencies so as to provide for the same number of ocean trips. Even so, the assistant postmaster favored a second ocean air line. The war had brought him around to this conviction, although only a few months before he had objected to the certification of Amex when the matter was first discussed. In January, 1940, this government official, J. M. Donaldson, wrote to the Civil Aeronautics Authority that he had changed his mind about the wisdom of the chosen instrument policy and now advocated the certification of a competitive service. He made it clear that he did not necessarily name Amex as the only possible candidate, but he did approve the authorization of a second carrier.[7]

Other agencies had already declared themselves on the monopoly-competition issue. Back in 1935 the President's Interdepartmental Committee had issued a statement after a conference with foreign air-line executives. The statement said that the committee had "endeavored to make all agreements on the basis of reciprocity ... and it is not the intention that any route shall be developed for the exclusive use of any one air line."[8] The U.S. Navy had also come around to the competitive philosophy after long adherence to the chosen instrument principle. Pan American Airways and the Navy had worked together so closely that at times they were almost partners. There were many former Pan American men in the Navy Department. Yet in spite of all this, the Navy now stood for competition in international air transportation. The Navy believed two companies would provide twice the trained personnel that would be needed in time of war. Indeed, the Navy was so sold on the idea that it loaned out its pilots to help Amex with survey flights when the company had trouble rounding up crews and equipment.

The new aviation law of 1938 also appeared to favor competition over monopoly. It provided for "competition to the extent necessary to assure the sound development of an air transportation system properly adapted to the needs of foreign and domestic commerce."[9] Senator Patrick A. McCarran declared that the competitive qualifications for international operations would be met by the rivalry of foreign air lines. That was understood at the time the law was drafted, said the Senator, who, as coauthor of the Civil Aeronautics Act, should have known what it was all about. Others denied that foreign competition had anything to do with our policy. Harllee Branch, former post-office official in charge of air mail and later a member of the Civil Aeronautics Authority, expressed a common sentiment when he told a Senate committee:

I feel first of all that this is an opportune time to get any services we have well intrenched before the Europeans settle down and inaugurate competitive services. I feel that if this company [Amex] is thrown out with a resultant loss of somewhere between two and three million dollars, it will be a long time before another company will come in and invest [that much] . . . on the chance of being authorized to operate a service, and it will probably close the door to any additional service across the Atlantic.[10]

Mr. Slater was especially persuasive on this point. The Government policy of fostering a single air line was understandable in the pioneering era, he admitted, but it was obsolete in 1939. He declared that if Pan American Airways had faced U.S. competition in Latin America it would not have dared to exact the high rates for passenger and mail traffic as disclosed in the CAB hearings. As for the saving that Pan American promised by means of adding frequencies to its own exclusive route franchise, wasn't it strange, inquired the Amex executive, that the offer had been made only when the favored company had been threatened with serious competition? Mr. Slater pointed out other instances where Pan American had lowered its rates in order to ward off opposition. He cited the record of Pan American when the post office asked for bids on the Bermuda run. Amex had just been organized at that time and Pan American executives were a little fearful. They had no idea just how dangerous Amex might be, but they knew they had to have the Bermuda base for future Atlantic operations. Indeed, the negotiations with the British were then pending, and Amex threatened to disturb equilibrium between the British and American operators. Accordingly, Pan American had offered to carry the mail for the ridiculous rate of 1/1000 of a cent a pound, it was charged. In that way Pan American believed it would be certain of winning the route. Of course it lost money at that rate—$20,000 a month, one official testified—but as soon as the threat of competition was ended, Pan American succeeded in boosting the rate on a *retroactive basis* to $1,700 a trip, Slater told the senators. Despite Pan American assertions that a single company could carry mail cheaper, competition was cheaper in the long run, he said, because a second carrier would provide the "yardstick of efficiency."

In the old days competition might have weakened the U.S. development of international routes, but since the passage of the Aeronautics Act of 1938 abuses of the competitive system could be checked by that body, it was suggested. The foreign competition upon which Senator McCarran depended as an antidote for possible greed was utterly inadequate, according to Amex standards. It was pointed out that foreign equipment was inferior, and would remain inferior long after peace had returned to Europe. Therefore, only a second U.S. carrier equipped with the best in planes and facilities, could stimulate the healthy rivalry that was necessary. For example, while Pan American awaited delivery of its new Boeings, Amex had ordered long-range transports from Sikorsky. That kept two competitive manufacturers busy—each seeking to produce a better plane.

Glenn L. Martin, who was a little irked with Pan American because it had ceased to buy from Martin, backed up Mr. Slater's contention that the competitive system would benefit the aircraft industry. Martin had made the Pacific clippers for Pan American after long and expensive research. No sooner had the experimental costs been written off, however, than Pan American began ordering from Boeing. No other air line needed big sea planes, so Martin was left with expensive and useless jigs and tools. The same thing had happened before, when Pan American switched from Sikorsky to Martin. That was bad for the industry, Martin insisted.

Trippe replied that Amex was scarcely the company to be accusing others of monopoly. According to Pan American's president, Amex threatened to become a far more dangerous monopoly than Pan American had ever been. Pan American, after all, was only after exclusive rights as a U.S. air-line operator over the Atlantic. But as Trippe described it, American Export (Steamship) Lines already had exclusive rights on the sea. If its subsidiary won similar rights in the air, there would be a "vertical monopoly" of ocean traffic. Mr. Trippe was asked if this did not apply just as well to Pan American, which instead of a steamship line, had profitable divisions in other areas to bear the financial shocks. This was denied. Mr. Trippe maintained that the vertical monopoly of a sea and air combination would win any demand, whereas calling on other divisions of an air line to help defray losses was only another way of spreading such losses a little thinner.

Pan American won greater sympathy when its spokesmen recalled the elaborate preparations for the Atlantic service. No one could deny the vision, courage, and abilities of the pioneers who developed the Atlantic and Pacific air tracks. They had risked fortune and even life to extend the high frontier. Was it then fair for another company to partake of the fruits of victory? Was not Pan American entitled to a modest profit after all it had done? Trippe held that the certification of a second carrier would cut Pan American's Atlantic revenue by as much as 25 per cent. Costs, however, would remain the same. That might be the difference between profit and loss. Indeed, the company's counsel argued that Pan American could not stand the financial strain, and he tried to show why.

In 1936, Pan American had had on order six Boeing flying boats valued at around $4,050,000. In 1939 the company bought six more of an improved model, costing about $5,100,000. Such an investment had been approved because directors expected a fair return. But the company had based its revenue estimates on mail payments of $21,600 for each of two trips a week; $13,800 for a third flight; $9,000 for a fourth; $8,500 for a fifth; and $8,000 for a sixth—providing it won the extra frequencies as requested. Any mail in excess of the 1,600 pound contract load was to be transported at the rate of $4 a pound. Since foreign governments had agreed to pay almost exactly the same amounts for the return trips, the company believed it could operate profitably.

War had changed this picture, said Mr. Trippe. As soon as the Nazis began their invasions, it became difficult for the American company to collect from foreign governments for return mail cargoes. As a stopgap, the U.S. Government authorized payment through the post office of funds to compensate for such arrears. But if foreign payments were not collected within a year, these U.S. advances were to be deducted from subsequent post-office payments. According to Trippe, foreign governments owed Pan American Airways $1,180,000 on July 31, 1940. That was the date on which legislation became effective granting the company temporary compensation. On the other hand, arrears were increasing at the rate of $100,000 a month, said Trippe, and it looked as though the company would lose heavily in the future. In any case, earnings were not up to estimates. And to provide for uncollectable debts, a reserve fund amounting to as much as 30 per cent of the net income had to be set aside. This not only cut into working capital, but also reduced what should have been slight profit into heavy loss. Pan American showed an operating loss of $171,000 for the period ending November 30, 1940. Yet on top of that, the company was now asked to share 25 per cent of what remained with a rival. It just didn't appear to be fair, as Trippe described it.

The trouble was that Trippe was too pessimistic. The difference between Pan American profit and loss on the Atlantic run was the amount set aside for the reserve fund to compensate for uncollectable foreign debts. If the company could get back any of that money from the conquered governments, there was nothing to worry about. Trippe made it appear that the arrears on postal payments were a total loss. U.S. postal officials replied that the payments were only delayed. For the curious thing is that no matter how much a nation suffers in war, it invariably makes good on its postal commitments. The posts are an international business surprisingly independent of national calamities. The foreign debts were arrears, not losses. Foreign capital impounded by the U.S. Government was sufficient to settle much of the debt. Most of the governments involved were ready to pay up. The delay was caused by the fact that negotiations had been transferred from the Post Office to the State Department. John E. Lamiell, director of the U.S. International Postal Service testified that in 1940 foreign governments had paid up $525,372, and he was certain that the balance would be paid in good time.[11] Mr. Lamiell was correct. By the end of the war the only countries behind on payments were Germany and Austria, and that was because postal services were completely wrecked during the occupation.

Pan American spokesmen had a better argument when they pointed out that there was no need for a second carrier after the beginning of European hostilities in 1939. By the President's proclamation of November 4, all the area around France and Great Britain was declared a Combat Zone, under the terms of the Neutrality Act. Pan American had to give up its terminus at Southampton for that reason. When Italy entered the conflict in June of the following year, the Mediterranean was also sealed off by proclamation. That left Lisbon as the only gateway to all Europe. Surely, Pan American officials insisted, there was no justification for authorizing *two* carriers operating to exactly the same point. Because Pan American had pioneer rights, Amex should be denied a certificate, it was argued. Under no circumstances could a duplicate service be described as one of "public convenience and necessity," as stipulated in the Civil Aeronautics Act.

Slater and his lieutenants were not convinced by this argument. It was true, they admitted that two air lines were not needed to serve Lisbon, but the duplication was a temporary condition imposed by the war emergency. The issue, they declared, was not one of economics, but of principle. It was up to the United States Government to decide at once whether it would adopt a policy of monopoly or competition on world air routes. War had so expanded the need for air transportation that there was plenty of business to support two companies over a parallel route during the emergency. Peacetime routes could be arranged to avoid inefficient overlapping. But the point was that Amex could not wait until the end of the war to find out its fate. If it did not get a certificate at once, it would disappear. No other company would again dare to challenge Pan American, because no other company would have the favorable opportunity and the resources of Amex. Failure to certificate Amex would therefore amount to a U.S. policy of monopoly, it was stated. Was that what this country desired?

That was what the members of the Civil Aeronautics Authority were asked when Amex filed application for a route certificate on May 9, 1939. The argument up to this time had been much more than a clash between two jealous private companies. It was the beginning of the struggle for postwar airways. It was the beginning of a new era in air transportation. And it was the test case as to America's future policy regarding world air commerce.

The American Export Case, as it was called, was therefore of great significance in the development of U.S. air transportation. The conduct of the case indicates clearly that all concerned realized its importance. Hearings, briefs, and exhibits fill 13 volumes the size of the New York telephone directory. Testimony alone covered 4,030 typewritten pages and the hearings lasted 37 days. Not until July 15, 1940, or fifteen months after Amex filed its application, was the decision announced. On July 12, 1940, the Civil Aeronautics Board handed its verdict to the President for his signature. Three days later the text was released to the press.

At first glance it appeared to be a victory for Amex. The air line was granted a *temporary* certificate to operate from the United States to Europe, although terminal points were not specified because of the "fluid" situation during the war. In justifying its findings, the Board had to explain a rather embarrassing statement made by the old Authority immediately after the passage of the Civil Aeronautics Act.* To reassure an apprehensive industry still groggy from the effects of the airmail contract cancellations, the Authority had announced in its first annual report that it was opposed to "uneconomic, restrictive competition and wasteful duplication of services."[12] How, asked Pan American objectors, did the decision in the American Export Case square with this earlier statement?

For an answer, the Board turned to the precedent established by the Interstate Commerce Commission in various railroad cases. The ICC had previously decided against applicants whose traffic would have been secured at the expense of existing carriers. This would appear to have been the issue in the Pan American–American Export litigation. Unlike the railroads,

---

*The President's reorganization plan for a streamlining of certain government agencies was carried out early in the summer of 1940. The distinction between the Civil Aeronautics Board, Civil Aeronautics Administration, and Civil Aeronautics Authority is described in a footnote on page 45.

however, the two air lines were to operate parallel services for only a temporary period. There was better precedent in the decision of the ICC handed down on February 15, 1940. Here it was held that "an additional service may be required in the public interest even though the existing operator is supplying ... what appears to be sufficient service, where there is lacking any worthy competitor ... and where available business is ample to support another operation."[13]

The Board held that there was more than enough business to justify two air lines in Atlantic service. The war had so strained the facilities of Pan American Airways that only passengers with top priority were able to be accommodated. Furthermore, the stream of traffic was likely to continue, the Board believed. But in the final analysis, said the report, statistics and precedent were of little importance. Decision had to rest on whether the United States wished to adhere to its traditional policy of supporting a single international air line, or whether it would foster regulated competition. It was pointed out that the Board had far less power over international operations than it had over its domestic air-line system. Regulation had been relaxed over international air commerce so that foreign governments would have no excuse for taking retaliatory measures. In that case, the Board argued, competition was all the more important for the public welfare. It was a check upon the abuses common to monopolies.

Even if the Board had full regulatory powers over international air routes, there was still a need for competition, the Board held. Regulation was a negative control. It merely prohibited an operator from continuing certain abuses. Competition provided the positive influence that would make for better service, the Board declared. For example, the ICC had regulated the railroads for fifty years, but passenger service had not improved materially until the busses and air lines forced the older system to offer more for the customer's money. Regulation only protected the public; competition served it.

"We are unable to find," said the majority statement in the report, "that the continued maintenance of an exclusive monopoly of trans-Atlantic American flag air transportation is in the public interest, particularly since there is no such public control of passenger or express rates... customarily provided in the case of a publicly-protected monopoly."[14]

In granting Amex a temporary route certificate, the CAB also had to decide whether or not the air line had to be completely separated from its steamship parent. Section 408 of the Civil Aeronautics Act specifically stated: "It shall be unlawful ...for any common carrier... to acquire control of any air carrier in any manner whatsoever." Senator McCarran, who, as coauthor, knew more about the law than anyone else at the time, said Section 408 had been inserted deliberately to keep air and surface carriers separate. The Board did not agree. All the members except one, Oswald Ryan, held that the word "acquire" meant only that a surface carrier could not take over an existing air line. That did not prevent a steamship company from starting a new air service, the majority insisted. Ryan, the lone dissenter, approved of granting a route certificate to Amex, but first, he insisted, the steamship and air line must be split. When the case came up in the courts, Ryan was upheld—but that is getting ahead of the story.

Pan American Airways, still jabbing away, despite these painful body blows, used this issue to delay the inauguration of service on the new air line. It carried the case to the United States Court of Appeals for the second district. The steamship company had been told sometime earlier that the aeronautics authority did not have the right either to deny or to grant approval for control of an air line by a steamship company. The aviation body held that it could merely interpret existing law, and that to decide such a question would be the same as establishing a law. But when the case was brought to court the jurists did not agree with this reasoning. The court decided that the CAB did have jurisdiction, and the dictum was that the Board must request the separation of the two carriers.[15] As a result of this decision, the Board believed it was forever forbidden from allowing surface carriers to develop air lines—a belief that was to cause it much grief in the years to come and was to make Pan American Airways all the more unpopular for having brought up the issue. At any rate, Amex had to refinance itself before it could be recognized as a certified air carrier.

While Amex was arranging for a separation from the parent steamship company there was one last problem it had to solve. Before it could begin service it had to assure itself of sufficient mail revenue to warrant the expense. The CAB could determine the rates that were to be paid an air carrier from postal revenue, but the appropriation for mail pay came out of the post-office budget, and that budget required the approval of Congress—more specifically the approval of the committees on appropriation. Thus, if the air-mail items were lopped by these committees, Pan American Airways might still retain the Atlantic airways for itself.

Everything possible was done, therefore, to kill the appropriations for Amex. It should have been a hopeless fight, for seldom had an applicant for appropriations had stronger endorsement. The Amex certificate had been approved by the Board and by the President. The Departments of State, War, Justice, and Navy had given their nods of approval. Most of the leaders in the aviation industry were in favor of competition on the world airways. The attempt to sabotage Amex by way of the appropriations committees in the House and Senate made the Government and the industry antagonistic to Pan American Airways—a matter of great significance in later years.

Pan American lobbyists performed efficiently, however. Even though Amex had requested only $1,200,000 as mail pay (small change in an era of astronomical budget figures), the petition was rejected. In April, 1941, the Senate Committee on Appropriations voted 13 to 12 in favor of granting funds to the new carrier, but on May 7 the Senate as a body voted down the committee's recommendation by the margin of 44 to 35 after a debate that lasted three days. The House committee also repudiated the CAB decision, although by that time Amex had pared down its original request by almost half a million dollars.

Raymond Clapper, a usually reliable commentator, wrote in his syndicated column of February 17, 1941, that the actions of the lawmakers smacked of "cheeseparing of a picayune expenditure in wartime economy." Wrote the editor of *American Aviation* in his March 1 issue:

If the House appropriations committee feels that it must re-try cases which already have been heard in great detail and decided by an agency created by Congress itself, Congress might as well abolish the regulatory agencies it has created. A certificate of convenience and necessity issued by the Civil Aeronautics Board is hardly worth the paper it is written on if one air line can go into the halls of Congress and persuade a Congressional committee to ignore a decision of one agency which has been endorsed by three other agencies and has the approval of the President. . . . The record of the hearings does no credit to the appropriations committee, nor to the air line which is seemingly so very much afraid of competition.

The irony of the Congressional action was apparent not long after, when a resourceful enemy was threatening our national existence. In 1942 Senator Walter F. George sponsored a resolution demanding to know why the air transport industry had not been geared to the defense needs of the country. L. Welch Pogue, chairman of the CAB, replied in terms that must have brought many a blush on capitol hill.[16] Did the Senator recall, asked Pogue, what the upper house had done in the American Export appropriations case? At that time, the CAB head recalled, the Army, Navy, and CAB had tried to show that a second carrier was needed. Such a move would have given the nation the experience, personnel, stimulus to industry, and communications facilities so badly needed in time of war. The George resolution accused the CAB of shortsightedness on the eve of war, but if the Senator cared to find out who was really blind at that time, he was advised to read over the hearings before the Senate Committee on Appropriations.

Turned down on mail payments, Amex might have been forced to give up the gallant fight, had it not been for the war. After Pearl Harbor the struggles of Pan American Airways and American Export Airlines were of only academic interest. All international operations were taken over by the Army and

Navy on a contract basis. Working for the Government, Amex had no need of mail payments, and the operation assured the company of future considerations. During the next four years the two rivals stopped bickering in order to work for a common cause. And in the meantime, the war changed all concepts of what international air transportation could be.

REFERENCES

1. From CAA hearings before Examiner F. A. Law on December 28, 1938, as printed in "The C.A.A. Record," *American Aviation*, January 15, 1939.
2. "Colossus of the Caribbean," *Fortune*, April, 1931, pp. 171 ff.
3. *CAB Docket No.* 298, (original copy), "Brief of Counsel."
4. *Ibid.*, "Brief of Henry J. Friendly" (Pan American's vice-president and general counsel).
5. See the statement of Admiral Emory S. Land in *Treasury and Post Office Departments Appropriation Bill, 1942*, Hearings on H.R. 3205 before the subcommittee of the Committee on Appropriations (U.S. Senate, 77th Congress, 1st Session), Washington, 1941, pp. 88 ff.
6. *Aircraft Yearbook*, New York, 1939, p. 189.
7. *CAB Docket No.* 238 (original copy) Exhibits 58 and 145. Hearings on this docket run from October, 1939, through January, 1940.
8. Reprinted in the *Annual Report of the Secretary of Commerce, 1937*.
9. *U.S. Statutes at Large* 52:977; *U.S. Code*, Title 49, Chapter 9.
10. See the statement of Harllee Branch, *Treasury and Post Office Departments Appropriation Bill, 1942*, Hearings on H.R. 3205, pp. 74-76.
11. See the statement of John E. Lamiell in *Treasury and Post Office Departments Appropriation Bill, 1942*. Hearings on H.R. 3205, pp. 225-27.
12. First Annual Report of the Civil Aeronautics Authority for Fiscal Year Ended June 30, 1939. (Washington, 1940) p. 2.
13. *United States Law Week*, Vol. 8, p. 431.
14. *CAB Annual Reports*, Vol. 2, pp. 16 ff.
15. Pan American Airways v. Civil Aeronautics Board, *Federal Reporter*, Second Series, Vol. 121, p. 810.
16. *Transport Aircraft Production*, Letter from the Chairman of the Civil Aeronautics Board transmitting in response to S.R. 228, (77th Congress, 2d Session, Senate Document No. 206).

A NOTE ON SOURCES

For the history and financial background of American Export Lines and its aviation subsidiary, see *Treasury and Post Office Departments Appropriations Bill, 1942*, Hearings on H.R. 3205 before the subcommittee of the Committee on Appropriations, United States Senate, Seventy-seventh Congress, First Session. The statement of Rear Admiral Emory S. Land is particularly revealing. Data on the economic factors involved in determining the advisability of authorizing a second carrier can be found in *CAB Docket No.* 238, original copy, popular title, "American Export Case." See especially the briefs of Pan American Airways, the Public Counsel, and American Export Airlines, as well as Exhibits 58 and 145 on the attitudes of postal officials, and Exhibit 144 on criticism of Pan American Airways. The CAB report on the case, including majority and minority opinions, can be found in *CAB Reports*, Vol. 2, pp. 16-54. The decision on the separation of Amex from its steamship parent appears in *CAB Reports*, Vols. 3 and 4; *CAB Docket* 319; and in "Pan American Airways v. Civil Aeronautics Board and American Export Lines," *Federal Reporter*, Second Series, Vol. 121, p. 810. For Pogue's answer to the George resolution, see *Transport Aircraft Production*, United States Senate, Seventy-seventh Congress, Second Session, Senate Document No. 206, 1932. The denial of mail payments is published in House Report No. 60, a report submitted to accompany H.R. 3205, House of Representatives, Seventy-seventh Congress, First Session, 1941. For comment all through this period on the Pan American-Amex controversy see editorials in *American Aviation, Aero Digest, Aviation,* and *U.S. Air Services*. Information for this chapter was also obtained from interviews with John E. Slater, who was in charge of Amex during this period; L. Welch Pogue, chairman of the CAB at the time; E. Balluder, a vice-president of Pan American Airways; and Harllee Branch, CAB member.

DON'T YOU KNOW THERE'S A WAR ON?

THE navigator of the Navy Liberator returning to his base at Parnamirim Field, Natal, Brazil, put his computer back in its leather case and noted in his log that he had just completed his fourth round trip to Ascension Island, lying midway between Africa and the bulge of South America. Back in 1939, when this same lad was entering high school, he had read of the daring ocean flights of the Pan American Airways pilots and he had visualized those intrepid airmen as the heroes of his age. Yet here he was, only four years later, directing the big planes across the lonely reaches of the South Atlantic to a plot of land that was only a pimple on the face of the sea.

That is an indication of what the war did to ocean flying. Between the white beaches of Cabo de Sao Roque and the lava runways of Ascension lay twelve hundred miles of heaving water. In 1939 veteran crews would have been assigned to such a hazardous route, and then only after long training. Four years later, hundreds of youngsters like the navigator were flying the run regularly. The young officer in the Navy patrol plane saw nothing remarkable in the flight he had just completed. He did not underestimate the responsibility put upon him, but he did not worry too much about the hazards. Sometimes during the long sweeps against Nazi submarines and blockade runners he hummed a verse that a wardroom commando had added to the famous war song:

Bless 'em all; bless 'em all;
The long and the short and the tall;
Our wives get a pension
If we miss Ascension,
So cheer up my lads, one and all.

But of the thousands of planes flying daily across the South Atlantic, only a few did miss Ascension. By dead reckoning, radio, radar, and celestial navigation the transports and patrol planes found their way to the bird-infested runways between the volcanic hills of the islet. When a plane did veer from its course, radio direction finders sought it and found it, or the powerful ground radar stations directed it home. Radio ranges and beacons took care of routine flying, and if the worst came to the worst, guide planes could be sent out to bring the lost birds home to roost. As a result, very few wives got the pensions promised in the song.

The technical advances in long-range air travel speeded up the progress of aviation by many years. Up to the end of 1939 only thirty-odd commercial aircraft had ever flown across the Big Pond. By 1942 the ocean air was crisscrossed by air routes. Curiously, the air offered the safest as well as the fastest means of transportation at that time. Enemy submarines, operating in "wolf packs," prowled the seas, closing off whole areas to surface travel, or making passage by water routes too hazardous for anything but emergency transportation. War was the acid test of the transport plane. During these years air liners proved their reliability and value, so that the public was ready to accept them casually when peace returned.

There was another effect of the war that was important to peacetime air commerce. That was the eradication of air lines controlled by enemy nations. Some of these operations were right in our own back yard, so to speak, and they offered serious competition to American promoters. Indeed, one of the first great victories over the Axis occurred thousands of miles from the battle zone when the United States moved in against German and Italian air lines in South America. The struggle took place long before the United States was officially at war. It would take too long to describe the full story of the "denazification" of the Latin-American air routes, but no history of commercial aviation would be complete without indicating the importance of the victory.

Brazil lay athwart one of the main aerial highways to the battle fronts. Over this airway flowed the personnel and materiel so desperately needed by the allied armies. The same route in reverse might just as well have served Germans and Italians. Looking back, it is easy to minimize the threat of Axis penetration, but to the military strategists of that day, the danger was of grave concern. With Dakar in enemy hands, the bulge of Brazil would have been the logical beachhead for an Axis attack on this hemisphere. That the enemy had this in mind is indicated by the activity in South America. For it will be recalled that both the Germans and Italians had important air-line operations in the area. They were a continual source of ideological infection and they were the germ of a possible fifth-column plague.

The incidental result of the U.S. victory in South America was that it left a vast area as the exclusive domain of western air-line promoters. This was important, too, because the foreign air lines were firmly established and might have been reorganized after the war. Core of the German system was Kondor Syndikat, which was part of the Nazi-dominated Deutsche Lufthansa network. Back in 1924 German air-line pioneers had actually tried to link up the South American and European systems. It was then that Dr. Peter Paul von Bauer and Fritz Hammer discussed with Lufthansa officials the possibility of an interhemispheric air line. They had discovered that Latin Americans were eager to grant attractive privileges to any foreigner who could help solve the acute transportation problem in the undeveloped area. In 1924 the Germans had not yet accepted the social and political philosophies of Hitler and so there was no reason for denying them such concessions. Accordingly, the Brazilians and Germans reached an agreement for the organization of Sindicato Condor (the Latinized version of the German title). The announcement was made by the

President himself in 1928, and the air line began operations at once, with Fritz Hammer as director. In ten years it grew from a route of 744 miles to a ramified system of more than 7,000 miles.

Condor was granted a small subsidy by the Brazilians, but the company never made any profit and soon was deeply in debt. By 1941 it had drained more than $2,700,000 from its parent company, Lufthansa.[1] Apparently this was of no consequence to the operators. The debt, in fact, was a device by which the Fatherland, through its creature, Lufthansa, could manipulate its South American offshoot for "patriotic" purposes. Condor was never expected to show a profit. It was primarily the German answer to the Good Neighbor policy that the United States was soon to promote. It was so effective that the Germans decided to expand services, regardless of cost. Fritz Hammer, for example, was detached from Condor in 1937 to organize a west-coast system called Sociedad Ecuatoriana de Transportes Aéreos, or SEDTA. He was killed in a crash the following year, but others carried on the work. The organization of SCADTA in Colombia has already been described, and there were many other smaller German-dominated air lines.

The Germans had one great advantage over their American rivals. Many of the Latin-American countries had laws restricting control and capitalization to citizens. Few Americans were willing to transfer their citizenship, but the Germans usually swore allegiance to their adopted countries. It was assumed in the homeland that a German was a German, no matter where he lived. Germans could therefore manage, or even own, Latin-American air lines, whereas American operators had to work indirectly, or by precarious arrangement with respective governments.

By 1940 the Axis air lines in Latin America were such a threat to hemispheric security that the United States began a counteroffensive. The U.S. expeditionary force was an organization known as the American Republics Aviation Division of the Defense Supplies Corporation (DSC). At first this agency met with little success. Brazilians resented the interference.

The thousands of German and Italian colonists had a strong influence in national policy and there were Brazilians who were not pro-Axis, but who hated anything smacking of Yankee Imperialism. Not until after Pearl Harbor did the U.S. strategy begin to produce results. Fuel supplies for the Axis air lines were dried up, and such companies as Condor found themselves on the Proclaimed List, with which no allied sympathizer would deal.

Soon Condor was in difficulties. By conserving fuel supplies and by stripping slightly damaged aircraft of needed accessories, the air line maintained a reduced schedule for many months but by the end of 1941 the planes were grounded. In January, 1942, Condor tried to get off the Proclaimed List by reorganizing with Brazilians in the key positions, replacing the suspected Nazis. The DSC refused to lift the ban, however, because Dr. Ernesto Hoelcke, a naturalized Brazilian, but a known sympathizer of the Nazis, remained as director-secretary and holder of the controlling stock. After Brazil declared war on the Axis the air line was completely "purified." In August Doktor Hoelcke was charged with treason and was forced to give up control of Condor. Later he was freed on the charges and was reimbursed, but he never regained his former position.

Brazil assumed the Lufthansa debt, reorganized Condor as Servicos Aéreos Cruzeiro do Sul (Southern Cross) and made it a completely Brazilian company. Off the Proclaimed List, and equipped with U.S. planes, Cruzeiro became a great air-line system — one of the world's best — and did much to build up good will between the United States and Brazil.

The "delousing" of Axis air lines in Latin America included a number of operations less important than Condor but still dangerous to hemispheric solidarity. There was Linee Aeree Transcontinentali Italiane, or LATI, as it was called. LATI had started out with an ambitious program just before the war and had made a nuisance of itself to the allies even before Italy became an enemy. Italian planes provided the Germans with a safe means of transportation for fifth-column agents to and from Latin America. On several occasions Italian airmen were known to have reported to submarine commanders the positions of allied convoys. LATI equipment was meager but good. The company had three Savoia-Marchetti SM-83 trimotor transports — slow, but reliable. In the liquidation of LATI by the Defense Supplies Corporation, these planes were taken over by the Americans until parts were no longer obtainable. Then they were discarded. As late as 1944 one of these beautifully constructed ships stood in the parking strip at Natal. It may still be there, a forlorn monument to a lost cause.

There was one Latin-American air-line reorganization that caused great embarrassment during the absorption of Latin-American systems by the Americans. That was the taking over of SCADTA by Pan American Airways — a story that would provide a plot for an unbelievable magazine yarn. It will be recalled that Pan American ended up with 80 per cent of SCADTA stock, following the negotiations to link Panagra with the trunk line at the Canal Zone. Pan American did not have control of the Colombian air line, however, because under Colombian law control could only be achieved by nationals. As a result, the original German personnel still ran the Colombian operation, and their jobs were guaranteed for ten years by the agreement. It is true that the Germans were not being replaced as they dropped out of the company for various reasons, and in time the situation would have been improved. The war made it desirable to rid SCADTA of Germans at once, but it took a long time to accomplish that end. Not until June, 1940, were the Germans completely pried loose. They had to be given severance pay, which was expensive, and substitutes had to be found. This was done through Pan American Airways. A new company supplanted SCADTA. It was called Aerovías Nacionales de Colombia (AVIANCA). Pan American Airways had a 64 per cent financial investment in the reorganized air line, but the Colombians were now active partners with the Americans and still retained nominal control. Discharged employes of the old SCADTA line at once started up a rival air line in the plains region of the country. It was reported that they were building air fields within three hundred miles of the Canal, but in May, 1941, the key officers were taken into custody and all their equipment was purchased by AVIANCA.

Liquidation of our Axis rivals left the United States alone in the Western Hemisphere as an air power. Several nations had small merchant air fleets, but all were dependent upon the United States for equipment and operational direction. The eradication of these potential postwar competitors brought up a serious problem, however. The United States could not wreck the foreign air services in Latin America without replacing them with equal or superior transportation and communication. With every transport plane needed on the battle-front supply lines, it was difficult to fulfill these demands. In some cases existing U.S. air lines had to take up the slack — not always willingly. To many a U.S. air-line executive in Latin America it must have appeared ridiculous for him to be operating his precious planes over "thin," unproductive, sometimes useless routes at a time when fuel and men and equipment were needed so badly elsewhere. It might have helped the morale of such operators to have known that this was the price of good will and Latin-American cooperation.

On the whole, the record of the Defense Supplies Corporation had been excellent. It had cleared up a source of Axis infection. It had eliminated dangerous rivals. And it had supplied a superior service in exchange. Credit for the success of the mission belongs to Francis L. Duncan, chief technical adviser of DFC who later took thirty experts with him to reorganize the Brazilian air system; William A. M. Burden, later assistant secretary of commerce; and Stokeley Morgan, later bureau chief in charge of aviation matters in the State Department.

Another great rival, this time a friendly one, was affected by the war. This was Great Britain, whose air-line development will be described in the next chapter. While the U.S. had been liquidating Axis air lines in Latin America, the war had been going badly for the anti-Fascist nations. In July, 1940, while the Civil Aeronautics Board was deciding the American Export case and the Defense Supplies Corporation was grappling with

Condor and LATI, the Nazis were advancing. France, Norway, and the low countries were conquered. And now the German war lords turned their eyes toward the British Isles. An epic battle was about to begin.

Early in the war the United States and Great Britain had reached an agreement whereby this country would supply all the needed transport planes while the British concentrated on military aircraft.* When the great air battle for the British Isles ended, the British were in no position to change that policy. All through August and September of 1940 the Heinkel, Junkers, and Dornier bombers roared in from Germany to soften up the indomitable British for the invasion that was planned. By night the Ju-88's and Messerschmidts hovered over London, spotting fires set by the day bombers and heckling the desperate groundlings. Nerves of the harassed people were near the breaking point. The few ships that got through the aerial barrage or the submarine barrier found the docks at Southampton, Portsmouth, and Liverpool increasingly useless. Only bright spot in all this death and carnage was the record of the British fighter pilot.

The Battle of Britain began on August 8, 1940. For eighty-four days the bombs fell without letup. Later it was admitted by the British that they were close to exhaustion and might have had to throw in the towel in another week. But the British fighters eventually drove back the enemy until it was too costly for the Nazis to maintain their fury. It was on August 20, while the battle still raged above him, that Prime Minister Churchill described the movements of this deadly combat to a House of Commons bowed down with fear and weariness. He spoke words of courage, not evading the issue, but confident of the outcome. Said he:

*State Department files contain no public record of any such agreement. See, however, *Hansard*, Lords, Fifth Series, May 10, 1944, Vol. 131, p. 691. The agreement was strictly a verbal contract between President Roosevelt and Prime Minister Churchill. It was reached just before the Battle of Britain. The only authority for this statement is the word of a well-known aviation figure, but the internal evidence and record of later events indicate beyond a doubt that there was such an understanding.

The gratitude of every home in our island, in our Empire, and indeed throughout the world, except in the abodes of the guilty, goes out to the British airmen, who, undaunted by odds, unwearied in their constant challenge and mortal danger, are turning the tide of world war by their prowess and devotion. Never in the field of human conflict was so much owed by so many to so few.

Great Britain won a battle that may some day rank with the decisive combats at Salamis, Lepanto, or Trafalgar, but, with her back to the wall, Great Britain had to make momentous decisions. What the British needed more than anything else were fast intercepter fighters to down the Luftwaffe, and then long-range fighters and bombers to carry the fight to the enemy's country. To produce enough fighter aircraft during the terrific punishment inflicted by the enemy would require every ounce of energy. There would be no place in the procurement program for the construction of transport aircraft. On the other hand the United States could supply such aircraft, and what is more, could deliver them by air. Air delivery would relieve shipping of a heavy burden. It would also avoid the long delays incident to crating equipment, loading it, unpacking it, assembling it, and testing it before final delivery. As a result of this arrangement, the United States emerged from the war with all the transport planes and with plenty of crews to operate them to any part of the world. We had the valuable but measureless advantage over our rivals of "know how" after the war, as a result of our agreement.

In addition to all the transports, the United States supplied a majority of the light, medium, and heavy bombers required for an offensive. These, too, were flown across the ocean. And as soon as the Bombers for Britain program was under way, the military leaders realized how much they owed to the private companies that had blazed the ocean air routes. It was the merchant airman who had proved that the northern route was practicable. It was the ocean air pilot who understood the lore of trans-Atlantic flying. It was the transport flyer who was largely responsible for pointing out the way for the Ferry Command.

In the days before the United States was a belligerent, Amer-

ican factories could supply aircraft to the allies, but they could
not deliver them because of the Neutrality Act stipulations.
The allies had to furnish their own crews. To obtain trans-
Atlantic ferry pilots, the British and Canadians appealed to
every airman not engaged in a war task. Battered old birdmen
who had won their wings in World War I drifted up to Dorval
Field near Montreal to see what all the excitement was about.
American youths who had caught the aviation fever while flying Cubs or Aeroncas under the Civilian Pilot Training course
were intrigued by the idea of being *paid* to fly. Overage Army
and Navy airmen found secret satisfaction in knowing that once
again they were needed in service. Hundreds of others headed
north, admitting frankly that the high wages offered were incentive enough. From this mixed group the British and Canadian transport pilots selected and trained many future ocean
airmen. A few weeks later the novice was ready to take command of his own transport or bomber. One morning he would
taxi on to the runway at a remote base in Newfoundland or
Labrador. Pushing forward on the throttles, he was off over
the cold, gray seas, bound for the foggy coast of Scotland.

To speed the bombers on their way a half-dozen bases popped
up like mushrooms out of the wilderness. Some of them were
destined to become airports on postwar routes. Others were
strictly wartime fields. In any case, their names became by-
words to pilots all over the world. There was Hattie's Camp at
Gander Lake, Newfoundland; Goose Bay in Labrador; and
Bluie West One in Greenland. Prestwick, destination of hundreds of trans-Atlantic planes, meant as much to the ferry pilots
as Shanghai, Liverpool, or San Francisco to the seaman. Next
step was to speed the process of return in order to increase pilot
utilization. This was accomplished by providing a westbound
shuttle service, operated for the most part by British air-line
pilots. By 1941, thousands of Americans were members of the
Short Snorter club, to which at that time only those who had
flown the oceans were eligible.

When the United States went to war there were hundreds of
qualified ocean pilots. Others had learned about the admin-

istrative, traffic, and maintenance techniques of long-range flying. They were learning, although few probably realized it,
how to take over the world commercial routes when hostilities
ended.

In all the confusion that followed our declarations of war,
the record of the air-transport men shines as an example of
what an ingenious people can accomplish under the drive of
necessity. Our enemies had counted on distance as their most
effective ally. They had told their peoples that the superior
resources of the United States would be of little avail, because
the war would be over before they could count. They were certain that our forces could not be landed because of the distance
of the battle lines from sources of supply. Space was indeed
our worst enemy, but the airplane was our weapon against it.
During the war whole armies were supported by transport
planes. Groggy China was kept on its feet largely by air-transport supply over one of the most hazardous air routes in the
world.

A typical U.S. wartime transport operation was the Cannon-
ball Express, operated by Pan American Airways. The Cannon-
ball flew on regular schedule from the United States to India
across 11,500 miles of ocean, desert, and mountains. It made
the entire journey in three and a half days, logging more than
two miles for every minute away from home. Equally impressive was the record of the 1340th Base Unit of the Air Transport Command (ATC). In one 24-hour period this organization completed 1,118 flights from India over the Hump of the
Himalayas to our Chinese bases. Ground personnel at Kunming are not likely to forget Big Push Day, August 1, 1945.
That was the thirty-eighth anniversary of the Army Air Force,
and to celebrate the event the transport planes dumped more
than five thousand *tons* of cargo in China. Not until the Berlin
air lift of 1948 did any performance approach the ATC record
of that day. Turnaround time was reduced from 105 to eight
minutes. Of course GI's received very little mail from home
during this test — mail bags didn't weigh enough to set load
records — but everyone else was impressed. The eyes of many

a shrewd observer were opened by this achievement, for it showed the potentialities of postwar air transportation.

Such efficiency was not achieved overnight. Every step had to be planned. The very mobilization of air lines was a feat. That can be credited to Colonel Edgar S. Gorrell, first president of the Air Transport Association when the ATA was organized in 1936. Colonel Gorrell met with Army and Navy officers to outline the role of the air lines in time of war. The British had tried to solve this problem by turning over air transportation to the Air Ministry — a solution comparable to letting the U.S. Secretary of War run the air lines. Colonel Gorrell had a plan which turned out to be more effective.

In the event of war civil air-transport operators were to *cooperate with,* rather than to be submerged by, the military services — and that is the way it worked out. True, the President did have power to seize the air lines in wartime, not only by precedent, but by his own Order No. 8974 of December 13, 1942. To the wartime traveler it appeared that the Army and Navy had used the Presidential decree, but there was a difference between the U.S. and British systems. Our carriers were under *contract,* not under domination by seizure. And our air lines continued to be operated by the men who had always managed them. Finally, the military authorities on the whole did not abuse their powers. They regarded the civil air-transport companies with respect and used them as training schools for the efficient air supply service that was soon developed.

It was at a meeting in Washington in July, 1942, that Harold L. George, then a brigadier general in charge of the Air Transport Command, outlined his plans to the air-line operators. He assured them that the Army would never absorb civilian operations, but would, on the contrary give them as free a hand as possible under the circumstances. He said he looked to the air-line leaders for the experience needed in building up the Air Transport Command, but he added that the Army would have to depend on the air lines at first to help in the supply problem. They were to fly everywhere — using their own pilots, navigators, and mechanics. This service was to be paid for by the Government at the standard rate.

As a result of this expansion, underwritten by the Government, many air lines emerged from the war stronger and better than before. Some of them earned profits for the first time, and had they been able to obtain more planes they could have shown impressive earnings. Lack of planes acted as a brake on reckless operations, however, and the shortage of equipment taught valuable lessons in maintenance and plane utilization that paid dividends after the war.

When the Japanese struck at Pearl Harbor on December 7, 1941, there were only 434 transport planes under U.S. air-line registry. Only 76 of these were in world service. This equipment was insufficient even then for the traffic of that restless era, but all the new planes were being snapped up by the military forces. This situation was rendered all the more acute when the Army and Navy took over 244 civil air transports to meet the emergency needs of the embattled Americans after 1941. Seventy of the transports were stripped of fancy accessories and were returned to the air lines to be used exclusively as cargo carriers. This of course did nothing to help the passenger traffic situation. And just to make things a little more interesting for the air lines, about a third of the personnel was put into uniform to work for Uncle Sam.

No one begrudged these sacrifices. A few operators declared that seizure of planes and personnel was less efficient than turning this skillful group over to organizations that had had experience in air transportation, but the outcry was not loud. There was even a bright side to the picture. Air lines could unload obsolete equipment on the Government at good prices. That made it easier when the time and opportunity came to buy new planes. That was why wartime financial reserves increased, despite the rise in costs. The air lines also discovered how profitable it was to run tight schedules with top load factors (actual pay load in relation to possible pay load). With high utilization of planes and with payrolls down a third, the air lines could not help but make money. Peace, not war, made the air lines suffer, but that is a later story.

One of the most important sources of revenue for the air lines in wartime was air mail. The dislocation of working families and the dispersal of thousands of lonely boys to all parts of the world increased mail traffic until operators could not carry it with their reduced equipment. Air lines reported in the summer of 1943 that they had collected more postal revenue in the previous six months than they had in all of 1941, the previous record year. What all this meant for the operators is indicated by the net profit of the domestic operators in that period. They reported net earnings of $31,958,072, or more than twice the net income of the corresponding periods in 1941 and 1942.[2]

But the air lines were more than mere carriers in wartime. On December 24, 1941, the heads of the various companies signed contracts with the Government to provide three important services: (1) transportation of the armed forces and military supplies to all parts of the world; (2) training military personnel in air-line operation, including navigation and maintenance; (3) converting aircraft in company shops so that they could be used for special military purposes. There was a fourth function, the most important of all, not mentioned in the contracts. That was the continuance of speedy communication between U.S. armament centers. Contractors, erecting the mushroom factories and industrial cities born of the war, rushed plans, emergency material, and essential orders by plane, thus saving thousands of man-hours every day.

Most of the air lines — domestic ones as well as the old international companies — began at once to carry out that part of their contract calling for air transportation to all parts of he world. There were four main routes: (1) the North Atlantic, either nonstop or by stages; (2) to China by way of Africa and India; (3) to the South Pacific via Hawaii; and (4) to the Aleutian bases by way of Canada and Alaska. During the first year of the war while the Army's Air Transport Command (ATC) and the Naval Air Transport Service (NATS) were still in the fledgling stage, contract carriers provided half the air transportation of the military forces. Hundreds of examples of their contributions could be cited, but typical was the successful struggle to keep supplies flowing to the Aleutian defenses.

When the Japanese fleet steamed in full force against the United States in May, 1942, it was divided into two task groups somewhere west of Hawaii. One division was turned back by the U.S. Navy in the great battle of Midway on June 4. The other task group sped north to protect landings on American islands in the Aleutians, long regarded as a weak section of our defense wall. Fortunately, the Navy had persuaded Congress to authorize a few bases before the war. These provided a little firm ground for the intricate footwork required to outmaneuver a determined foe until the United States gathered its strength for the knockout blow.

It was said after the war that the Japanese were playing out of their league and that their Navy was incapable of carrying out the ambitious tasks assigned to it. In June, 1942, such wiseacres were not as certain as they were later. The enemy had landed on our shores for the first time since 1812. Holding them at bay with the resources at command had responsible departments in Washington worried. On June 3, the day before the decisive Midway battle hundreds of miles to the south, Japanese carrier planes attacked the U.S. base at Dutch Harbor. That meant that a task force, or possibly something bigger, was in the vicinity. Nine days later Japanese troops established a beachhead at Kiska and Attu. Clearly, the U.S. had been knocked off balance.

In the boys' adventure books it is Dick Dare of the U.S. Marines who arrives at the crucial moment. In the summer of 1942 Dick Dare was the U.S. air-line operator. Ten contract carriers were assigned the task of taking help to the defenders of the Aleutians. Flying every plane that could be lifted into the air, these ten air-line companies brought in sufficient supplies and troops to stop the enemy advance. They brought in ammunition, food, medicine, and technicians. Dutch Harbor was the terminus. From this point NATS ferried the precious cargoes to the battle fronts — one veteran NATS pilot leading two greenhorns imported hastily to man the three-plane sections.

One air line flew in a complete hospital in two days, when the building at Nome burned to the ground. Other air lines brought in saw mills, diesel engines, electric power plants ,and road equipment. All of this transportation was accomplished under the worst flying conditions most of the pilots had ever experienced. It was so cold sometimes that oil had to be heated and thinned with gasoline before it would flow into moving parts. The cold was hard on pilots and passengers, too. Once a pilot reported distractedly over his radio that his ship appeared to be disintegrating under some mysterious force. Later he discovered that the "force" was only his load of soldiers stamping their feet in unison to keep warm. A crewman confided in one of his letters home that in addition to all the inoculations regularly administered to GI's "going out," the Aleutian defenders were given a special injection — a shot of antifreeze solution. They could joke about such things, but the remarks indicated the seriousness of the flying problems.[3]

Amazingly, all this hazardous flying was accomplished with a safety record that would have done credit to peacetime operation. Airmen had learned another lesson — that with proper maintenance and precaution terrain and cold were incidental. But that was learned only from experience. The air lines had met the test. As Secretary of the Navy Frank A. Knox declared publicly at the end of the campaign: "The retaking of the Aleutians would have been postponed for months if air transport had not been able to fly in men and cargo quickly and in great quantity."[4]

By the end of 1942 the Army, Navy, and Marine Corps were operating their own transport services with a nucleus of former air-line administrative and flying personnel. The Naval Air Transport Service (NATS) was authorized by the Secretary of the Navy on December 12, 1941. NATS service was inaugurated in February, 1942. The Army's Air Transport Command (ATC) was an outgrowth of the old ferry service, but was made a separate unit in July, 1942. The Marines had their own supply service in South Pacific Cargo Air Transport (SCAT). Later there were "combat cargo task forces" and troop-carrier divisions that took some of the load from the older transport services. Altogether, these transportation organizations surpassed anything ever dreamed of by prewar airmen.

ATC alone delivered more than 40,000 aircraft abroad by January, 1945. It was flying 28 million miles a month in transport service and another 32 million as a ferry agency. To put it graphically, ATC was flying the equivalent of 70 trips around the world every 24 hours. Every 19 minutes an ATC plane started across the Atlantic. Operations of this one air carrier were *twice* as extensive as all the rest of the air lines of the world *combined*.

Although the operations of the old commercial carriers were thus dwarfed by military air transport before the end of 1943, the air lines continued to play an important part in the war effort. C. R. Smith, head of American Airlines, was a deputy commander of ATC. George Gardner of Northwest Airlines was in charge of ATC foreign operations. Harold R. Harris, formerly of Panagra (later vice-president of American Overseas Airlines) was chief of staff. Roy Ireland of United Air Lines supervised priorities. Lawrence G. (Larry) Fritz of TWA was boss of the North Atlantic division. There were scores of other air-line executives just as deserving of mention, but the list will indicate the contribution made by the air lines to military administration.

To many of the operators who had kept their eyes within the borders of the country, flying the world routes was a revelation. They discovered there was no reason why they could not expand beyond the continental rim. After all, they had found, what lay below was of minor importance. It apparently made no difference to a plane whether it flew over the Sahara desert, the Greenland icecap, or the wide blue sea. Time and again that fact was proved. Some of the old domestic carriers were flying more miles in a month than the pioneer international air line heretofore had flown in its entire history. American

Airlines, a prewar coast-to-coast carrier, had completed 1,200 Atlantic crossings as a contract carrier by the end of 1943. A year later this figure mounted to more than 5,000. American Airlines served every continent, including 27 countries and 90 foreign cities. If it could do that in wartime, why could it not do the same in peace, its chiefs began to ask each other?

Other commercial operators had similar records. They began to talk openly of world routes after the war. Croil Hunter, president of Northwest Airlines, announced he would apply for a route to Asia when the war was over. Northwest had specialized in Alaskan flying, and believed the Great Circle route by way of the Aleutians could be flown easily after the experience of the war years.

Meanwhile, Pan American Airways was making extraordinary contributions toward the coming victory. In 1942, with only 5 per cent increase in equipment, the company flew 46 per cent more route miles than it had during its previous record year of 1941. One of its Boeing Clippers had established a record of six ocean crossings in 10 days. A pilot captain, J. H. Hart, had performed the unbelievable feat of crossing the Atlantic 12 times in 13 days. But the company's greatest wartime achievement was the building of the African air track — the life line to the "desert rats" of the beleaguered British Eighth Army.

The British had pioneered the African routes, and at first they resented the arrival of the Americans because they suspected that Trippe intended to keep what he had won in war. The British could not object too loudly, however, because they were desperately in need of air transportation but lacked the equipment. All they could do was to swallow pride and to vow that after the war things would be different. Pan American Airways was the U.S. air line best fitted to develop African routes, because the company had had experience in the operation of flying boats and had operated already in Africa. A part of Pan American's "circular route" to and from Europe touched the coast of Africa. The Clippers returning from Lisbon took

The building of the African air track compares in daring and the African–South American route to avoid headwinds.

resourcefulness with the development of the Atlantic and Pacific airways. The feat was all the more marvelous because of the speed with which it was completed. Despite the pioneering of the British, the wartime African operations involved complete reorganization. Imperial Airways, which had first flown the African routes, had perfected a curious operation. It used land planes for the long over-water hops from England to its West African base, but it changed to seaplanes for the routes crossing the continent. That may sound odd, but it had been carefully thought out. Imperial used land planes where it could, because it had found them to be more efficient. It used seaplanes on the trans-African runs because it was too difficult to build runways in the jungle, whereas seaplanes could land on rivers and lakes. This system was all right for prewar operations, but if the allies had to deliver war planes to the armies in Egypt, and to ferry planes and supplies across the continent, airports were needed. Pan American Airways took over that work.

On August 18, 1941, President Roosevelt announced that Pan American had been designated as the company to develop a ferry and transport service to the Middle East by way of Africa. Two months after that press release, planes were being delivered over the new route. To airmen all over the world, this was sheer magic. It was 7,000 miles from the United States to the African gateway in Liberia. But the gateway was 4,300 miles from the Cairo terminus, and in between was a trackless waste that explorers had penetrated only after months of tedious trekking. Every mile of the route was subject to unusual flying conditions; the intense heat of deserts that burned up men and machines; the Harmattans and Khamsins — dust storms and searing blasts.

Nevertheless, company engineers started right in. Franklin Gledhill, a vice-president of Pan American Airways, conducted the first surveys. Two weeks after the President's order had been released, he was flying in supplies to his ground crews. Gledhill attacked the problem as a general would have planned a campaign. An expeditionary force of three ships unloaded a complete air base at Bathurst, British Gambia. From this main camp, "task forces" were dispatched into the wilderness by air to hack out runways. As soon as a strip could receive a transport, supplies and machinery were flown in. Modern villages, radio stations, and airports soon dotted the route where before the bushman's hut had been the only man-made structure. At the end of the year a steady flow of planes and equipment was streaming across Africa. By that time, the airway was being pushed to Cairo, Karachi, Calcutta, and Kunming. There was really no end to it. No undertaking in the glorious days of early American railroading ever offered more adventure, color, or test of ingenuity than did the building of the African airway.

There was something to be gained after all this work, of course. Africa had offered slight inducement to American aviation promoters because the cost of developing an airway was not justifiable. But with the Government paying all the construction bills for airports, Africa offered more opportunities for the commercial airman. Pan American had already shown its interest by trying to reach down as far as Capetown from its African bases at Portuguese Guinea and Liberia. The state-owned air lines of South Africa had blocked that invasion, but soon Pan American won rights from the Belgians to go as far south as Leopoldville in the Congo region. With control of the West African gateways, Pan American might have won a new empire, as it had in the Pacific area. At any rate, it had pioneer equities in Africa when the time came to take over peacetime routes. Indeed the CAB did grant Pan American a route license on August 12, 1941. It was temporary, but it indicated the shape of things to come.

Another great wartime service of Pan American was the operation of its affiliate, CNAC, China National Aviation Corporation. The air line was already a legend among airmen long before the United States became an ally of the Chinese. For years the Japanese had tried futilely to destroy it. Japanese fighters roamed unmolested in China's skies in those days, and the pilots had orders to shoot down CNAC planes on sight. In spite of such opposition, CNAC not only continued to operate, but even expanded under the very noses of the Japanese invaders.

Most of the Pan American personnel in China signed up with CNAC when Japan invaded the country. They had to, or the State Department would have been placed in the embarrassing position of trying to protect U.S. nationals who were acting as belligerents. Under these Old China Hands, CNAC began to show a profit during the long, undeclared war that preceded the world conflict. In 1941, after four years of Japanese aggression, the air line was flying more than 2,000 miles of routes with load factors seldom under 100 per cent. Equipment was rather primitive — some DC-3's, three old DC-2's, and half a dozen old Curtiss Condors, vintage of about 1930, purchased from California's famous aviation junkman, Charles Babb.

No airline ever operated under such weird conditions. Most operators tried to assure customers that planes never took off except when weather permitted. Not so CNAC. The worse the weather, the more flights it scheduled. Most of its flying was by night, over airways traversing enemy skies. If rain or clouds darkened the moon, that was only added protection against lurking Japanese fighters. Considering the flying hazards, the operation was surprisingly safe. One air liner was shot down with the loss of crew and passengers, but that was before the company began night flying. Another brush with the enemy ended more happily. One of the DC-3's was forced down by a Japanese fighter pilot but landed safely in a rice paddy. The enemy pilot circled the aircraft but apparently decided it could be salvaged, for he refrained from strafing it. Then friendly coolies made a temporary runway. Before dawn a CNAC relief plane landed with a spare wing strapped to the underside of its fuselage. This was attached to the grounded transport, but since it was a DC-2 wing, it did not match with the DC-3's undamaged member. Nevertheless the lopsided craft was taxied on to the makeshift runway. It took off safely and returned to its base to fly again another day.

The main route of CNAC was from Hong Kong, the British stronghold, to the Chinese provisional capital at Chungking. Here the route turned south to Rangoon and Calcutta. Over this aerial life line flew famous statesmen and newspaper correspondents, spies, businessmen, military leaders, and charming adventurers merely out for the ride. There was always a CNAC transport on the ramp when help was most urgently needed. When the Japanese closed in on Peiping, capital of the old empire, it was Pilot Foxy Kent who took the last Chinese cargo out in a CNAC plane. Pilot Kent reached his ship disguised as a coolie and he took off in a hail of bullets, "just like in the movies." In 1938, when Hankow, the temporary capital, fell to the enemy, it was CNAC that brought out the last government officials, including the Generalissimo and Madame Chiang Kai-shek. CNAC was in the thick of the fighting in Burma. It was here, in the retreat from Rangoon, that a CNAC DC-3 broke all known records for a plane of that type. Designed to carry 14 passengers, the stripped-down Douglas that day brought out 74 passengers and 592 pounds of gear.

Guiding hand of CNAC was the same William L. Bond who had been sent out in 1928 to manage the Curtiss-Wright interests. Retained by Pan American, he was key man in China when the fighting began in earnest in 1937. He learned about war the hard way — by personal experience. On December 8, 1941, he was awakened by the captain of the Pan American trans-Pacific air liner, *Philippine Clipper*. The United States was at war, the pilot announced, and the British were fearful that the Clipper would be the target for a Japanese air attack. The two decided to hide the plane at a nearby lake until the company wired orders, but as the men ran for the waterside the air-raid sirens began screaming. Overhead appeared a squadron of enemy fighter planes. The leader peeled off into a diving attack on the resting transports. When it was over, CNAC was minus the Clipper, three DC-3's, and four Condors. With the few remaining aircraft Bond began evacuating key personnel. There were scores of important officials who insisted on being carried first, but the manager knew he had to save his air line, or it would never perform the tasks that would be so essential in the critical days to follow. Using his own judgment as to priorities, Bond evacuated four hundred passengers in two nights, together with sufficient spare parts, tools, and fuel to keep the line running indefinitely. All this was accomplished while the enemy was occupying the city — sometimes under the gunfire of the Japanese batteries.

CNAC then became more a military than a commercial operation. It received a few more planes and began to fly supplies over The Hump. Chinese pilots began to supplant the old American employees, but a few of the old timers remained to train the native airmen and some of them were still flying for the company nearly a decade later. It was profitable to fly for CNAC — and exciting, too. A pilot could earn up to $1,600 a month on the tough runs. For this pay the CNAC airmen risked their lives daily. Foxy Kent was killed making an emergency landing during an air raid on Kunming. Others were lost while crossing the mountain barriers. Many others had narrow escapes. The ATC pilots growled that they ran the same risks for a fraction of the pay given CNAC pilots, but few of the complainers understood what the air line had been through during its short, exciting history.

CNAC has been singled out because its story is helpful in describing wartime activities of transport companies. There were operations all over the world with similar histories. British, Dutch, and French airmen all had yarns to spin about their own wartime air routes. The Americans had more to tell largely because they had more men and planes in the air. The contributions of the transport operators was recognized by the National Aeronautical Association when it awarded the Collier Trophy to the air lines for their gallant war services.*

And what was air travel like during these harrowing years, when the United States and its allies had carried the war to every part of the world? Thousands of officers and enlisted men will recall only too vividly what it was like. They will remember the metal bucket seats, as uncompromising to the human anatomy as something out of the torture chambers of the Span-

---

*The coveted Harmon Trophy was not awarded between 1940 and 1946, but in 1947 Trippe accepted the trophy in the name of Pan American Airways for its contributions during the war years.

ish Inquisition. Many a soldier and sailor taking his first long journey by air emerged at his destination groaning that this sort of travel was "for the birds" — a phrase meant to convey the utmost in displeasure. For those who have not experienced this modern way of marching off to war, the routine trip of Ensign Watertight Hatch may be revealing.

Ensign Hatch is on his way to join NavGrChina (Naval Group, China) at Kunming. He has been transported across the Atlantic in a four-engined Douglas DC-4 operated by one of the contract air lines. The plane is what the trade calls a plush job, meaning that it has real seats, unlike the similar Army C-54's. As our hero disembarks at Cazes Field, Casablanca, he reflects that it has been a speedy and enjoyable trip. But at Cazes the air line turns over its passengers and cargo to the tender mercies of the Air Transport Command.

Ensign Hatch is hustled off to a confiscated orphan asylum now serving as a transient hostel. He is told that he is now on alert. This means that Ensign Hatch and others of his ilk cannot leave the vicinity of the building even to visit the Old Medina, which, by report, presents much to admire. After four days of close confinement, during which the only exciting event has been the rationing of one warm can of beer a day and a nightly movie starring such luminaries of the twenties as Bebe Daniels, Laura LaPlante, and Rin-Tin-Tin, Ensign Hatch has become what the convicts call "stir-crazy." At 2000 hours on the fourth day the squawkbox in the yard announces that Ensign Hatch, together with half a dozen other befuddled compatriots, is to report on the double to the Operations Officer. He is also informed that the carryall will be around in half an hour to pick up passengers and gear for transportation to Cazes Field. Impatient to be off after four days of thumb twiddling, all the passengers assemble, fully packed, five minutes after the announcement. One hour later the carryall still has not arrived. The senior officer present, a colonel of engineers with a jaw like one of his Stillwell Road bulldozers, steps up to the field telephone to chew out whoever is responsible for this outrage. But every time he asks for Transportation, the WAC operator gives him Transient Mess, and the Arab boys there are only amused at his queer expressions. Finally he pulls rank and "unloads" on the poor duty officer.

The carryall, it develops, has been commandeered by a visiting general who had planned a swimming party that day. A jeep is being sent around, however, and Transportation is sorry for the delay. Forty minutes later the jeep arrives. It is five miles to the field and it takes the jeep three trips to complete its assignment. It is now fifteen minutes short of midnight. By the time all the orders have been checked it is 0100. The hour's lapse does not matter, because by this time Engineering has reported that the magnetos are out on the battered C-47 assigned to the haul. Repairs must wait on receipt of parts from the supply depot, which supposedly operates twenty-four hours a day. By now the entire group of passengers has reached that torpid state where anyone with energy enough to generate an idea can become leader. All therefore listen approvingly as Ensign Hatch demands transportation back to barracks and bunks.

"Sorry," answers the young wrap-legging at the operations desk. "You'll have to stand by for a while. There's a possibility that we may be able to ready a C-46 in an hour or so. We'll let you know."

The canteen in the corner has now closed for the night and an expenditure of three nickels in the coke machine, together with much shaking of the device, has convinced the tired pilgrims that the sign over the slot does mean "out of order." They collapse on the few wooden benches scattered around the waiting room. This arouses a young chaplain, who notices the colonel's collar insignia. He comes forward eagerly, explaining he has been keeping a vigil for three days with the hope that the plane for Algiers may finally arrive, and he ends his sad recital by pleading, "Maybe you could get things started, colonel. Isn't there anything you could suggest?" The colonel adjusts his musette bag as a pillow and looks up glassily. "The only suggestion I have, padre," he answers, "is that you look around for a quiet corner where you can pray."

At 0300 all the lights go out. When they come on again in half an hour, Operations is only a name-plate over a vacant counter. There is a PFC on duty at Priorities, however — a pimply-faced youth whose main occupation is exploring his ear with a toothpick while wondering how he ever had the misfortune to draw such a billet. He looks up sourly as Ensign Hatch approaches. Asked what is being done for the war effort at this point, Priorities looks at the one gold bar on the Ensign's overseas cap and shrugs his shoulders in annoyance. On threat of putting the dog-face on report, Ensign Hatch finally gets word through to Engineering. O happy day! A C-46, last three numbers 711, is now ready for loading at the parking area south of the tower.

The glad tidings arouse new hope in the bleary-eyed. All thirteen passengers grab duffle, seabags, and kits and totter on to the field. A half-hour search fails to reveal the Commando, last three numbers 711. Eventually one of the line crew putters up on a scooter to announce that the C-46 has been recalled to the shops with a fuel leak discovered in the warm-up.

Ensign Hatch and the colonel return to the waiting room. The young chaplain is leaping like a mountain goat over his piled-up gear. "I took your suggestion, colonel," he cries out in exultation, "and my prayer was answered. I don't know why I didn't think of it myself. I'm off for Algiers in fifteen minutes." But for the others the hour brings no comfort. At the end of that period Ensign Hatch again confronts the sleepy Priorities attendant. The officer demands transportation back to the barracks, but his voice cracks with weariness and lacks any real authority. He is told that nobody — but nobody — can have transportation back to the barracks unless a flight has been cancelled. The flight is still scheduled. The PFC has no authority to cancel it. And for emphasis he points to a sign advertising the direct consequences for those who disobey this edict.

"Great frozen hotboxes," growls the colonel, "the enemy sure must be stupid if we are beating him with this kind of a setup." He turns to Ensign Hatch "C'mon, admiral, let's you and me to hell with this outfit. They can't do any more than send you to Portsmouth, and right now that looks good to me."

The two eventually get back to the barracks by hitching a ride with the shore patrol. They find that their quarters have been reassigned to a new batch of arrivals, also on the alert, and besides, there is no more bedding. At 0600 they are aroused from the seat cushions under the writing table by an "urgent." It calls for immediate appearance at the field. Nothing is said about flouting of orders, and Operations, now back at his desk, even remarks cheerfully that a "special" is about ready to depart for Tripoli, where they can pick up the C-87 from Gib to Cairo. At 1000 the thirteen somnabulists are herded on to the tarmac. Sure enough, a scabby C-47 is waiting with engines turning over. This looks like the real thing. The passengers clamber aboard. All the seats have been removed to make room for the cargo, but one contortionist might be able to squeeze into the slit left on one side, where a few bucket seats have been unfolded. All the passengers finally adjust themselves to this space. The more experienced air travelers eye the rubber Mae West life jackets (the route is straight across the desert) because they can be inflated to form cushions. As soon as the ship is safely airborne there will be a dash by the smart passengers for the narrow deck space aft of the lashed-down cargo. There one or two lucky fellows will be able to lie down in some comfort, if they can stand the odor from the nearby "head."

All this is not for Ensign Hatch, however. Ten minutes before departure Priorities runs out with a slip of paper in his hand. Ensign Hatch is to be off-loaded. He has only Class III orders and a lieutenant commander on his way to buy liquor for the wine mess at Port Lyautey has taken his spot on rank. The story has a happy ending, however. Realizing that this thing can go on indefinitely, not only at Cazes, but at Payne, Abidan, Drigh Road, and Dum Dum, Ensign Hatch takes the easy way out. He looks up Communications and rides to his destination without interruption, chained to sixty-five pounds of classified matter (official correspondence).

That was air travel in wartime. Ensign Hatch realizes that under emergency conditions service is a luxury. He knows the military transport people are performing miracles in supplying the distant fronts with men and materiel. He does not object to being dumped out sweating, or half frozen, at isolated air strips all over the world. What he resents is the utter contempt for persons as human beings. He is tired of having all his queries answered by the standard "Don't you know there's a war on?" Ensign Hatch knows there is a war on. He is not traveling for the fun of it. But sometimes he wonders if the transportation people haven't confused him with the enemy. If the military transport services don't care a damn about Ensign Hatch, it can also be said that the feeling is mutual. When Ensign Hatch comes home from the conflict, he is convinced that the only air war he favors is one between private air-line operators fighting for the passenger's dollar, with service as a weapon.

REFERENCES

1. William A. M. Burden, *The Struggle for Airways in Latin America* (New York, 1943), pp. 13, 42, 75.
2. Office of War Information, *The First Complete Report on the Air Lines of the United States at War* (Washington, no date), p. 6.
3. A colorful account of these operations is given in Hugh B. Cave's, *Wings Across the World* (New York, 1945).
4. OWI, *The Air Lines of the United States at War*, p. 4.

A NOTE ON SOURCES

The *Thirtieth Annual Report of the Secretary of Commerce, 1942*, includes information on wartime air transportation and the mobilization of the air lines. A good description of wartime operations is given in *The Air Lines of the United States at War*, prepared by the Office of War Information, no date. See also Hugh B. Cave, *Wings Across the World*, New York, 1945. The *Aircraft Yearbook*, New York, 1940–48, also supplies data on this period. A contemporary account of the building of the African air track is Don Wharton's "Our New Life Line to the East," *Saturday Evening Post,*

August 1, 1942. Valuable information for this part of the chapter was also furnished by correspondence from C. G. Grey, the famous British aviation writer. The operations in China are described by Theodore White in "China's Last Life Line," *Fortune*, May, 1943. More on this subject was taken from the Pan American Airways' *Annual Reports*, 1939–48. The section on the denazification of the Latin-American air lines is based on the thorough report of William A. M. Burden in *The Struggle for Airways in Latin America*, New York, 1943. Best report on the economic and political aspects of air transportation is Oliver J. Lissitzyn's *International Air Transport and National Policy*, New York, 1942. Data for this chapter were also gathered from interviews with Stokeley Morgan, formerly with Pan American Airways and the State Department; American and Brazilian officers at Belem, Natal, Recife, and Rio de Janeiro; and with ATC personnel on the round-the-world air route. The recently published volumes of Wesley Frank Craven and James Lea Cate, *The Army Air Forces in World War II*, (2 vols., Chicago, 1949), were also available before this book went to press, as were H. H. Arnold's *Global Mission* (New York, 1940), Oliver LaFarge's *The Eagle in the Egg* (the history of the Air Transport Command) (Boston, 1949), and James Lee's *Operation Lifeline* (Naval Air Transport Service) (Chicago, 1949).

BIRTH OF A BOAConstrictor

PENDING the outcome of the war, progress in commercial aviation appeared to have been halted. All the international air lines were under contract to the military forces. Domestic operations were frozen by lack of equipment. And the situation was all the more static because of the Civil Aeronautics Board moratorium on new route applications while military needs were so pressing.

Despite this seeming preoccupation with matters other than commercial, the air-transportation industry was building up pressure for a tremendous postwar boom. By 1944 the CAB had received more than a hundred requests for new international routes or for extensions of old airways. Many of the domestic operators hoped to bid on world routes after the war and dozens of enterprises existing only on paper were designed to engage in international air commerce. The dormant civil aviation of the war days was like the elephant in C. G. Grey's story of the schoolboy. Asked by his teacher where the elephant was found, the moppet replied that because of its large size the elephant very seldom was lost. The commercial air lines could not be lost either, even in the dense jungle of wartime restrictions.

Many of these potential applicants had only a hazy notion of what postwar international flying would entail. Even the big domestic companies, with personnel experienced in ocean flying, had no idea of the political and economic problems that would come up after the war. They had overcome the technical obstacles to long-range operations, but they had no inkling of the more frustrating opposition that was to rise when the artificial war situation gave way to a renewal of national jealousies and intrigue.

For the war years were in many respects a golden age in air transportation. Oddly enough, war had brought peace to the world airways. In the air the world was unified as it never could have been on the ground. The airman saw his dreams come true. For five years he was able to fly anywhere and everywhere with little or no hindrance. There were none of the bothersome delays at national borders that had plagued the prewar operator. Indeed, borders ceased to exist, as far as the airman was concerned. Nor was he bound by the onerous regulations imposed on pilots and aircraft by peacetime commercial rival nations. Planes were flown in war under Standard Operating Procedure, with no regard whatever for artificial load limits, declarations, and inspections. It was too good to last. As one writer described the situation:

On war service prodigious feats have been performed . . . [but] full account may not . . . [have been] taken of the circumstances under which those feats were performed. War ignores economics; it is forced to. . . . Commercial air transport cannot begin where military transport leaves off. With the return of peace, operating costs will have to approach more closely to the value of the services rendered; peacetime standards of safety and comfort will have to be restored; there will be stricter control and more stringent regulation. The war has merely shown us what is technically possible when cost and safety are secondary considerations.[1]

The undercurrent of restlessness was not confined to America during this lull in air-commerce development. Every battered European state had its quota of visionaries who dreamed of an aeronautical resurrection. People deep in the mire of defeat could still lift up their eyes to see a bright future in the clean, cold air. Commercial aviation offered an immediate opportunity to regain self-respect lost during the captive years.

The French, for example, guarded as a symbol the huge,

ungainly, six-engined flying boat, *Lieutenant de Vaisseau Paris,*
with which they had started a program of trans-Atlantic flight
surveys in 1939. A sister ship had been unintentionally destroyed by the British in the bombing of Friederichshafen, but
the *Paris* had been hidden by the Maquis. (Apparently they
completely dismantled the big boat, for it is incredible that a
plane of this size could otherwise have escaped the eyes of the
conquerors). Reassembled after the war, the *Paris* helped re-
kindle pride in despondent hearts.

It was clear, however, that America's only serious rival in
the air war was to be Great Britain. To the British, postwar
air commerce was both a challenge and an opportunity. It was
a challenge because war had wiped out the resources required
for its rebirth. It was an opportunity because it was a means
of binding together the crumbling empire. Air transportation
was thus much more than a commercial venture for the British.
It was an arm of the government and it was a people's bid
for regaining some of their waning pride. "I hold the view,"
cried Viscount Bennett to a House of Lords debating postwar
aviation in 1943, "that if we are not to sink to the level of a
second class power we have got to have an air transport service
now. By 'now,' I mean just that — now." [2]

The great fear of the British was that they would not be
able to match U.S. transport-plane production. On the other
hand, they could block Americn expansion by their control of
strategic bases along the world routes. Many of the British
bases had no commercial value. They furnished no traffic or
trade. Nevertheless they were as essential to the merchant air
fleets as the isolated coaling stations were essential to shipping
men in the great days of the Empire. Now these bases were to
become valuable bargaining points. For example, American
planes flying to Europe had to pass over Newfoundland or
Labrador, at least until longer-ranged planes were developed.
Egypt, India, the Straits Settlements, Malaya, and Australia
were other areas where British influence could be used against
American air lines. Only in the Pacific did the United States
enjoy similar bargaining advantages. U.S. denial of the Ha-

waiian Islands could have prevented the British from connecting Australia and Canada by air line. On the other hand, this airway was less valuable to the British than the Atlantic route was to us. Indeed, it was possible for the British to reach any part of the empire without crossing the Pacific. Clearly, the advantage lay with the British. It looked as though the Americans might emerge from the war all dressed up in fine equipment but with no place to go. If the British were not dressed up with planes in the latest style, they had only to wait until their own aircraft industry could catch up. But that was the trouble — there was no time for that. The British desperately needed air transportation during and after the war. The upshot was that the two countries had to work out agreements for their mutual benefit. That was inevitable, but it was not easy to achieve because both countries had old, established air lines, proud of their records, and jealous of their rivals. Furthermore, the programs of expansion were diametrically opposed to each other.

U.S. international aviation policy is of fairly recent origin. The British have been following the same pattern since 1917. That was the year when a powerful German army almost broke through at Arras. Great Britain had never been in greater danger. But the British, no matter how hard they are pressed, always keep one eye on the future of their commerce. This is as true today as it was in 1917. Commerce is as essential to the British as political independence. That is why Lord Northcliffe appointed to the Civil Aerial Transport Committee of 1917 the best men he could find.

The committee was to investigate possibilities of commercial aircraft after the war, and the report of the group actually was published before the British had a single civil air line worthy of the name. Five planks were put down for the future platform upon which to build a British air-transportation system. The committee insisted that the nation had full sovereignty of the air space above the land. This was a means of keeping out unwelcome foreign operators and was the pattern followed by most of the other nations at the Paris aviation conference in

1919. The report also suggested cooperation with foreign transport companies so as to provide reciprocal exchanges of privileges in the respective countries. It also advocated the development of a strong aircraft industry, for which civil aviation was to be the principle market in peacetime. The committee recommended the establishment of "Empire Routes" to all members of the British Commonwealth, "for both economic and political reasons." Finally, the report asked for government assistance until civil aviation was capable of supporting itself.[3]

This program has been followed, on the whole, ever since that day. Liberal, Conservative, and Labor Governments have all agreed on the general principles first enunciated in 1917 and 1918. There have been violent verbal battles in Parliament over the *interpretation* of British policy, but except for an occasional lapse, the plan of the Northcliffe committee has been the chart for British civil air transportation.

The first air line in Great Britain began service August 26, 1919, when Air Transport and Travel, Limited, sold tickets for air travel between London and Paris. By 1920 three other companies were competing for channel traffic, serving cities in France, Belgium, the Netherlands, and Germany. All maintained surprisingly reliable schedules. The record shows that 96 per cent of the scheduled flights were completed, and the accident toll was very low. Soon foreign air lines, notably the French, appeared as rivals. The French operated a parallel enterprise between the two capitals, and because the air line was very heavily subsidized by their government, the French could undersell the British. Failure of the British Government to provide a similar subsidy was one of the few lapses in the program outlined by the Northcliffe committee, and the British thereby learned a lesson. By February of 1921 Secretary of State for Air Winston Churchill observed wryly that the only air lines using London's Croydon Aerodrome were those of the French, Dutch, and Germans. All the British companies had failed.

The bad record of British civil aviation touched off another exposé. Lord Londonderry, who was to be the Great Agitator for civil aviation during the next twenty-five years, sponsored an investigation. Result of the study was a small "vote," or subsidy for British operators. Thus encouraged, four private operators resumed services to the continent. By agreement, each took a separate route. Despite the subsidy and the allocation of exclusive spheres, the companies lost money. It was soon apparent that regional monopoly was not the answer to the problem.

Slowly the British muddled their way to a solution. Under Sir Herbert Hambling, a committee studied air transportation from the ground up and concluded that all civil aviation should be under one management. The British maintained a quarter of a century later that experience had proved the superiority of the chosen instrument over competitive services. Others say that, as a test of competition, the British system previous to 1924 was not at all conclusive, considering the stage of aviation at that time.

At any rate, the single company that emerged was called Imperial Airways. It was born on April Fool's Day, 1924, a fact that was called to the attention of its backers on more than one occasion. By the terms of an agreement with the government, Imperial received a subsidy in return for flying a million miles a year. Because this formula did not produce larger and better equipment, it was soon revised to make horsepower the measurement of subsidy. On this basis Imperial began to expand rapidly.

It should be pointed out that the United States was far behind Great Britain in civil aviation at this period. Although the U.S. Post Office Department was developing a fine air-mail service, there was not a single scheduled passenger service of any importance in this country. It was to be three years later before Pan American Airways appeared on the scene, and by that time Imperial was reaching around the world.

In 1926 the British Air Ministry authorized the development of the All Red Routes (on most maps the component parts of the empire are shown in red). This was an ambitious program to knit together members of the British Commonwealth, as recommended in 1917. Imperial was to receive a subsidy for five years to pay the costs of expansion, and the Government sent representatives to foreign countries for the purpose of obtaining the necessary landing rights. By 1939, when Imperial first faced Pan American Airways as a rival, Imperial was the longest air line in the world.

Main artery of the system was the "Kangaroo Route," connecting Great Britain with Australia by way of Egypt, India, and Malaya. From this airway the "Dragon Route" branched off to Burma and later to China. Almost as important as the Australian service was the "Springbok Route" from London to Capetown via Cairo. From this airway a branch line crossed the center of Africa to Takoradi on the west coast.

It was an ambitious undertaking, all the more difficult because Imperial was charged with a heavy task in 1937. This was the development of the "all up," or "Empire Air Mail Scheme," by which *all* first-class postage was to be carried by plane. Imperial thus became far more important as a communications implement than as a transportation service. Unfortunately, the program strained the resources of the company to the breaking point.

Bigger loads of mail required bigger aircraft. If the company continued to use land planes, it would have to replace its ancient tumbrils with larger, modern equipment. But that would mean the construction of better airports along the entire route. That was too expensive. Imperial turned to the flying boat as a solution to the problem. Seaplanes could be made large enough to carry the bigger mail cargoes, yet they did not need the elaborate base facilities of land craft. The seaplane "carries its landing field on its bottom." It was also easier to obtain concessions from foreign governments for seaplanes, because they did not have to fly over strategic areas to land. Seaplanes could be restricted to the coast, like foreign shipping. But the shift from land to sea planes committed Imperial to a type of equipment that was losing favor among progressive operators. In any event, the change of equipment called for a complete revision of the old empire routes designed for land planes.

In addition to technical problems, Imperial also had to solve others. Countries along the main route asked excessive tribute in exchange for concessions, and this money was often handed to Imperial's local rival to help it fight the British operators on unfair terms. France and Italy long blocked the extension of the London–Cairo division. Even the smaller nations took turns at twisting the Lion's tail. The picture of an Imperial Airways plane with Undersecretary of State for Air, Sir Phillip Sassoon, being detained at Basra, "under guard of half a dozen barefooted, ragged, verminous Persian soldiers . . . was enough to make our gracious Queen Victoria turn in her grave," C. G. Grey, the noted British aviation pundit said disgustedly.[4]

Operators of the various Commonwealths also "put the squeeze" on Imperial. Indian Transcontinental Airways held up the New Delhi–Calcutta section of the Imperial route until 1933, when its request for a share of the traffic was granted. Imperial had to buy an interest in an Australian air line, Quantas Empire Airways, before it could reach Brisbane from Singapore. Both the British and Australian companies were held up, in turn, until they signed an agreement with Tasman Empire Airways to share traffic and costs on the New Zealand route. Indeed, it was not until 1940 that the British reached Auckland, and by that time, Imperial had disappeared.

The task appears to have been too great for a company bound so tightly by the early air-ministry agreement. In 1939 Imperial got the axe, following the recommendations of an investigating committee. There was something rather sad about the end of this pioneer air line. It had established a fine reputation for reliability over difficult routes. Its safety record was enviable. It had been operated as economically (in a loose sense of the word economical), as any contemporary air line. Indeed, that was the main cause of the complaint against it.

The Cadman Committee, which reported on the Imperial Airways case, brought out that George Wood Humphreys, the managing director, "had a commercial view of his responsibilities that was too narrow."[5] As a chosen instrument of the government, Imperial should have been less concerned with profit and loss than with the fulfillment of its function. Its function was partly transportation, but above all, it was created to tie the commonwealth together by means of cheap, fast communications, and to supply a market for aircraft manufacturers. Another important duty of the air line was to train flight crews for defense purposes. All these services cost much more than an air line could earn from commercial traffic. Britons were willing to support a losing company, even in the dire depression days, if it met the above needs. Imperial was accused of failing in its primary duties.

Critics maintained that it was so obsolete from an equipment standpoint that the training value to crews was seriously lowered. Up to the very end it was still carrying passengers in huge, boxlike biplanes of the Hannibal and Hercules class. Aerodynamically these ancient stringbags were masterpieces of inefficiency, complete with what one writer refers to as "built-in head winds." Cruising speed was around 100 miles an hour. These ships were good enough for the short London–Paris hops, but they were uneconomical for the long hauls. Such operation was bad for the aircraft industry. Not only did Imperial fail to provide the outlet for the designer, but the obsolete planes themselves were bad advertising for British plane-makers.

The policy of Imperial was not altogether the fault of Humphreys, it should be noted. Under the terms of the Imperial–Air Ministry agreement, the air line could buy only British equipment. Unfortunately, most of the better British designers were concentrating during this period on the production of military aircraft. Imperial had to take what it could get. Toward the end of its career it did have some respectable planes on order — and a few in operation. But most of the time Imperial was hopelessly outclassed by its rivals. The Dutch were bound by no such restrictions as the Air Ministry forced upon Imperial. The Dutch company went out and bought the best planes it could find for its purposes, regardless of where they were made. Royal Dutch Airlines (KLM) could beat Imperial's schedules to the East Indies by from two to five days as a result of this policy.

The company that succeeded Imperial was called British Overseas Airways Corporation (BOAC). It was organized "to secure the fullest development of efficient overseas air transport services at reasonable cost." [6] BOAC was a public corporation. Members were to be appointed by the Secretary of State for Air. A vestige of private enterprise remained, in that stock was to be sold to individuals. Stockholders would be guaranteed dividends by the government, but they had no right to sell their shares or to dictate policy.

The British Overseas Airways Act was approved in August, 1939, just before the outbreak of the European phase of the war. Transfer from Imperial management was not completed, however, until April, 1940. By that time the war was well under way. Thus, the company organized to advance British claims for commercial air routes never did have a chance to function in its intended peacetime capacity. Under the articles of incorporation a civilian body was to have managed the air line. That was impossible in war. In fact, BOAC was as much a part of the armed services after 1940 as our own ATC. The later criticism of the air line should be weighed with this in mind.

For more than five years BOAC ad-libbed its way on the war stage. It was continually readjusting itself to conditions over which it had no control. Two of its best planes, *Cabot* and *Caribou,* which had pioneered the Bermuda and Atlantic routes, were destroyed by the enemy in the ill-fated attempt to invade Norway. Technically these planes were under the Royal Air Force Coastal Command, but the planes and crews were strictly BOAC. The loss of these planes prevented the company from beginning Atlantic operations, as planned. It was that way all along — a steady battle against unforeseen attacks, and the revision, *re*revision, and *re-re*revision of plans that could only have been stopgaps in the first place. Yet the wartime record of BOAC is as inspiring as that of any flying unit, including anything the Americans could exhibit.

"Victory," said Prime Minister Churchill, "is the beautiful, bright-colored flower. Transport is the stem, without which it could never have blossomed. Yet even the military student, in his zeal to master the fascinating combination of the ancient conflict, often forgets the far more intricate complications of supply." [7]

In the days when Great Britain was fighting desperately and alone, BOAC was a central stem, or perhaps more accurately, a vine. The main stalk had its roots at Durban, South Africa. The longest tendril reached to Sydney, Australia. It was a U-shaped plant, curving through sixteen countries; working up through East and Central Africa to Khartoum and Cairo; thence over the old Kangaroo and Tiger routes to Palestine, Iraq, India, Burma, Siam, and Singapore; and finally, across the Sunda Sea to Australia. The shape of the airway had been determined by the fortunes of war. Strategists had foreseen the break with Italy and had rerouted the London–Cairo link across French territory in such an event. But no one expected France to fall so quickly. The loss of direct access to the United Kingdom from Africa left a severed BOAC to squirm for itself. Yet so carefully had plans been worked out that nine days after the Italian declaration of war, the so-called "Horseshoe Route" from Durban to Sydney was in full operation.

With the collapse of France and the denial by the Italians of a direct airway to Egypt, BOAC had to fly a hazardous route between London and Cairo. British transports avoided enemy patrols by flying far out to sea on the first leg of the trip to Lisbon. From that point the route hugged the coast of Africa to Lagos, under the shoulder of the continent ("Beware beware the Bight of Benin, where few come out and many go in"), then cut straight across the old trans-African airway to Khartoum and Cairo. It was the last section of this route that Pan American took over just before the United States went to war.

Over this route flew the transports loaded with all the vital machinery of war. British fighter pilots for General Montgomery's Big Push were hustled to the front by BOAC. Every type of warrior and technician arrived by air to swell the ranks of the "desert rats." There was even a song about them:

Soldier blokes and sailor blokes a'wingin'
    in to war;
A bloke to write it up and tell 'em what
    the fightin's for.
Some are calculatin' the distance to a drink,
But what I want to know is — what does
    the pilot think?
Is she dropping down too fast?
Hades, will the petrol last?
What does the blinkin' pilot think,
    a'sailin' through the sky?

Canadians, Australians, and Americans, too, all had a part in the ultimate African victory. While Generals Wavell and Auchinleck were struggling back and forth with General Rommel's Afrika Korps, a steady stream of planes, supplies, and men were being funneled into Egypt over the long air route. By the time General Montgomery started the decisive Nazi rout at Alamein in November of 1942, the British had overwhelming air support. This included entire squadrons of American planes delivered over the trans-African route. BOAC had an important part in this vast aerial undertaking. It brought in leaders who could rally the Free French of Equatorial Africa. It landed agents at obscure desert landing strips. It supplied garrisons isolated by the disruption of old services.

In other parts of the world the air line performed just as valiantly. When the Japanese cut the Malay section of the Horseshoe Route to Australia, BOAC repaired the damage as a spider mends its web. It ran a new strand around the affected area — in this case a 3,000-mile thread from Ceylon to the west coast of Australia — the longest scheduled water hop ever maintained. While continuing with its service of supply, it evacuated key personnel from Malaya. It helped maintain isolated pockets of British resistance until help could be sent. And more than any other agency, BOAC was responsible for the efficiency of the Atlantic ferry service.

Neutrality laws prevented the U.S. from delivering planes to belligerents, but British and Canadian crews bore the early brunt of transporting the big bombers to the United Kingdom.

BOAC trained the greenhorn ocean pilots that were soon to fly the planes across. It returned them to North America when they had handed over their planes to the theaters of war. For many months it provided the only regular transport service across the North Atlantic. BOAC brought Prime Minister Churchill home from the Washington Conference of January, 1942 — which was evidence of the confidence placed in the air line by British officials. It operated a nightly service to Sweden and Russia, carrying agents and dispatches through the center of the Nazi blockade.

This was British Overseas Airways Corporation, the air line that was to be the greatest rival of American operators in the struggle for postwar air routes. It was a hard-hitting, able, and gallant antagonist — an organization of fine tradition, and one that was ready to meet all comers. Among American pilots who had served with the British, it was customary to deride "them crazy Limies." The British airmen were accused of everything from sloppy flying to incompetent operation of equipment. No doubt the British said the same of American pilots. Mostly this was based on the same instinct that makes one gorilla beat his chest when another is in the vicinity. The record of two wars proves that the British certainly are not inferior in the air. One senses their efficiency in watching them perform their tasks. They carry into the air the same traditions that have made them great upon the sea. Air crews observe customs and protocol incomprehensible to those who have no experience in an exacting profession. They speak with pride of the planes they fly, calling them by name rather than by number — *Cleo, Corsair, Caledonia,* and *Golden Hind.* This spirit was shown by an incident that took place on a westbound crossing of the Atlantic during the war.

In mid-ocean one winter night Captain O. P. Jones, the black-bearded master of the Boeing flying boat, *Berwick,* was working up his log at the pilot's seat. The binnacle light took that moment to burn out, and so Captain Jones turned over the controls to his co-pilot and moved back to the engineer's desk, where he could work under the reading lamp. Engineer Stack made room for the captain by sitting on the floor with his feet through the hatch. At that moment, all four engines cut out simultaneously. Any airman can tell you what happens to a pilot's insides when he hears the motors stop. (It was discovered later that, in this case, the co-pilot had accidentally pulled the master engine switch while adjusting the trim of the plane.) *Berwick* dropped eight thousand feet before the motors were brought back to life again. But before striding forward to the rescue of the frantic co-pilot, Captain Jones closed his log book with deliberation, placed the pencil carefully in the little loop designed for it, and turning to the engineer, remarked: "Strangely quiet, isn't it, Mr. Stack," — an expression that made the rounds of the hangars like "I hain't impressed" or "Sighted sub sank same." The formality and understatement tell why it would be foolish for Americans to underestimate the British on the peacetime commercial air routes.

REFERENCES

1. Sydney E. Veale, *Tomorrow's Airliners, Airways, and Airports* (London, 1945), p. 12.
2. *Parliamentary Debates (Hansard)*, House of Lords, Fifth Series, February 10, 1943, Vol. 125, p. 1008.
3. *Reports of the Civil Aerial Transport Committee* (Cmd. 9218), London, 1918.
4. C. G. Grey, *The Civil Air War* (London, 1945), p. 201.
5. Air Ministry, *Report of the Committee of Inquiry into Civil Aviation* (The Cadman Report, Cmd. 5685), London, 1938.
6. Ministry of Information, *An Outline of British Pioneering in Civil Air Transport,* London, 1945.
7. Air Ministry, *Merchant Airmen* (London, 1946), p. 71.

A NOTE ON SOURCES

For a summary of the technical aspects of commercial aviation at the end of the war, see Sydney E. Veale, *Tomorrow's Airliners, Airways, and Airports,* London, 1945. A full discussion of British policy and early history of aviation can be found in *Reports of the Civil Aerial Transport Committee with Appendices* (Cmd. 9218), London, 1918. Supplementary to this account are the following pertinent documents: Air Ministry, *Agreement . . . providing for . . . the Imperial Air Transport Company, Ltd.,* (Cmd. 2010), London, 1923; Air Ministry and General Post Office, *Empire Air Mail Scheme,* (Cmd. 5676), London, 1938; Air Ministry, *Report of the Committee of Inquiry into Civil Aviation* (The Cadman Report, Cmd. 5685), London, 1938; Air Ministry, *Report of the Committee to Consider the Development of Civil Aviation in the United Kingdom* (The Maybury Report, Cmd. 5351), London, 1937; *Parliamentary Debates (Hansard),* Fifth Series, Vol. 125, House of Lords, February 10, 1943; Air Ministry, *Civil Air Transport Subsidies Committee* (Cmd. 1811), London, 1923; Air Ministry, *Agreement with Imperial Airways, Ltd.* (Cmd. 2574), London, 1926; *Hansard,* House of Lords, Vol. 127, April, 1943; Air Ministry, *Merchant Airmen,* account of British Civil Aviation 1939–1944, Ministry of Information, London, 1946; C. G. Grey, *The Civil Air War,* London, 1945; Brigadier General Sir Osborne Mance and J. E. Wheeler, *International Air Transport,* (especially chapters seven, eight, and eleven), London, 1944; Oliver J. Lissitzyn, *International Air Transport and National Policy,* (especially chapters one through sixteen), New York, 1942. Information from this chapter was also obtained from correspondence with C. G. Grey and from interviews with British operations personnel at Cairo, Karachi, and Calcutta.

TO ARMS; HERE COME THE BRITISH

BOAC was to be the weapon of the British in their fight for a share of postwar air commerce, but even its sponsors were not certain as to how it should be used. It was called a "chosen instrument" of the government, although it did not have an exclusive franchise to operate on empire airways. True, BOAC did have the sole right to government aid (which was the same as an exclusive franchise, practically speaking) but any other air line could fly parallel routes, if it could find some way to finance itself. Government mail payments applied only to the international routes, however. Local and trans-Channel services remained outside the coils of BOAC. Furthermore, the British chosen instrument was to work in cooperation with other Commonwealth air lines — in effect, in competition with them. Was it actually a monopoly, then, as opponents maintained?

"At any rate," said Lord Beaverbrook in defending the company before the House of Lords in 1944, "it is still what it was. It is fixed by statute, and until Parliament decides to repeal the statute, the chosen instrument is just what it used to be. Well, do you want to keep it? If not, what do you propose in its place?" [1]

At the time the Lord Privy Seal asked this question the British had already made the decision. They had committed themselves to the chosen instrument, but not without misgiving. The Honorable W. R. D. Perkins, a Conservative, inquired of the House: "Are we really wise in concentrating after the war on one chosen instrument? Would it not be better, in view of what is going to happen after the war, to have at least two, or possibly three, chosen instruments?" [2]

The quotation implies that in the United Kingdom, as in the United States, national policy in regard to international aviation was under close scrutiny at this time. Extreme opposition to the prevailing policy was expressed by Frederick Montague in the long debate on civil aviation. Mr. Montague had been Undersecretary of State for Air and Parliamentary Secretary for the Ministry of Transport. His remarks are therefore of special interest.

If civil aviation is to be used for the sowing of more dragon's teeth, then to hell with civil aviation as far as I am concerned ... My only point was that if we are to undertake a fierce commercial competition with America, and America turns all her resources upon that competition, we cannot hope to beat America. . . . Therefore I deplored the tendency to suggest, as some honorable members seem to be doing, that we must go in for competition on commercial lines which would not help in the cause of civil aviation in this country or in the world and would certainly not help the cause of international peace.[3]

Mr. Montague's did not appear to be the popular view. In both the United States and in Great Britain, merchant airmen prepared for the civil air war. Both nations sought the most effective means of encouraging their respective enterprises. Great Britain turned to the chosen instrument; America to regulated competition. But the point is, in neither country was opinion unanimous. In the long run, the positions taken by the two nations were determined by economics and by tradition. The British believed they had given competition in air commerce a fair trial and that it had failed the test. And so they concentrated all their resources in one international air carrier.

In the final analysis, what the British were defending was not so much their air *routes* as their aircraft *industry*. They were interested primarily in protecting their own international airways against foreign competition so as to provide a certain outlet for their own manufacturers. To the Americans there was something sinful about this policy of sacrificing the spur of competition for the benefit of selfish interests. Americans were likely to depict British aviation leaders as Colonel Blimps, sitting around in overstuffed club chairs and calling for government restrictions whenever a progressive foreign operator threatened to take business away by means of superior equipment that these plutocratic Britishers were too stingy to provide. The British, on the other hand, saw the American as an extravagant and ruthless rival, spending recklessly and wasting irreplaceable resources. The British looked upon the American policy in the air as little short of anarchy. What the British wanted was law and order in the air lanes.

The British had good reason to be apprehensive of American competition. In 1938 the empire had accounted for about 18 per cent of the world's total air traffic. U.S. air lines at that time were carrying about 45 per cent of the total air commerce. But whereas more than half the total of British operations was international, only one-ninth of U.S. air traffic passed beyond our borders. By 1943 this proportion had changed. The British were then flying only 12 per cent of the world's air commerce, while the Americans accounted for 72 per cent. In five years American international air transportation had increased so rapidly that our operators were carrying twice the volume of the combined British and European air traffic.[4] U.S. domestic air lines alone carried more than 50 per cent of the world's air traffic, and Americans were carrying more than one-fifth of the international air commerce.

No one expected the United States to hold that lead after the war. Indeed, it was possible that the British would eventually fly more route miles, simply because they had more scattered areas to serve. But route miles are not an accurate measure of air commerce. They tell no more about air traffic than rails across the desert tell about train schedules. Only ton-miles (one ton carried one mile is a ton-mile) can serve as a traffic yardstick, and on this basis, the United States was likely to remain ahead. Americans had the equipment, the money, the resources, and above all, the traffic required for successful operations. Thus, although British and American routes were nearly equal in extent in 1943. BOAC plane frequencies were only about one-third those of the U.S. international carriers.

The British made the first move to regain some of this traffic immediately after the completion of the successful Tunisian campaign, and the first evidence that the tide might be turning in favor of the allies. Now, said Lord Rothermere, publisher of the London *Daily Mail,* and former director of Imperial Airways, the time was ripe to develop a postwar civil aviation policy. The cornerstone, he declared, must be a working agreement with the United States. The most important part of that agreement, he believed, would be a contract verifying the understanding reached by President Roosevelt and Prime Minister Churchill for the United States to supply Great Britain with needed transport planes as soon as the emergency was past.

This was a delicate problem and should be settled before victory complicated the problem, added Lord Strabolgi. "Otherwise you will get some isolationist saying ... in Washington that 'the British are trying to get transport planes from us under Lease-Lend and will enter into cutthroat competition with our American lines after the war'."[5]

The British hoped to whittle down the advantages of the Americans by means of a world aviation authority. They held up the U.S. Civil Aeronautics Board as a model for such a world organization. Americans liked the CAB, but they were not enthusiastic about the British suggestion. Indeed, they saw through the scheme at once. In an international CAB made up of representatives from all the United Nations, other countries, less favored than the United States, could outvote the American members. In other words, the Americans, who were "fit, willing, and able" to bring the benefits of air service to all parts of the world sooner than anyone else, would be held back by the less fortunate nations until their air systems had been perfected. What the American wanted was a modified form of free competition so that his advantage in equipment could be realized before the others could build up to it. This was a curious inversion of philosophies, for Great Britain, traditionally committed to free trade, was now sponsoring strict regulation on an international level, whereas the United States, long an exponent of regulation in transportation, was now arguing for international free trade, or at least a modified form of it.

The British had made this stand after realizing that they would have to battle for peacetime routes while they were in an enfeebled condition. The cause of the complaint could be diagnosed as a pronounced swelling of their national pride, aggravated by an unbalanced diet of transport aircraft. Since this condition of transport plane starvation was the result of the agreement between Mr. Roosevelt and Mr. Churchill providing for the concentration of British industry on combat aircraft, Britons believed it only fair for the Americans to feed back equipment — and more, that the Americans handicap themselves in the coming race. That was the sporting thing, since the lack of British transport planes was no fault of the British — or was it?

The record of Imperial Airways showed that the British had failed to perfect adequate equipment long before the Roosevelt-Churchill agreement. British aircraft builders simply did not have time for civilian production in those days. As a result, Imperial was outclassed by all its rivals. On the other hand, the British had proved during the war that they could build marvelous planes and engines when they put their minds to it. The Spitfire, Mosquito, and Lancaster, as well as many other successful craft, showed what British designers and engineers could do. British Rolls-Royce engines powered the fastest U.S. fighter plane. Radar devices, power turrets, and turbo-jet propulsion were other British contributions to aviation. The same ingenuity turned to commercial uses might produce the efficient transports the nation needed. It would take time, that was all.

With the first glimmering of victory, the British aviation leaders began to agitate for a revival of the air-transport industry. Spurred by the clamor, Prime Minister Churchill appointed his Lord Privy Seal as head of the Civil Air Transport Committee (CAT). The new chief of civil aviation was Lord Beaverbrook, a go-getting newspaper publisher and member of the inner circle of the government, known as the War Cabinet Committee. CAT's chairman had three main responsibilities. He was to coordinate other agencies of the government concerned with aviation matters. He was to work out international and empire agreements relating to air routes. And he was charged with organizing a new ministry of civil aviation.

At the same time, Lord Brabazon of Tara was authorized to study the equipment needs of the industry. Soon this subcommittee announced its program for supplying transport aircraft. One of these new planes was to be called the "Brabazon"—a 100-ton transport capable of cruising at 250 miles an hour over the longest sections of the world routes. Since it would take two years to produce even a prototype of such a monster, two smaller, faster, plane types were to appear first. These were planned as the Tudor I and Tudor II. It takes time to produce any type of transport, however, and the British realized it would be several years before their industry could meet the foreign challenges. Peter Masefield, civil air attaché in Washington in 1946, estimated it would be 1950 before the British could hope to catch up. Then, said he, "We will have planes the equal of any in the world." [6]

That was a long time to wait. Meanwhile, civil air-transport plans were delayed by war priorities. Lord Brabazon summed up the impatience and frustration of the air-transport industry when he spoke· out at a luncheon in 1944 commemorating the twenty-fifth anniversary of British commercial aviation. Sir Archibald Sinclair, Secretary of State for Air, and the man held responsible for restricting civil aircraft production, was also present. Lord Brabazon, who is noted for his blunt expression, left no doubt as to his contempt for the way bureaucrats were stifling air transportation. He declared that air transportation was either important or unimportant to the war effort. If unimportant, it should be ignored altogether. If important, and he pointed to the American record, why was not the empire building up its fleet, now that the "fight or die" days were over? Six hundred bombers converted to transport use would suffice until the Brabazon Plan materialized, he insisted. That was only a "fortnight's output" for British factories. Turning to Sir Archibald, Lord Brabazon blurted: "You are being maneuvered off the earth by what is happening. If you are playing for a fall, you are going about it the right way. That is all I have to say to you, Mr. Secretary of State."[7]

Lord Brabazon may have been a little pessimistic. The British were slowly working out a postwar aviation policy. If anything, they were ahead of the United States on that. True, there was uncertainty at the start. A small but determined group known as the Little Englanders insisted that the entire empire should be sealed off from foreign competition. They might eventually have been willing to grant foreign operators rights to refuel, or to make repairs at British bases, but they would certainly have refused any commercial privileges, such as the right to discharge or pick up traffic. There was plenty of precedent for such restrictions. Most nations have denied "cabotage" to foreign shippers — cabotage being the right to engage in commerce between points *within the national borders*. Foreign vessels, for example, cannot pick up cargoes in New York for discharge in New Orleans. In like manner, the Little Englanders would merely have extended cabotage to include all territory in the far-flung British Empire.

Americans did not dispute the right of the British to deny cabotage privileges to foreigners on route between the British Isles and the colonies. To object to that restriction would have meant that the United States, in turn, would have to open up routes to foreigners between the United States and such places as Hawaii, Puerto Rico, and at that time, the Philippines too. But when the Little Englanders demanded exclusive rights on routes between the mother country and the Dominions, they were talking to an unfriendly audience. For the Dominions insisted they had the right to regulate their own foreign commerce. They might even some day wish to restrict British air lines. Most Commonwealth operators therefore had little patience with the philosophy of the Little Englanders.

The truth is, the policy of the Little Englanders would have injured British air commerce far more than it would have protected the individual operator. For if the empire shut its door on American air lines, it would thereby lose the richest traffic market in the world. American tourists, carried by U.S. air lines expert in such promotion, would bring in more money to the empire than would be saved by shutting out competition. The Little Englanders, therefore, not only met stiff opposition from the Dominions, but also from the planners at home.

It was a more moderate school that slowly formulated British air-transport policy. This group believed in protecting the internal lines. It would not allow uncontrolled competition on the Red Routes connecting the members of the Commonwealth. On the other hand, there was no objection to having foreign operators serve British points after a fashion, so long as the interlopers behaved seemingly. The moderates had no patience with Americans who demanded exclusive rights to the British bases built up with lend-lease money. They looked upon lend-lease as a mutual defense expedient that in no way changed the sovereignty of the territory—and they were entirely right. They also believed in the right of inter-empire cabotage regulation as a means of commercial protection. But they would have bargained some of these rights for recriprocal privileges.

From this divergent opinion emerged a postwar policy. It was first announced while the bombs were still falling on British cities. Captain A. G. Lamplugh, who was interested in working out a program as head of the largest aviation insurance company in the empire, saw that stability could be achieved only after British aviation began to operate under a plan. In September, 1942, he gathered together a group of aviation friends. All were noted for the freshness of their ideas and for their frankness in expressing them. They met casually for frugal suppers and remained to chat far into the night. One member of this group was Peter Masefield, secretary of the committee and author of the two Lamplugh Reports. Masefield, an aeronautical engineer, later became Lord Beaverbrook's special adviser. His reports, therefore, assume an importance that would not otherwise be attached to such unofficial documents.

The Lamplugh Reports helped to coagulate opinion into official demand for the organization of the new Ministry of Civil Aviation, of which Lord Londonderry was parliamentary advocate. Undoubtedly the reports spurred the investigation of civil aviation ordered by the Prime Minister under the supervision of The Beaver. Finally, they helped reduce the U.S. and British problems to a common basis for discussions on a governmental level.

The first Lamplugh report appeared in May, 1943. It recommended as "urgent" the immediate crystallization of a government policy on civil air transport, with particular reference to monopoly and subsidy. Also "urgent" was international cooperation on landing rights and the use of air bases. It asked for a separate ministry for civil aviation on an equal basis with the military body. As its "cornerstone for future peace" the report emphasized the necessity for a "complete agreement" with the United States.[8]

The second report was published a year later, after Masefield had become Lord Beaverbrook's adviser. It re-emphasized the need of international understanding on traffic regulations, navigational aids, and the establishment of cooperative weather stations. Significantly, it asked for a "reconsideration" of the chosen-instrument policy, to which the government was already committed. It suggested instead a plan that sounded very much like the American system of regulated competition. Clearly the committee was trying hard to reach an accord with United States opinion. That of course subjected it to the charge of being pro-American, but apparently the idea was merely to work out a kind of truce between the American and British factions. Upon the relations of the United States and Great Britain, the report concluded, would depend whether the airplane was to be a curse or a blessing to society. The seeds were now planted, it declared. They would produce rivalry and dispute, or good will and cooperation.[9]

Before the British Commonwealth could come to terms with the United States it had to present a united front. This was not as easy to achieve as one might suppose. That one of the Dominions, at least, had no desire to be "taken in" by the United Kingdom civil aviation program is indicated by the visit to the U.S. State Department of the Canadian Ministry Counselor, L. B. Pearson. On September 28, 1943, Pearson informed U.S. officials that the Canadians had been invited to London for an aviation conference on the following week. He declared that his government was not much interested in the meeting, but he had at last agreed to send a representative "to explore the subject," yet to make no commitments. Pearson said he was certain his government did not desire an Imperial transport agreement—that is, an inter-Commonwealth pact. He was informing the State Department of this attitude so that there would be no later misunderstanding as to Canada's part in the discussions. Pearson wished to assure the U.S. officials that the London Conference did not imply, necessarily, that the Commonwealth was "ganging up" on the Americans.[10]

This must have been something of a relief to our aviation spokesmen. Had the members of the Commonwealth reached an agreement on air transportation, they might indeed have forced the United States to modify plans. The Dominions Conference in London was decidedly only "exploratory," as Pearson predicted, however. Indeed, it was something of a farce. In his usual slap-bang way, The Beaver had whisked along the delegates so fast that most of them did not even understand the issues that were up for discussion. After two and a half days of secret session the representatives were homeward bound again. If there had been "complete agreement," as Lord Beaverbrook later announced, it could only have been complete agreement to disagree. It is significant, however, that the Dominions Conference was the first international meeting to bring into the open the issue of the "Five Freedoms."

The Five Freedoms was a phrase that was to be bandied about in the following months wherever operators and statesmen gathered. It is the popular name for a set of privileges that a government may grant a foreign air line. These five freedoms, or "privileges," as they should be called, include the following: (1) the right to cross through the air space above a foreign territory without stopping; (2) the right to land for fuel, repairs, or for strictly non-commercial purposes; (3) the right to discharge passengers and cargo from the home country at the foreign airport; (4) the right to pick up passengers and cargo at a foreign airport for transportation back to the home country; and (5) the right to discharge passengers and cargo from the home country at a foreign airport, and then to pick up traffic bound for a third, fourth, or any number of other countries.

Most of the countries were ready to be argued into the first two concessions—the Two Freedoms—without much trouble. Eventually, even the third and fourth freedoms were generally acceptable. But the fifth freedom was not very popular in Europe. It was favored by the Americans and it was recognized by our good neighbors in Central and South America. The Five Freedoms became part of U.S. civil aviation policy because it was believed that unrestricted traffic was the only means by which Americans could take advantage of their special aviation assets to build up a truly world-wide service. For example, if an American plane started out from La Guardia Field with fifty passengers, half of them would probably get off at Heath Row, in London. Half of the remaining passengers might disembark at Paris. Others would drop off at airports along the world route. By the time the plane reached India, only one or two of the original passengers, or more likely, none at all, would still be aboard. An air line had to be able to pick up passengers along the way, if it expected to operate economically on international airways. That was just what the air lines of the less favored nations feared at first. It looked to them as though the international U.S. company would snatch all their traffic, if the fifth freedom were to be permitted.

The British led the opposition to the plan. They held that an air line reaching half way around the world could be operated profitably by what they called the telescope principle. They denied that they needed fifth-freedom traffic to fly successfully to, say, Buenos Aires from London. Instead, they would schedule as many flights to the first stop, Rio perhaps, as traffic would support. Half as often they would schedule a plane all the way through to Buenos Aires. It would carry the traffic accumulated for the less popular run. Planes would thus fly loaded, regulating frequencies according to the traffic needs. The British saw no reason why the Americans could not do the same on the long world routes. They said the U.S. argument for fifth-freedom traffic was groundless, unless, as they suspected all along, the Americans intended to operate more planes than the traffic justified. This, they maintained, nullified all the American talk about economies. Of course what the British had in mind was just as selfish. Under the telescope plan, U.S. air lines could take only U.S. traffic to India. American planes could not pick up passengers in London for the Indian flight. That traffic would go via BOAC, which the British believed was fair enough. Such a plan did not please the American operators at all. The U.S. method for building up a route was to provide service that was always a little more lavish than the traffic warranted.

Shortly after the Dominions Conference, President Roosevelt and Prime Minister Churchill reached their own private understanding on civil aviation. The Lord Privy Seal declared in Parliamentary debates a few months later that he and the President had "reached a considerable measure of agreement" on freedom of the air, "subject to certain conditions."[11] Probably the two had discussed only the Four Freedoms. Certainly Mr. Churchill's record did not indicate any sympathy for the American plan, nor did the statements of other British leaders at the time.[12]

There was only one way that the British could have been lured into accepting the fifth-freedom principle. The price would have been an agreement with the United States for the imposition of quota restrictions to guarantee a share of the international traffic to each nation. As the British reasoned, there were three ways of maintaining international routes fairly and economically. One was by limiting subsidies, so that the wealthy nations did not have undue advantage. On the whole, the United States aviation representatives would have approved of that, but until we were assured of our world routes, subsidy, or the threat of it, was one of our best bargaining points. Less acceptable to Americans were the two other means suggested by the British for controlling world air traffic so as to prevent one country from taking all the traffic. One of these suggestions was the quota system, arbitrarily limiting each nation to a percentage of world traffic. The other plan was by international regulation of fares. If the British could be certain of a proportionate share of air traffic, or if they could be certain that fares would be sufficiently high to bring in enough revenue they believed they could hold their own against American operators. No doubt they were right. If Americans could pick up only so much traffic and could not offer service at lower cost than competitors, there was very little threat to the British even if fifth-freedom traffic were to be agreed upon. Obviously, the Americans had little use for such schemes, but the British were enthusiastic over the possibilities.

"I repeat these principles," Lord Beaverbrook told the House of Lords in the spring of 1944, when he was outlining British civil aviation policy. "The elimination of uneconomic competition, the setting up of national quotas in international air transport, [and] equilibrium between transport capacity and the traffic offering on any international route. These must be the foundations of any enlightened approach to this subject in the future."[13]

This was the situation as the British prepared to demand a full share of world air commerce at a proposed meeting with the Americans in the fall of 1944. They were definitely on the defensive. They knew they must have protection by regulation —regulation by agreement with the Number One air power of the world. For them salvation rested upon the principles of internationalism, a word then in vogue. On paper, internationalism appeared to be a noble concept. Others were not so certain. "I wish it could be realized that internationalism is not an answer to anything," one of our most thoughtful statesmen confided to his diary. "Either it means arbitrary action, or it engenders action on some principle of law and equity."[14]

All right, replied the British, then just what alternative did the Americans propose?

REFERENCES

1. *Hansard,* Lords, Vol. 131, May 10, 1944, pp. 694, 787.
2. *Congressional Record,* Appendix, Vol. 89, Part 9, December 17, 1942, pp. 498 ff.
3. *Hansard,* Commons, Vol. 390, June 1, 1943, pp. 92, 127.
4. Grover Loening, *Air Transportation in the British Empire,* a brochure prepared for the Defense Supplies Corporation, (Washington, 1945).
5. *Hansard,* Lords, Vol. 125, February 10, 1943, p. 1000.
6. Interview with Peter Masefield, civil air attaché, British Embassy, Washington, D. C., June 27, 1946.
7. "Civil Aviation's Birthday," *Flight,* August 31, 1944, p. 233.
8. *First Report of an Independent Committee on the Future of Civil Aviation* (The Lamplugh Report), London, May, 1943. See source note on p. 121.
9. *Second Report of an Independent Committee on the Future of Civil Aviation,* London, May, 1944.
10. From the private journal of A. A. Berle, Jr.
11. "Foreign News Supplement," *American Aviation Daily,* Series B., December 8, 1943.
12. *Hansard,* Lords, Vol. 130, January 19, 1944, p. 462. Lord Beaverbrook cited a speech of a U.S. Government aviation spokesman and added, ". . . complete freedom of the air in the present state of the world might result in commercial anarchy."
13. *Hansard,* Lords, Vol. 131, May 10, 1944, pp. 694 ff.
14. From the private journal of A. A. Berle, Jr., assistant secretary of state until November, 1944.

A NOTE ON SOURCES

Most of the material on the development of the British civil aviation policy has been gleaned from the long series of debates in Parliament. This material can be found under "Civil Aviation" in *Hansard,* Fifth Series, House of Lords, Vols. 125, 126, 127, 130, 131, and House of Commons, Vol. 390. An economic comparison of British and American aviation appears in a brochure by Grover Loening, *Air Transportation in the British Empire,* published by the Defense Supplies Corporation, Government Printing Office, 1945. The following citations from contemporary periodicals also may be useful: an editorial, "America's Lead," in *Flight,* September 28, 1944, p. 329; the London *Times,* December 18, 1942, comment on aviation debates; "Civil Aviation's Birthday," in *Flight,* August 31, 1944, pp. 161 ff.; "Debates Clarify British Postwar Air Policy," *American Aviation,* June 1, 1944, p. 17; and "Foreign News Supplement," *American Aviation Daily,* December 8, 1943. The development of British civil aviation policy begins with the *First (and Second) Report of an Independent Committee on the Future of Civil Aviation* (The Lamplugh Reports), May, 1943, and May, 1944, respectively. Lamplugh is a British insurance broker who made an independent investigation. Because Peter Masefield, later Beaverbrook's secretary, was a member of the group, the investigation had some significance, but as a private undertaking, it is not listed in the Commands. See also Air Ministry, *International Air Transport* (the first "White Paper") (Cmd. 6561), London, October, 1944. Information for the chapter was also obtained from interviews with Peter Masefield, attaché for the Ministry of Civil Aviation, British Embassy, Washington, D. C.; L. Welch Pogue, chairman of the Civil Aeronautics Board during the period described; and Adolf A. Berle, Jr., assistant secretary of state at the time.

FREE AIR AND HOT AIR

I F YOU wish to avoid foreign collision, you had better abandon the ocean," Henry Clay warned the House of Representatives in 1812.[1] Had the War Hawk statesman lived in the modern era, he might just as well have added "and the air, too." In 1944, as in 1812, Great Britain was the nation with which we were "colliding," and the issue at stake was "freedom of the air," just as it had been "freedom of the seas" in 1812. These were glib phrases imperfectly understood by most Americans. They were used to stir up public reaction when they often had no meaning at all.*

The pattern of commercial history has been as unchanging as the law of supply and demand. First, a new area is grabbed by a daring promoter. Then this area is exploited as the material prize of discovery. Next, the exploiter tries to perpetuate his advantage by demanding special privileges in order to keep out possible rivals. If the enterprise is controlled by an individual, he tries to set up a monopoly for himself and his heirs. If the enterprise is controlled by a nation, it establishes a trade

---

*It is curious, for example, that the New England states were opposed to the War of 1812 and voted solidly for DeWitt Clinton, the peace candidate for President, although these states, where shipping was an important industry, might be supposed to have been interested in freedom of the seas. On the other hand, the West and South, with little direct interest in shipping, were all for war with Great Britain. The point is that various groups used the expression "freedom of the seas" as a catchall for all sorts of anti-British feeling.

empire and denies commercial rights to other nations. This sweeping exercise of self-interest usually leads to a final phase: so much antagonism is aroused against the favored exploiter that rivals "gang up" to force concessions. Invariably the monopoly or trade empire crumbles under the pressure. Such was the fate of the great charter companies responsible for so much colonization in the heydey of British mercantilism. Such was the fate of the European nations that once controlled vast trade empires. But, sometimes, before such a cycle begins over again, nations discover that the strain of preserving artificial trade barriers has brought them to the verge of ruin.

The right to use the waste spaces of the world for unhindered commercial transit was an important issue in 1493 when Spain and Portugal were leading maritime nations. Each had claimed large areas of the world by right of discovery and exploration. Each country sought to establish exclusive trading spheres for the benefit of its merchant princes. In this conflict for control of trade empires the peace of the world was threatened by the greed of the two maritime nations. For this reason the Vatican tried to settle the dispute between Spain and Porugal by arbitration. Pope Alexander VI was no doubt certain that he had brought about peace in his time when by papal bull (*Inter Caetera*) in 1493 he drew his "demarcation line" separating the commercial spheres of the two rivals. There were two revisions of this agreement. The second, in 1494, known as the Treaty of Tordesillas, split the commercial world between Spain and Portugal. In the Western Hemisphere the line extended south from the tip of Greenland. Everything east of that line was reserved for Portuguese exploitation; everything west of the line was to be the land of opportunity for the Spaniards. The treaty was not concerned with the sovereignty of the allotted areas, which were not necessarily to be under the flags of the respective rivals. It was only an agreement whereby the commercial rivals promised to respect each other's fields of interest. The truce might have been effective had Spain and Portugal continued as the dominant maritime nations. Unfortunately for them, they were soon challenged by other nations, notably the

Dutch and the English. These haters of Papists, Spaniards, and regimentation refused to recognize a treaty that did not "cut them in" on the commercial pie. The Dutch were particularly aggressive in their demands for unrestricted commerce, and as part of their program of rebellion they insisted on ready access to all parts of the world—the right to travel freely on the high seas. In 1604, therefore, they announced a revolutionary concept of international trade.

Daring Dutch seafarers had started to tap the wealth of the fabulous East Indies. This was in the Portuguese sphere and the Dutch were treated as poachers. Disputes arose on those distant seas — disputes that could be settled only by cannon and cutlass. In one of the many engagements the Dutch captured a Portuguese caravel and brought it home under a prize crew. There was an argument over disposition of the spoils and the verdict hinged upon whether or not the Portuguese had the right to seal off extensive areas from foreign commercial penetration. In the Dutch prize court that day a new doctrine was announced—the doctrine that the high seas were available to all peaceful traders. This was the beginning of the battle for freedom of the seas.

The Dutch argument was presented by a brilliant student of international law named Huigh van Groot, or Grotius, as he is known to the jurists. Grotius had already discussed some of his ideas on international law in a significant work entitled, *De Jure Belli et Pacis* (*Laws Relating to War and Peace*) but the book by which he is most generally known was his *Mare Liberum* or *Freedom of the Sea*. According to Grotius, the waters of the open ocean belonged to *all* nations. Therefore, to hinder traffic on the high seas was to violate international law.

Curiously, the British, later the strongest defenders of the free seas concept, were at first violently opposed to the doctrine. This opposition was largely the result of the intense rivalry between the British and the Dutch, but it was mainly based on the fact that the British commercial dominance was not apparent at the time. For in general it follows that the nation with the greatest trade resources is the nation most in favor of

free seas. Even the Spaniards and Portugese might have come
around to this philosophy, had they not been so evenly matched
as rivals. At any rate, the British had no use for freedom of the
seas when Grotius first expounded his views. Answering the
"open sea" challenge of the Dutch jurists, the Englishman,
John Selden, wrote *Mare Clausum,* which took exactly the opposite view. For two hundred years the British advocated the
"closed sea" principle. Not until the British were secure on
land and sea did they reverse this stand officially. In a great
decision handed down by Lord Stowell in 1817, the Court of
Admiralty recognized freedom of the seas as a governing policy
for the Empire.

This discussion of freedom of the seas is not at all irrelevant
to the argument on freedom of the air. The two doctrines
actually are very different, but they are always being compared
with each other. At any rate, the policy of freedom of the seas
suited the British in the nineteenth century as freedom of the
air suited the United States in the twentieth. Lord Stowell's
verdict suited the British in 1817 because they insisted upon
going everywhere with their great merchant navy. By 1817 the
British had little to fear from any other martime power.
Britain had made herself mistress of the seas by means of her
merchant fleet.* That the British sponsored freedom of the
seas, then, not so much as a principle, but as an economic
doctrine is verified by the way they worked out air policy gen-
erations later. They did not follow the same course in air
commerce as in sea commerce because the economic factors
were different.

With no powerful nation to act as sponsor, freedom of the
air languished until about 1944. A few faltering steps had
been made in that direction, it is true. In 1902, a year before
the first airplane flight at Kittyhawk, M. Paul Fauchille had
introduced a resolution at the Brussels Institut de Droit International asking that freedom of the air be *considered* by the
legal body. Response was favorable, but when members met

---

*It was not the British Navy that made Great Britain a sea power. The
merchant fleet built up that power, and the Navy was merely its guardian.

again in 1906 they had had time to ponder the potential dangers of the machine the Wrights had given the world. Air sovereignty—national control of the air space within borders—was accepted in 1906 as a much safer doctrine. The closed sky concept was generally recognized from then on.[2]

After World War I aviation leaders tried again to open up the skies to peaceful aircraft. The opportunity to work out an international agreement was presented at the Paris Peace Conference. A special subcommittee was even appointed to draft a "convention," or set of international regulations governing air commerce. The war had demonstrated the threat of aircraft to national security, however, and as a result there was little relaxation of the closed sky restrictions. All that the delegates would concede was what they called "the right of innocent passage"—a pretty phrase, but meaningless to the air merchantman. All it granted was the right of *private* aircraft to fly over the air spaces of signatory nations. Even this concession was criticised. The United States would not even sign the Paris Convention on aviation, although in 1928 it did finally agree to a similar convention drafted at Havana. Unfortunately no one paid much attention to the Havana Convention.

The only way an American operator could push out the air frontier was by making private, or unilateral agreements with the governments of each country along the proposed route. That was how Pan American Airways developed most of its Latin-American system. Where air transportation was a necessity such agreements were easy to obtain. But in Europe, where every air line was an agency of its government, negotiations of this type were difficult to work out. Jealousy, fear, and the relative unimportance of air transportation held back route development for years.

It is unfortunate that freedom of the air means many things to many persons. For that reason it is difficult to arrive at agreement. To some it may mean only the unhampered transit of aircraft through the air spaces outside national borders—spaces comparable to the open ocean. Others assume that freedom of the air means the right of commercial aircraft to fly to any point in the world. Somewhere between these two extremes lies the generally accepted policy. Few would deny the right of aircraft to fly peaceably in the spaces above oceans. Even at the height of British dominance, freedom of the seas was never understood as the right to navigate inland waterways or the coastal waters of foreign countries. Freedom of the seas extended only to the waterway ports. There was no more reason for allowing foreign aircraft to wander all over our skies than there was for letting foreign vessels ply our rivers and lakes unchecked. What the open sky advocate had in mind when he used the phrase was not indiscriminate flying by foreign aircraft, but access to designated airports along prescribed airways.

That was more than most military men were ready to concede. They were afraid that air transports were only potential bombers, ready to deliver a paralyzing surprise blow at the bidding of an unscrupulous ruler. At first there may have been some slight justification for this fear. Bombers in the early days were about the same as air transports fitted with racks and guns. They were like war vessels in the days of John Paul Jones, when the difference between a merchant and a navy ship was in the number of cannon aboard. Today this difference no longer holds. There is no more similarity between the modern air transport and bomber than there is between the *Queen Mary* and the *U.S.S. Missouri*. Air transports may be implements of war, it is true. They are to air power what the merchant marine is to the navy, but no one suggests scuttling our commercial vessels just because they supply the training, personnel, and transportation necessary in wartime.

Others have been afraid of espionage, if foreign aircraft are allowed to fly within national borders, even though restricted to specified air lanes. One might as well forbid foreign shipping in our great harbors for fear foreign spies might photograph vital dock facilities. Such fears are exaggerated. Espionage does not depend upon such obvious devices. The Japanese, for example, had never flown commercially within a thousand miles of Pearl Harbor, yet they knew all about our strength and disposition when the time came to strike.

The real fear of international air transportation is based on possible loss of trade advantages. An American exponent of the closed sky doctrine might argue this way: "If the United States has the greatest traffic possibilities and resources in the world, why should we let foreign air lines take passengers and cargoes out of this country at the expense of our own operators? Was it not enough that the foreigners reaped rich profits from the passengers and commerce our air lines were capable of bringing them?" The answer, the spokesman would tell you, is to keep our rivals out of our skies.

But air sovereignty can work against us as well as for us. It has given small countries as well as large nations the power to disrupt world air commerce. Thus, Imperial Airways had to delay extension of the Kangaroo Route to Australia because the Italians, Turks, and Persians insisted on tribute of one kind or another before their governments would grant transit rights. The United States, by refusing to let foreigners use Hawaii as a base, blocked any plans the Australians or Canadians might have had for a connecting air route. In retaliation, Australia denied U.S. air lines similar rights. As a result, Pan American was unable to complete the Pacific airway planned in 1935. It was that way all along—blocking, hagging, retaliation, stalemate.

Up to 1943 the international aviation policy of the United States was mostly negative. We upheld sovereignty of the air both by law and by deed, although not always by word. Domestic routes were as tightly sealed off from foreign competition as were the Japanese or Russian airways. Our national policy on flag-line operations was, by and large, that of the chosen instrument—Pan American Airways. The Government had no objection to letting Pan American make its own agreements with foreign governments. The United States was thus relieved of any obligation to grant reciprocal privileges. Not until 1939 were we jolted out of complacency by the inauguration of trans-Atlantic service. For the first time it was necessary to grant reciprocal privileges in order to start U.S. operations. Agita-

tion for competitive air lines further emphasized the need for
a national policy on international air commerce. For when
more than one company engaged in operations unilateral agreements (a contract between a private company and a foreign
government) were impracticable. When two private companies
tried to win concessions from a foreign government, they could
be played off against each other, to the great profit of the
foreigner. To gain a franchise, one operator would have to
underbid the other, and in the end he might have to be rescued
by a subsidy from his home government. Only with an official
policy could U.S. air lines develop the world routes. The
trouble was that most Americans did not know what they
wanted in the way of such a policy.

Up to the very moment when British and American aviation
representatives met for the first time, public opinion in the
United States was still confused on the issues involved. There
were several schools of thought. Each was certain that it had
the answer to America's needs in the postwar air. One door
out of this maze opened the way to imperialism. This was a
vista that Americans might have found to be attractive because
of the dominant role we were destined to play and because
of our obvious advantages over competitors. Our opportunities
were well summarized in the freshman speech of Representative Clare Booth Luce in February, 1943. The sentiments of
the glamorous Connecticut congresswoman might have passed
unnoticed, had they not been broadcast in the colorful phrases
that had helped to make Mrs. Luce a popular author and play-
wright. Because she so well expressed what many Americans
were thinking, her words were widely circulated by editors and
radio commentators. Said she:

Our American pilots . . . know that America, which produced the
Wright brothers and Lindbergh and Rickenbacker, and scores upon
scores of air pioneers and heroes, has not only the tools, but the
technical genius and the industrial capacity — in short everything it
takes — to let American pilots and passengers go anywhere in the
world. For the postwar air policy of these hundreds of thousands of
young airminded Americans is quite simple. It is: "We want to fly
everywhere. Period." [3]

It was clear that the new congresswoman saw postwar international air transport in a far different light than did the men who were slowly developing our official policy. It is not so clear, however, just what it was that she saw. Apparently she was advocating the old air-sovereignty concept established at Paris in 1919, which would have preserved our own skies for the exclusive benefit of our own airmen. On the other hand, Mrs. Luce took it for granted that American operators had a right to fly through the air spaces controlled by other nations. How this contradiction was to be effected she did not say. Possibly she meant to work it out by an exchange of rights. In fact, she later modified her statements to indicate such a train of thought, but her revisions were never official enough for publication in the *Congressional Record.*

The plan advocated by Mrs. Luce was similar to that of the British moderates, but it was more an answer to than an endorsement of them. Mrs. Luce is the wife of Henry Luce, whose magazines, *Life, Time,* and *Fortune* sometimes irked the British by what Matthew Josephson has termed "strident calls for the 'American Century'." [4] It so happened that Mrs. Luce also reflected the ideas of her friends in Pan American Airways. Mr. Luce and Mr. Trippe had gone to the same college, and were neighbors in Connecticut. Samuel F. Pryor, one of the top vice-presidents of Pan American Airways, was also important in the state Republican organization that had backed Mrs. Luce for office.

Mrs. Luce had asked for the floor in Congress after reading two reports, one by a prominent American and the other by a British aviation official. The American was Henry A. Wallace, then vice-president of the United States. The Britisher was the Right Honorable Captain Harold H. Balfour, His Majesty's Undersecretary of State for Air. Wallace, looking at the future through the eyes of an idealist, had suggested in a magazine article that the way to peace in the air was through an international aerial police force controlled by the United Nations. Since these airmen would receive only infrequent calls to duty in Wallace's brave new world, it was suggested that they fly the world's transport planes as part of their training. The plan as elaborated had more merit, perhaps, than so brief a summary might indicate. At any rate, it was far ahead of any official policy contemplated in this country, or in such places as New Zealand and South Africa, where aviation thinking was so advanced that most Americans could not even see the outlines. Mrs. Luce remarked in her speech that she had often admired Mr. Wallace's lofty views. But, she added: "One usually finds that the higher the plane Mr. Wallace puts his economic arguments upon, the lower it turns out American standards of living will fall. Mr. Wallace's article . . . is on a very high plane indeed. In it he does a great deal of global thinking. But much of what Mr. Wallace calls his global thinking is, no matter how you slice it, still 'globaloney.' Mr. Wallace's warp of sense and woof of nonsense is very tricky cloth out of which to cut the pattern of the post-war world." [5]

The best insurance against future wars, said the Congresswoman, would be American dominance in the air. Freedom of the seas, said she, had not prevented two world wars, so why expect any more from freedom of the air? Mrs. Luce was answered by a speaker who was just as able, but unfortunately not as glamorous to the press, as the Congresswoman. He was Representative J. W. Fulbright, former president of the University of Arkansas. He replied: "I submit that the only substantial benefit this nation can realize from the war is the assurance of a peaceful world, based upon a world-wide system of collective security. Such a system can be achieved only with the genuine cooperation of our gallant allies. The narrow, imperialistic policy of grab, advocated by the honorable lady, carries within itself the seeds of its own destruction." [6]

Representative Fulbright declared that Mrs. Luce's premise could only be effected by asking all and granting nothing. What the Congresswoman was actually suggesting without saying so, declared the Arkansan, was the seizure by the United States of the strategic world bases while our partners were absorbed in a war of survival against the dictators. For without bases, Mrs. Luce's plan could not be carried out. Instead of

preventing war, as the Congresswoman promised, a narrow
policy such as hers would be certain to start another war. It
was true, he admitted, that freedom of the air and the opening
up of this country to foreign operators would not of itself assure
peace. Freedom of the seas had indeed not prevented two
devastating wars. But if that were to be the argument for
abandoning plans for an open sky throughout the world, one
might as well argue that since freedom of speech and freedom
of religion had failed to prevent wars, we should do away with
them, too.

Mrs. Luce replied to Mr. Fulbright a few days later. She
complained that he had "misinterpreted" her comments. If
he had, he was not the only student of politics to have been
confused by the lady spellbinder. To the rescue of Representative Fulbright came the nation's leading woman quidnunc,
Dorothy Thompson, who wrote in her column: "Mrs. Luce's
speech is not in the least clear, and she can easily challenge
Representative J. W. Fulbright . . . to 'give a precise quote in
which I said America must control the skies of any other nation.' There is no precise quote. It is not a precise speech,
but a lot of American Century double talk." [7]

Mrs. Luce also spoke for a specific group when she tore into
Captain Balfour, one of Britain's most important aviation
officials. She even had his speech to the House of Commons
reprinted in the *Congressional Record* so that her colleagues
could read what perfidious Albion was fulminating against the
defenseless Americans. A reading of the entire Balfour speech
in *Hansard* (British record of parliamentary debates) dis-
closes no such sinister motives as were attributed to it. Had
the same speech been made in Congress it would have been
too mild for comment. What had happened was this:

Mr. Perkins, Conservative member from Stroud, had risen
to state that he was alarmed at the way Pan American Airways
had been spreading to all parts of the world. He was particularly concerned with the way the Americans were pushing across
the heart of Africa, a route dear to the RAF and to veterans of
the old Imperial Airways, now employed by BOAC. Perkins

asked if Pan American Airways was to be given a permanent franchise in this British sphere. He pointed out that the American company was supreme in South America and the Pacific. He had no objections to that, because the British also had dominant areas, too, or would have, in normal times. But Perkins wondered if it weren't about time for the two nations to keep each other's lusty aviation offspring out of each other's back yards.

Captain Balfour replied that the British Government had been forced to let Pan American take over the African routes because of the importance of the desert campaign and the shortage of British transports. In exchange for this service, certain concessions had had to be made by His Majesty's Government. Of course there had been denunciation at this surrender of British interests, but the captain insisted that he had acted out of necessity. His sole purpose was to win the war without delay. Americans had the equipment and the British had none; that was the crux of the matter. But, added the speaker, waving his finger emphatically, it was well understood on both sides of the Atlantic that the turning over of the African routes to the Americans was only a temporary measure. With the return of peace. Britain would again demand her rightful place "in every possible way."

"I presume," interjected Earl Winterton, "that when my right honorable and gallant friend says that he means that 'in every possible way' . . . it will be represented to our American allies and friends that the fact that they are running particular services through particular parts of the Empire during the war does not mean they will have any right to do so after the war?"

"That is well understood," answered Captain Balfour. "To use a colloquialism, we have agreed on the highest level with the Americans that as regards routes they are running which may have commercial values, 'all bets are off' at the end of the war." [8]

The "all bets are off" phrase was picked up by Mrs. Luce to show how the rapacious British were ready to mow us down in the air when the shooting on the ground was over. Perhaps too much is made here of the Luce speeches, but they show the interest with which Americans and British were watching the race for postwar air routes. By the time all this Luce talk had been discussed, world routes had come to mean more than mere transportation. Civil aviation involved a philosophy that sooner or later would have to be threshed out at a peace table.

On the one hand were the Imperialists, who believed that by winning the war America had a "manifest destiny" to dominate the air. We had provided the weight of supplies that had crushed the enemy. Our aircraft literally had darkened the skies. Clearly we were the ones chosen to claim the high frontier. Anyone who objected just did not know what was good for him, said the Imperialists. They pointed out that as British dominance of the seas had brought a measure of peace and security to the world, so American dominance of the airways would bring the blessings of the American Century to all the benighted peoples beyond our borders. This was a philosophy gilded with self-righteousness — the kind of policy Americans have followed enthusiastically before. As the Imperialist saw the picture, the United States would have been derelict if it had shirked the responsibility of maintaining order above the land when, by the same token, we were expected to preserve the peace below. Was U.S. power to be stratified in terms of land, sea, and air, asked the Imperialist?

"There is nothing basically wrong with a benevolent imperialism, such as the United States could provide," wrote one editor. "There is nothing basically wrong with an imperialism that raises the standards of living, creates more opportunities, and brings a better way of life to more and more people. If we think enough of our own way of living to fight for it and wreck our economy in helping others fight for it, why should we apologize and shy away from extending that way of life to other and larger areas?" [9]

This is a frank statement of imperialistic policy. Kipling extolled it as "the white man's burden," but it has been recognized through history. The weakness of the policy is that it is claimed by too many. In every strong nation there are editors saying the same thing. A Russian writer could just as well have penned the above quotation — and with the utmost sincerity. But what happens when the editors and the policy-makers of two such countries meet?

The Imperialist would probably admit that one or the other has to give way. His solution would be to make his own country so much stronger that there can be no serious challenge. This was the rallying cry of the "America Firster." But at the point where the Imperialist carries his philosophy over into the development of world air routes, there is a curious contradiction. For now the Isolationist emerges as one of the most vociferous allies of Imperialism. As one writer put it: "He will admit that America can no longer find security within its own boundaries, but the alternative, as he sees it, is not subordination of American sovereignty — in common with other sovereignties — in the interest of world order, but the indefinite expansion of American sovereignty.. If America can be threatened by bases thousands of miles across the sea, the new Imperialist declares, America should control such bases. If the civil aviation of other powers is competitively dangerous to American interests, all and any methods should be taken to crush it." [10]

The red herring of the Imperialists is that America is mere putty in the hands of foreign diplomats, and that the only way for us to go forward is under our own power. The Imperialist often believes that the moment the United States depends upon negotiation with the wily Europeans, it will be the loser. He frequently argues that the United States is no match for other nations skillful in the sorceries of international diplomacy. The fear of the "infant status" of American diplomacy almost always crops up in any discussion by this group. As Colonel J. Carroll Cone, a vice-president of Pan American Airways, told the aviation writers at their convention at Chicago in June, 1945, if America persisted in its trend to internationalism it would be exploited by neighbors who had the advantage of "nearly a thousand years of schooling and experience in international manipulation."

The myth of American impotence in foreign diplomacy is as old as the nation. It won preponderant acceptance after World War I. We were told then that our Government had been "taken in" by the British, by the munitions trust, by the foreign delegates to the peace conference, and by other ulterior agents. The League of Nations was held up as a horrible example of our naïveté in world diplomacy, although history appears to have shown that it was our public, not our diplomats, who were to blame for that bungling.

The fact is, America has little to fear in the diplomatic arena. We have so much to bargain away that we would not even have to be shrewd in our dealings. But we have more than our bargaining power. In the knowledge of diplomatic technique the Europeans are more experienced, it is true. They have made a deeper study of the fine points and they appreciate the importance of protocol. One has only to look at the appointments of our State Department — which usually does not appear to understand that a great physician or historian is not necessarily a great statesman. Even conceding all that — the fact remains that on major issues the United States has fared surprisingly well for an "infant status" nation of diplomats.

A quick glance at our diplomatic relationships through the years will show that our international representatives have given an excellent account of themselves — even when pitted against the shrewdest statesmen in Europe. Our "infant status" was no handicap to us at the time of the Louisiana Purchase, the Florida boundary dispute, the Monroe Doctrine, the Northwest boundary settlement, the Alaska purchase, the Open-Door policy in China, or the various negotiations over the Panama Canal — to name only a few issues. Indeed, just before Colonel Cone made his address at Chicago, the United States had taken over a string of bases stretching from Argentina to Trinidad in exchange for a hundred obsolete destroyers, a swap that would have won the admiration of a David Harum. It is difficult to pick out a major diplomatic negotiation in which Americans have not acquitted themselves well as master horse traders.

The other philosophic extreme was represented by such idealists as Henry Wallace, who saw salvation in exchanging national sovereignty for a kind of international confederation. How such control was to be distributed, or who would direct the world aerial police force, build the planes, allocate routes, or determine membership in such a world authority, Wallace left for more mundane minds to work out. He sounded like a crackpot to many aviation planners. And yet the Man in the Moon — the purely objective observer — might have looked down on the world and concluded that men like Wallace made more sense than did the Imperialists, that is, if America had to choose between the two extremes.

Mrs. Luce wanted Americans to fly everywhere — period. The British, Dutch, Scandinavians, and scores of others also wanted to fly everywhere — question mark. How would a program of American supersovereignty recognize such claims? By driving out that competition by means of superior resources? That could be accomplished, perhaps, but it would mean that inevitably the rest of the world would gang up on the United States. Might not the United States gain more by cooperaion than by aggressiveness? That had been our solution to other problems of the war and the peace. The end of the war found the United States calling upon all her allies to work out their destinies intelligently around the peace table. Was international air transportation to be an exception — the contradiction of our professed intention of guaranteeing freedoms and a fair share of world commerce to others? If so, there was no room for the Imperialist in such company.

To the politician, whose career depended upon tangible results, this program was impractical. It was unthinkable that the United States would give up its prerogatives, trade advantages, or national sovereignty for the sake of international welfare. That was too much to ask of the pseudo-statesman. Men had reached the stage where they were willing to die for their country, but they were not yet prepared to suffer even mild discomfort for the sake of the world in general. As a churchman put it:

It is impossible to have today, or in any near tomorrow, world government . . . because between the nations there is no unity of cultural aim, no shared conviction as to what life is about, no willingness to see mankind as other than atomistic and competitive . . .

Each nation serves a particularistic ideology, follows its inherited prejudices, advances its own small self interest . . .

United Nations . . . is only a trading place for international deals. . . . That is all we deserve to have in the way of international agreement; it is all we really wish. If the United Nations tried to become a true world government it would not last a week; it would be a government without the consent of the governed and as such would immediately be repudiated, by Americans as quickly as by any other group.[11]

But did the United States have to choose between the two extremes of Imperialism and Internationalism? There was one school that thought not. This group was represented by what we shall call here the Merchant Airman. He was willing to concede the necessity of some international cooperation and was therefore willing to sacrifice a certain amount of his independence in exchange for order on the world airways. He remembered the chaos in his own country following the cancellation of the air-mail contracts, and the tonic effect of regulation that followed under the Civil Aeronautics Act of 1938. On the other hand, he had no patience with an international plan that would punish the efficient operator by limiting traffic for the sake of a weak rival. The Merchant Airman took this much from the Imperialists — that America had the resources and skill to develop a service of benefit to all the world. As Mrs. Luce had put it, he did want to fly everywhere — period; or more accurately, he wanted to fly wherever there was a good economic reason for doing so. He realized that he could do that only by sharing some of his own advantages — his traffic and his routes. He also knew that cutthroat competition was dangerous. For that reason he was willing to accept certain restrictions, providing those limitations met his test.

That test involved the purposes for which such restrictions were to be imposed. If such restrictions were applied for the development of air transportation, then the Merchant Airman was in favor of them. If they were imposed for the protection of a weak rival, the Merchant Airman was not interested in them. What he had in mind was a vast transportation system, not just a medium of communication or an outlet for national manufacturers. Under the spur of competition he would order better and better planes carrying bigger and bigger loads at lower and lower rates. The more passengers, the lower the fares; the lower the fares, the more passengers — that was the way he asked for it. Any limitation on plane performances, frequencies, fares, or traffic would only slow up the process. If carried very far, such restrictions could wreck the proposed program.

In the final analysis, as John Parker Van Zandt has pointed out, it all narrows down to a contest between the "ins" and the "outs." [12] Both groups are willing to submit to controls, but on entirely different principles. The "outs" demand restricted competition, but only after they have been given a quota of operations. The "ins" ask restrictions that will preserve the *status quo*. And if the "ins" have been operating successfully under a laissez-faire policy, they may even ask for restrictions against restrictions.

This contest between the "ins" and "outs," or "haves" and "have-nots" is fought all the way up the line. It was indicated in the attempt of the U.S. domestic air lines to muscle in on the business developed by the original international carriers. The domestic operators, as the "have-nots," toward the end of the war used all the old arguments of the competitive school to break down Pan American Airways' dominance of the ocean air routes. While so arguing, they followed the same policy as Pan American in keeping rivals out of domestic areas in which they had established exclusive services. On this basis, to accuse Pan American of selfishness in its attempt to block international competition by other carriers would be to let emotion run away with reason. Pan American in this case was an "in." It reacted as the "ins" have always reacted where the *status quo* is threatened.

The same explanation could be made of our international policy. In the postwar air-commerce pattern, the United States was a "have" nation. It had the equipment and administrative machinery to begin flying world routes immediately. The other nations, as "have-nots," were thus committed to a united front against the one nation that had all the aces. They unpacked all the old shibboleths to justify their policies, and we did the same in pressing our advantage. The idea was ably expressed by L. Welch Pogue, chairman of the Civil Aeronautics Board after the war, speaking to the annual meeting of the National Aeronautics Association at Minneapolis. Said he:

It would be the height of naïvete to contend that the United States desires an 'open sky' primarily to improve the welfare of mankind. By the same token, it would be unfair to contend that the refusal of Great Britain or any other nation to conform to our views is necessarily reprehensible. Once again we are confronted with an attempt to rationalize an international problem on the notably fallacious and dangerous theory that since the 'open sky' principle would conform to the requirements of the United States, it would be acceptable to the rest of the world — regardless of any political or economic incompatibilities that may exist. This line of reasoning is usually accompanied by carefully chosen slogans concerning human progress and liberty, which have the effect of putting the nations that would oppose it in the position of being antisocial. The natural concomitant of such tactics is friction, which in the long run produces nothing better than angry and unsatisfactory compromises.[13]

With all these conflicting concepts confronting the aviation planners of the world, it would have been impossible to work out an international program for civil air transport that would have pleased everyone. If the great, broad view of an international authority working for the common good appears to be the logical answer, one must stop and reflect a moment. One must ask whether, after all, such a concept is not motivated by the "outs," who see this as the only means of stopping the progress of a more fortunate rival. If the realism of the Imperialist appears more attractive, let it be recalled that realism has failed invariably to bring the security promised. And anyway, the trend has been away from "enlightened self-interest," a popular phrase in 1943 that was only "the white man's burden" in a cellophane wrapping. If the student is sympathetic to the motives of the Merchant Airman, he should imagine himself for a moment as a foreign air-line promoter, pitted against hopeless odds in a competitive race.

If, somehow, these divergent philosophies could be woven together by men of good will, it would be an achievement of world moment — an encouragement to a war-weary world striving to find a formula for peace. Solving the international aviation problem would be important from a commercial and economic standpoint, but the solution would be far more important as an example of how the nations might work out other differences. That has already been pointed out by such thinkers as Sir Osborne Mance. "Without some advance in this direction," he wrote, "the prospects of a prosperous development, not only of international aviation, but of security generally, are not very bright." [14]

"The air," declared another authority, "will become more and more . . . not only a scene of commercial activities, but of political developments, and the question of air routes will soon emerge as one involving some of the primary objects of the external policy of nations." [15]

As the war burned itself out, four courses were open to American airmen. They could adopt the fortress policy — a sealing off of the country at the rim, allowing no competitors within our borders. By this program we would have confined our international operations to those nations demanding no exchange of privileges, or to areas where our influence and power made expansion possible. Or we could continue the old, ponderous ritual of individual treaty, delayed indefinitely by the elaborate horse trading known as diplomacy, until eventually we achieved a spotty international system. That would have meant, of course, that we should have lost the advantage that was ours at the end of the war — the advantage of owning all the available transport planes. A third way was to adopt Mr. Wallace's "everybody's brother" concept by recognition of a central authority which would maintain discipline in a happy family of nations. Somehow this course did not ring the bell in our postwar stage of national maturity. It was too grandiose and it was a threat to initiative, because rivals could outvote the United States. Finally, we could take a stand for American *leadership* in world aviation — a leadership so certain of its own strength that there could be no fear of foreign competition. This plan presupposed no restrictions for protecting weaklings or for hampering progress, but it did presuppose an exchange of privileges and a modification of air sovereignty.

This was the plan the Merchant Airman would follow. He did not necessarily demand dominance by the United States on the world air routes — for there is a nice distinction between leadership and dominance. He did not require exclusive control of world bases, or a monopoly of air transports. Nor did his program include the right to fly everywhere — period, regardless of the wishes of our neighbors. All it included was an exchange of concessions so that American operators could fly anywhere there was trade opportunity. If that involved sharing traffic with foreigners — even a certain amount of our own traffic — the Merchant Airman was willing to take that chance, secure in his belief that in fair competition he could hold his own with anyone. On the other hand, sharing traffic did not mean that the Merchant Airman was willing to discard national sovereignty entirely. He would only modify that sovereignty to permit the establishment of prescribed routes, ports of call, and flying regulations for foreign air lines within our borders.

There were dangers in such a policy. Labor costs might put us at a disadvantage in foreign competition. In the manufacture of the limited number of giant air liners required to conduct international services the United States would lose the advantage of mass production. Mass production had made it possible for Americans to compete with other air powers having lower wage standards. Airplanes, like automobiles, could be made cheaper in the United States because of economies effected by manufacturing skill. But on custom-built products, where handwork accounted for most of the labor, America was handicapped by high wages. U.S. shipbuilders had learned that lesson. There was also danger that in a system of free enterprise a foreign operator, supported by his government, could undersell Americans, without concern for his financial loss.

Against such threats the United States had one overwhelming defense — its wealth. If foreign nations took advantage of lower wages to produce cheaper aircraft, our builders could still lead the way. For the cost of an airplane is not computed in wages alone. British, French, or Dutch craftsmen could undoubtedly assemble equipment as well as the best American workmen, and at less cost, but aircraft superiority in the long run depends upon design, research, and the endless testing of new devices. The United States had the resources to turn out superior aircraft, if it was willing to pay the price. It could experiment ceaselessly, and afford all the costly wastage. In so doing, it could produce the planes that all other nations would prefer, regardless of price.

The Merchant Airman believed that he also knew how to defend himself against foreign operators who tried to edge him out by underselling him through government subsidy. In a subsidy battle no foreign nation, or combination of nations, could stand up against our wealth, if we chose to answer subsidy with subsidy. In a pinch, the U.S. Government could take over the private air lines, if such action were forced upon us by any foreign nation foolish enough to challenge us to that extent.

All the Merchant Airman asked was a chance to show what he could do. The Merchant Airman was no one company. Probably few promoters held all the ideas described as those of the Merchant Airman. He was an imaginary figure representing one important group. But it was for him that the policy-makers sat down with foreign statesmen to work out a world plan for air transportation. How could they achieve the aims of the Merchant Airman without arousing the jealousies and resentments of foreign diplomats? The task was not an easy one.

REFERENCES

1. Speech on the increase of the Navy, U.S. House of Representatives, *Congressional Record*, January 22, 1812.

2. For a discussion of this phase see John C. Cooper, *The Right to Fly* (New York, 1947) pp. 17-122.

3. *Congressional Record,* Vol. 89, Part I, February 9, 1943, pp. 759-64.

4. Matthew Josephson, *Empire of the Air* (New York, 1943) pp. 12-14.

5. *Congressional Record,* Vol. 89, Part I, February 9, 1943, pp. 759-64.

6. *Ibid.,* 1012.

7. *Ibid.,* A-725.

8. *Hansard,* Commons, Vol. 385, December 17, 1942, p. 2153.

9. Editorial, "U.S. Imperialism in the Pacific," *American Aviation,* March 1, 1943, pp. 1, 10.

10. Keith Hutchinson, "Imperialism of the Sky," *The Nation,* April 17, 1943, pp. 551-53.

11. Bernard Iddings Bell, preaching at a Lenten service in Chicago, as reprinted in *Time,* April 29, 1946, p. 29.

12. Van Zandt, *Civil Aviation and Peace,* Washington, 1944.

13. Delivered before the Aviation Day meeting of the Greater Twin Cities Chapter, National Aeronautic Association, at Minneapolis and Saint Paul, April 9, 1943.

14. Osborne Mance and J. E. Wheeler, *International Air Transport,* London, 1944.

15. Daniel Goedhuis, in *International Airways,* a symposium edited by Alberta Worthington, New York, 1945.

A NOTE ON SOURCES

The history of the early progress in international air commerce is described by A. A. Berle, Jr., in "Freedoms of the Air," *Harper's,* March 1, 1945, pp. 327-34. See also William A. M. Burden, "The Future of Air Transport," *Atlantic Monthly,* December, 1943, pp. 51-62. The standard reference on policy and aviation economics is Oliver J. Lissitzyn's, *International Air Transport and National Policy,* New York, 1942. Some of the philosophies discussed in this chapter have been derived from an unsigned article, "Logic of the Air," *Fortune,* April, 1943, pp. 72 ff.; E. P. Warner, "Atlantic Airways," *Foreign Affairs,* April, 1938, pp. 467-83; the same, "Airways for Peace," *Foreign Affairs,* October, 1943, pp. 11-27; speech of Clare Booth Luce, "America in the Post War Air World," *Congressional Record,* Seventy-eighth Congress, First Session, Vol. 89, Part I, February 9, 1943, pp. 759-64; Henry A. Wallace, "What We Will Get Out of the War," *American Magazine,* March, 1943, pp. 23, 98-104; "Remarks of Rep. J. W. Fulbright," the above-cited *Congressional Record,* Vol. I, Part 9, p. A-725; speech of Captain Balfour, *Hansard,* Fifth Series, Commons, Vol. 385, December 17, 1942, pp. 2153 ff.; Emanuel Celler, "Imperialists of the Air," transcript of an address over the Blue Network, February 27, 1943; John C. Cooper, *The Right to Fly,* New York, 1947; and John Parker Van Zandt, *Civil Aviation and Peace,* Washington, 1944. One of the best summaries of the "enlightened self interest" themes is given in Arthur E. Traxler's "International Air

Transport Policy of the United States," *International Conciliation,* December, 1943, pp. 616-36. The best answer to the imperialists is given by Keith Hutchinson in "Imperialism of the Sky," *The Nation,* April 17, 1943, pp. 551-53. An outline of the various organizations that have influenced international aviation is given in John Jay Ide's *International Aeronautic Organizations and the Control of Air Navigation,* a lecture published by the James Jackson Cabot Professorship of Air Traffic Regulation and Air Transportation, Norwich University, as revised in May, 1938. An interesting comparison of international aviation and international postal agreements is given in Agnes A. Gautreaux's unpublished brochure for the Office of Air Transport Information Division, Economic Bureau, Civil Aeronautics Board, dated September 16, 1943, and entitled, "The Universal Postal Union." One of the best general discussions of international aviation is to be found in a symposium of noted authorities writing in "Aviation Transport," a special edition of *Law and Contemporary Problems,* School of Law, Duke University, Durham, N. C., Winter-Spring, 1946. Another worthy summary by various authorities is given in *International Airways,* a symposium edited by Alberta Worthington, New York, 1945. Information for this chapter was also obtained from interviews with L. Welch Pogue, chairman of the Civil Aeronautics Board during this period; John Parker Van Zandt, formerly with the Brookings Institution, later an editor of *American Aviation;* Gill Robb Wilson, aviation editor of the New York *Herald Tribune;* Stokeley Morgan, formerly with Pan American Airways and the State Department, and later president of Air Carriers Supply Corporation, Washington; and Blaine Stubblefield, Washington representative of the McGraw-Hill Publishing Company, publishers of *Aviation, Aviation News,* and *Air Transport.*

THE PRESIDENT SAID...

HALF the government agencies in Washington appear to have had some part in the development of our international aviation policy. The Civil Aeronautics Board and the Departments of State and Commerce of course played leading roles, but many other official groups appeared on the program. Congress, through its subcommittees, has always exerted a strong influence on aviation decisions. The War and Navy Departments were interested in civil aviation because of its potential value in war time, and each submitted reports on the subject from time to time. The Post Office Department, once the sole policy-maker, continued to wield power as a dispenser of mail payments. The Director of the Bureau of the Budget kept a close watch on aviation matters because he had to pass on appropriations set aside for air-line development. Even the Justice Department got in on the show, through its antitrust division. In fact, it was the Justice Department that submitted one of the most interesting reports on postwar international air transport. Most of the negotiations for world routes centered around certain key figures, however.

Outstanding advocate of the open-sky concept was Adolf A. Berle, Jr. A brilliant lawyer drafted by Franklin D. Roosevelt as one of the original brain-trusters, Berle was for one brief interlude the most important figure in international air commerce. He was the protégé of Felix Frankfurter and a favorite of Cordell Hull, the Secretary of State. As an assistant in the department, Berle did much of the diplomatic spade work needed to begin the cultivation of our civil aviation policy. He was close to the President and knew just what his chief hoped to win in the negotiations with foreign aviation officials. Berle's identification with the New Deal made him unpopular with many of the American aviation leaders. He was certainly on Pan American Airways' "go-to-hell" list. And yet he produced more results in the short time he was in control of aviation policy than anyone in office before or since.

Opposed to Berle and his philosophy were three important legislators. One was Senator Patrick A. McCarran of Nevada. The senator was not supported by many of the merchant airmen. They believed that he followed too closely the policy of Pan American Airways, which had its own proposals for postwar air routes — proposals that rival operators would not tolerate. The Senator had strong public backing, however, and as the coauthor of the excellent Civil Aeronautics Act of 1938, he enjoyed a certain respect of the industry.

Closely associated with Senator McCarran on aviation policy was Senator Owen Brewster, junior member from Maine. Senator Brewster emerged from the aviation battles as an extremely able in-fighter. He was aggressive, shrewd, and a great spokesman for the Pan American Airways line of reasoning.

Senator Josiah W. Bailey of North Carolina withdrew from the Washington arena because of ill health, but during the critical period of policy-making, he was a man of great influence. Less outspoken than Senators McCarran and Brewster, he was nevertheless definitely in the camp of the conservatives who were helping to work out our future in the air. All were members of the subcommittee on aviation of the Senate Committee on Commerce. Senator Bailey was, in fact, chairman of both committees. With Senator Brewster and others he represented the United States at the important Chicago aviation conference. And since his committee heard most of the testimony for and against the course finally taken by the Government, Senator Bailey was a force in aviation matters up to the time of his death in 1946.

Somewhere between Berle and the senators stood Lloyd Welch Pogue, chairman of the Civil Aeronautics Board. Pogue was an Iowan who had learned about aviation while practicing law in New York. He had risen to his responsible post while still a young man, as assistant and general counsel for the old Civil Aeronautics Authority. Pogue appeared to have little sympathy with the restrictive views of the Pan American–McCarran–Brewster school, but on the other hand, he was alarmed by the apparent willingness of the Berle group to sign away our valuable concessions through multilateral, or general agreements. What Pogue appeared to advocate was the open-sky principle, but an open sky achieved by means of bilateral, or individual negotiations with foreign nations. Under this plan, he believed, the United States could use its air sovereignty as a strong bargaining point.

Several others were more or less in agreement with Pogue's philosophy. William A. M. Burden, the assistant secretary of commerce in charge of aviation matters, was perhaps a little to the left of Pogue. Harllee Branch, the former newspaper man and assistant postmaster general in charge of air mail previous to his appointment as a member of the Civil Aeronautics Board, veered more toward the conservatives. He took issue with Berle on more than one occasion, but never openly attacked the spokesman of the State Department. Edward P. Warner, the erudite veteran CAB member, was too good-natured to get himself embroiled in violent argument with proponents of either extreme, but in general, his philosophy appeared to be similar to Pogue's. These men, and a dozen others almost as well known, prepared to work out our policy as the war came to a close. Their purpose was to get our merchant air fleet on to the world routes just as soon as the pressures of war would permit. To do that, it was necessary to begin preliminary negotiations with Great Britain, our biggest potential rival for air commerce, and controller of essential world air bases.

The leaders of the two nations had discussed this problem on several occasions. Both President Roosevelt and Prime Minister Churchill saw the need of immediate understanding. By 1943 they had reached agreement in their own minds. It was then their problem to sell their ideas to the planners of the postwar air world.¹ Shortly after the United States became a war partner of the British, Wayne Chatfield Taylor, then the undersecretary of commerce, had suggested to Pogue that a committee should be appointed to co-ordinate all the activities of the various government agencies as they affected wartime air transport. At that time the CAB was swamped with the work of mobilizing the air lines. When Pogue brought up the suggestion at a Board meeting, his colleagues refused to let the chairman take on any additional duties. Pogue and Taylor then went to the President and persuaded the chief executive to appoint a special committee to study air transportation. President Roosevelt was reluctant. Previous co-ordinating committees had not been notably successful. In the end, however, he appointed an Interdepartmental Committee on Aviation, with Berle as chairman of the over-all committee and Pogue as head of the working subcommittee.

Both men prepared reports for the President. The subcommittee held long hearings throughout 1941 and 1942, but when the combined report was sent to the President by way of the State Department nothing happened. The CAB then made an independent report on the situation. This, too, was pigeonholed. Berle was blamed for failure to bring the reports to the attention of the President, but the fault apparently lay with other advisers in the State Department. Strong pressure was brought to bear by those opposed to the open-sky policy advocated in the reports. Secretary of State Hull probably was as much at fault as anyone. He meant well, but he was never one to grasp an idea quickly. His office was a true reflection of the State Department mood at that time — the ancient Victorian furnishings, the big, grandfather clock sleepily ticking away, and the general air of somnolence were all in keeping with the personality of the department head.

Late in 1942, after the Interdepartmental and CAB reports had been filed away and forgotten, the Army and Navy made similar independent surveys. The recommendations were about the same in each case. These reports were routed through the usual channels, and when they disappeared into the State Department limbo, Assistant Secretary of War for Air Robert A. Lovett protested noisily. He made such a fuss that the Department was forced to release *all* the reports.

The President undoubtedly was impressed by the documents, particularly in their agreement on international policy. All the reports denounced the restrictive policies of the imperialistic school. All recommended that the United States abandon the policy of isolation. All recognized the need for surrendering some of our air sovereignty for the benefit of the world. On this point they had as a guiding principle the Atlantic Charter, which promised "to further the enjoyment by all states, great or small, victor or vanquished, of access on equal terms to the trade and to the raw materials of the world which are needed for their economic prosperity." [2]

From these reports the President drafted his own proposals for postwar air commerce. His views are outlined in a memorandum of a meeting held at the White House on November 11, 1943. Present were Undersecretary of State Edward Stettinius Jr.; Mr. Lovett; the President's assistant and adviser, Harry Hopkins; Mr. Berle; and Mr. Pogue. All these men represented executive agencies interested in air commerce, and it is interesting to see how all of them later followed almost to the letter the recommendations of their chief. The President's words were so significant that day, therefore, that they merit comment. The following verbatim account is the first published report of that meeting: [3]

The President requested the five men above-named to meet him at two o'clock yesterday.

He stated that he had begun to discuss aviation policy with Prime Minister Churchill at Quebec and he expected to go on doing so at their coming meeting. He had considered the various problems of policy and wished to state the policy he wanted followed. Reading from a memorandum which he said he had himself prepared, though he took the points out of order, he gave us the following oral directives:

(1) Germany, Italy, and Japan were not to be permitted to have any aviation industry or any aviation lines, internal or external. This involved policing these countries.

Their external traffic would be handled by the lines of other countries. Internal aviation could be handled by a company or companies to be formed by the United Nations. The participation of former enemy countries (Germany, Italy, and Japan) in aviation was to be limited to the maintenance of airfields, local servicing work, and detail of that kind.

As for flying, the President said that he did not want them to be in a position to 'fly anything larger than one of these toy planes that you wind up with an elastic.'

(2) As to aviation in other countries: The President felt that each country should have ownership and control of its own *internal* aviation services. He recognized that there might be exceptions in backward countries unable to organize aviation themselves. But Brazil, which he took as an illustration, was quite competent to run its own internal aviation. He did not wish Americans to own or control their (Brazil's) internal aviation; nor did he wish them to hire Americans or other foreign companies as managers of their internal aviation. He had no objection, indeed, he hoped that they would hire American individuals, and of course he hoped they would buy American equipment. But he wanted the internal aviation to be the development of the country itself.

(3) Regarding the handling of American aviation, he stated that he had decided that American overseas aviation should not be handled by a single line. The scope of international aviation was too great to be trusted to any one company or pool. He said that certain companies — to speak frankly, Pan American — wanted all of the business, and he disagreed with Trippe.* He was willing to agree that on its record, Pan American was entitled to the senior place, and perhaps the cream of the business; but he could not go along with the idea of their, or anyone's having all of it. This meant a multi-company operation [of world routes].

He said he still felt — though he was open to argument on the subject — that the plan he had outlined . . . [to Mr. Pogue and to Mr. Berle] two years ago, of various companies having 'zones,' still appealed to him; thus there might be a company for the western side of South America, another having the eastern side, one company

---

*Another member of the group that day, not Berle, tells an interesting aside about this mention of Trippe and Pan American Airways. Stettinius, the undersecretary of state who was present that day, was a brother-in-law of Trippe. Stettinius left the room just before the mention of Pan American was made by the President. He left to make some arrangements for the reception of Cordell Hull, who was arriving by plane from Moscow. There was a pause until the door closed behind the Undersecretary. President Roosevelt then made his remarks about Pan American Airways. He was talking about another item when Stettinius returned from his errand.

having the North Atlantic; another the Mediterranean; and so forth. In answer to a question of Bob Lovett's he said that there might be a shift of equipment from one group to another as seasons required this . . . [Mr. Berle] thought Mr. Pogue's idea of competitive terminals by the competitors draining different fields of traffic probably could be harmonized with this general idea. The President said that he agreed that his idea would have to be applied flexibly.

(4) Regarding the possibility of Government participation in the lines, he said there remained open the question of ownership by the Government of an interest in the various lines contemplated under this policy. But he said he thought there was no need of such ownership under the proposed plan, except as the Government might have to own, initially, lines going to places in which traffic could not support such a company. This would be covered by his idea that the Government should run such lines until private enterprise was prepared to take over.

(5) The President then spoke of subsidies. He said in general he thought the traffic could be made to pay its own way except in connection with certain routes on which the traffic was not enough to make the line a paying proposition. Using the illustration of the United States to South Africa [route], he said it probably would not be a paying proposition. He therefore wished that we would apply the same policy which he had worked out for shipping lines after the last war, namely: to have the United States Government use its planes and its men to run Government lines — but always on the understanding that if ever a private line was prepared to bid for the route, the Government would promptly retire from the business.

(6) As to air and landing rights, the President said that he wanted a very free interchange. That is, he wanted arrangements by which planes of one country could enter any other country for the purpose of discharging traffic of foreign origin, and accepting foreign bound traffic. Thus, if Canada wanted a line from Canada to Jamaica, with stops in the United States at Buffalo and Miami, they should be able to discharge traffic of Canadian origin at Buffalo, and take on traffic at Buffalo for Jamaica; but they should not be allowed to carry [passengers] from Buffalo to Miami.

He considered that each country would have a number — in the United States a quite large number — of airports available for such foreign traffic.

In addition to that, he thought planes should have general right of free transit and right of technical stop — that is, the right to land at any field and get fuel and service, without, however, taking on or discharging traffic.

This, he pointed out, would dispose of any need for a United Nations authority to manage airfields.

The President said that there might, however, remain airfields in respect of which the traffic itself would not pay the cost of upkeep. Liberia, for instance, might have to maintain a field for the purpose of a line between the United States and South Africa; but there would not be business enough to make it a paying proposition. There might be United Nations contributions, or arrangements might have to be made for the lines which used the field to pay part of the cost.

(7) In answer to a question from Lovett, the President said that he thought there should be no general party or conference about aviation until the time was right to call a United Nations conference. Talks with Britain and other countries could be handled quietly as a part of the preparatory discussion.

(8) The President considered that there would have to be a United Nations conference on aviation and probably a United Nations organization to handle such matters as safety standards, signals, communication, weather reporting, and also to handle the problem of competitive subsidies or rates. The impending return of Secretary Hull from the Moscow Conference was then announced, and we broke up.

The President's statement on international air commerce started the ball rolling. Within a month the diplomats of the two leading air powers were corresponding in an effort to find a common hypothesis upon which they could begin discussions. The British proposed a bilateral or face-to-face negotiation for allocation of world routes, but the Americans insisted on including the Canadians in the discussions because of the significance of the Canadian corridor on the Atlantic routes. It was also suggested that the President favored inviting Russia, China, and Brazil to such a meeting because of their strategic positions on the world air map. The British agreed, but insisted quite logically that all members of the empire had as much right to participate as countries like China and Brazil. On March 7, 1944, Michael Wright, first secretary of the British Embassy in Washington, informed the State Department that his Government was ready to go ahead on that basis. He suggested that the conference be held somewhere in North Africa and that fourteen nations be invited to send delegates.

Mr. Berle replied that such a conference would require considerable preparation. He also maintained that a formal meeting would antagonize members of the United Nations not included in the invitation. Mr. Wright went back to talk this over with his superiors. He returned the next day to say that it was too late to back out of the proposed conference but that "with a little cobbling" the two leading air powers might yet work out some plan.[4] In the meantime Lord Beaverbrook had announced that he would not be able to leave London.* As a result of these discussions the two nations agreed to hold a series of individual meetings, first with each other, and then with other nations concerned in air commerce.

That was the way it worked out. The British and Americans met in London. The Americans and Canadians talked over their problems at Ottawa. Even the Russians were invited to a conference — at Washington. Later, our aviation policy planners met with officials from several other nations. All these conferences were admittedly "exploratory." The main purpose was to discuss the various plans then proposed for peaceful settlement of differences. It was expected that a common course could be worked out afterward.

Because some critics complained later that the division of the world was decided by the British and Americans without consulting Russian spokesmen, it is pertinent here to point out how carefully American officials tried to keep the Soviets informed of international developments. For example, while envoys were discussing aviation matters in London and Ottawa, Joseph C. Grew — former ambassador to Japan —, Mr. Pogue, and Mr. Burden were sitting down with Russian representatives at Washington. There was evidence that the two nations might work out their differences. Certainly it was to the advantage of all concerned to have Russia as a party to world agreements. The Soviet spokesmen were therefore given all the information available — even data of no particular concern to them. When Secretary Hull announced his appointments to the London Conference and suggested the agenda for that meeting, President Roosevelt wrote across the memorandum:

---

*Lord Beaverbrook was faced with a rebellion in his ranks and did not dare leave for fear his absence would be the signal for a *coup d'état*.

"O.K., but let the Soviets know." [5] Brazilian, Indian, French, and Dutch representatives sooner or later met with the American officials. The complaint that the British and Americans ignored their allies when drawing the world air map is therefore unfounded.

The most important of these bilateral or face-to-face conferences was the one held in London with Berle and Warner as the U.S. delegates. The meetings were held at Gwydyr House during April of 1944. Lord Beaverbrook was the host. Although the conversations were strictly unofficial, they were important because they were conducted on a high governmental level. Berle spoke as the *alter ego* of President Roosevelt. Warner represented our highest aviation authority, the Civil Aeronautics Board. Lord Beaverbrook was the leader of the dominant group in Great Britain concerned with civil aviation. Thus, when the delegates sat down together they were ready to bargain, even though they were not authorized to make any commitments for their respective governments. They got their heads so close together, indeed, that from time to time they banged them.

Just before the meetings began Wayne Parrish, the cherubic looking but shrewd editor of *American Aviation,* published the full report of the Canadian proposal, or draft, on international regulation of civil aviation.* The Canadians were playing postwar air commerce across the board. That is, they were prepared to gain regardless of how the world plan eventually worked out. Their preference was an international controlling authority with power to regulate the air lines of any nation. The British could follow that all right. On the other hand, the Canadians were willing to play with the Americans by advocating minimum restrictions on traffic. They were still working on other compromises when the London Conference was called. Parrish's announcement of their plan caused them great embarrassment, coming as it did just before the meeting. They had kept us well posted up to that time on their plans. There

---

*There is an interesting side light on the way in which this draft found its way into print. Wayne Parrish obtained a copy of the Canadian

is every evidence, indeed, that our top aviation officials were in on the Canadian plans all along. A year before, C. D. Howe, the Canadian Minister of Munitions and Supply, had suggested a modified version of the 1944 Canadian Draft Plan.[6] Nevertheless, the scoop by the American editor was a surprise to most of the aviation planners in this country and abroad. The premature publication of the Canadian plan forced Howe to explain himself to his own government, so that further details were added by the time the British and Americans concluded their talks. The Canadian Draft Plan had been kept as an ace up the sleeve. Its publication warned our delegates of what they had to guard against. It also told them that there was no Commonwealth united front in aviation.

Lord Beaverbrook requested at once that the Americans agree to the proposed Canadian Draft, or at least to accept in principle the suggestion for an international regulatory authority. Our spokesmen turned down this proposal flatly. Under such a plan, they pointed out, the United States (which had the most to contribute to world air commerce) would be outvoted by rivals jealous of our might. They could even maneuver the United States out of the picture at the very time air transportation was most needed. By such a plan the United States would lose most of its bargaining power. It was pointed out to Lord Beaverbrook that such a regulatory body would be bad for everyone at that stage of the negotiations. For until the nations had their own over-all authority to prescribe the limits of internationalism, a world aviation authority could be only a futile debating society, the Americans believed. It was certain that Congress would never turn over its regulatory powers to an international body, particularly when the codification of those regulations had not yet been made. That would have been like signing a blank check.

Draft Plan from a subordinate in the British Air Ministry. The editor spent all night writing down the provisions of this draft in his diary. Parrish writes in a very fine hand, and the material was difficult to read in his little notebook. That probably explains why, on the return trip to the States, it was passed by the censor, customs inspectors, and British Intelligence.

Unfortunately, this part of the London Conference was clumsily reported in the American press. The original report was all right, but only part of it reached the American reader, who, after all, had to make the final decision. Actually, our representatives had emphatically turned down the proposal for the world regulatory body, but they had suggested instead, as a kind of compromise, the setting up of an international group with *advisory* duties. When Lord Beaverbrook reported his progress in civil aviation to Parliament on May 10 and 11, 1944, he mentioned this suggestion and stated that the negotiations with the United States were "entirely satisfactory." Those words were interpreted over here as proof that our delegates were playing into the hands of the British by acceding to the request of our rivals for a world authority. That was the very thing we did not wish. Had the full text of the Beaverbrook speech to Parliament been printed in the U.S. press, it would have been clear that our delegates had given away nothing. Even The Beaver was careful to point that out to his countrymen. He had said: "According to the American plan, the proposed authority would start on a *non-executive* basis, *with no power or means of enforcing its regulations,* [italics mine]. I hope I have made quite clear the position taken by the United States of America. It proposed an international authority on a non-executive basis, with no power or means of enforcing its regulations, at least during the interim period." [7]

Instead of giving way to the British, the Americans had forced Lord Beaverbrook to give up a cherished program. That was also brought out in his speech.

"But make no mistake," he said, "we did not give up the Canadian Draft Convention [plan] without reluctance. We should have preferred it. Mr. Howe, the Canadian minister, had produced an admirable document, building up his structure for the regulating authority on the principles agreed at the Commonwealth conversations." [8]

Because of American stubbornness, the British had to give up the Canadian plan in favor of the Balfour report presented previously in October at the Dominions Conference on Aviation. This plan prescribed regulation of air navigation only — a control that almost all aviation planners were willing to concede — but the Americans had gone one step further. They had unofficially accepted the Halifax agreement by which both governments were bound not to enter into discriminatory negotiations with other nations. That was as far as the Americans would go. They had hardly sold out to the British, as charged in some quarters.

In August, 1944, Lord Beaverbrook and Peter Masefield came to Washington to continue the aviation talks started at London. The British were now insisting upon holding a conference where the preliminary agreements could be made official. Americans had little interest in such a meeting at that time. It is interesting to note that Berle was later blamed for acting hastily when he issued invitations for an aviation meeting at Chicago in the fall of 1944. He had no desire for such a meeting. The British literally forced him to it. If he did not call the conference immediately, the British were prepared to issue their own invitations. They might thereby have achieved the united front of empire members. That would have been a real threat to U.S. plans for postwar civil aviation. The Chicago meeting was premature, no doubt, but that was not the fault of Mr. Berle. The pressure on him is indicated by a message from Lord Beaverbrook delivered by the British Embassy to the State Department on August 29, 1944. It read:

1. I have now had an opportunity of consulting my colleagues on the subject of your proposals to me of August 3d elaborated in your telegram of August 23d [a suggestion that the operators of the United States and of the United Kingdom 'move out' on a friendly basis on world routes, with negotiations to follow].

2. We ask for postponement of your project for moving out on to the civil air routes of the world.

3. We still feel that the next step should be to hold an international conference on the basis agreed between us in London last April at the earliest date convenient to us both.

4. If, for domestic reasons, you should find it difficult to hold a conference in Washington at the present time, we shall understand your position and stand ready to call a conference ourselves in London." [9]

Spurred by the British, then, the United States invited fifty-four nations to be present at an international civil aviation conference at Chicago late in October. Before the delegates assembled the British published a statement of policy, or White Paper, stating the principles for which they would fight at Chicago.[10] The purpose of this document was to allay suspicion in Great Britain that the Americans were winning the civil air war and to make clear to the Americans just how far the British were prepared to go in meeting the U.S. counterproposals. For the most part the White Paper was the same old tune with a few new cadenzas. It stated that the British were now willing to accept the first four freedoms (the right to carry traffic between the two countries). While the fifth freedom (the right of an operator to pick up traffic in a foreign country bound for still another foreign country) would not be denied specifically, it was a privilege to be accorded only by direct, or bilateral, negotiation, not by an international (multilateral) pact. Such negotiations would give the British an opportunity to impose the restrictions they believed necessary to protect less favored operators against the strong U.S. competition. The White Paper recommended that these restrictions be enforced by an international aviation authority, with the actual supervision under regional "panels" or boards. It was suggested that at the appropriate time all this power to control would be placed under the World Security Organization of the United Nations, with voting powers to be determined on "an equitable basis."[11]

The Americans were also prepared to state their aims as the delegates gathered at Chicago. The U.S. delegation was appointed by the President. Members were Mr. Berle, chairman; Mr. Pogue and Mr. Burden, representing official aviation agencies; two senators, Josiah Bailey and Owen Brewster, leaders in aviation thinking in the upper house; two representatives, Alfred L. Bulwinkle and Charles A. Wolverton, also well versed in aviation matters; Rear Admiral Richard E. Byrd, for the armed forces; and Fiorello H. LaGuardia, the articulate little mayor of New York. Stokeley Morgan of the State Department served as secretary-general of the delegation.

It has been charged that these delegates arrived at Chicago utterly confused about the course the United States should take on international civil aviation. On the surface it did look as though no two delegates could agree on anything. On the other hand, all had followed civil aviation matters closely. They understood the fundamental issues. Where they clashed was in the area not previously explored. Of course not all the issues could have been foreseen, and it was necessary, then, for the delegates to thresh them out at the meeting. In working out such unforeseen problems they did at times give the impression of bewilderment. Nevertheless it is true that our delegates were well briefed before they arrived at Chicago. The U.S. Interdepartmental Committee had agreed upon the agenda. This was known to the delegates. So were the President's views. We even had a White Paper of our own outlining official policy.

It is a curious fact that our equivalent of the British White Paper was a product of the Justice Department, which would ostensibly have little interest in aviation. We called our White Paper the Biddle Report, after the Attorney General. Actually, it had little influence upon our delegates at Chicago. They relied more on the reports of the Interdepartmental Committee and the Civil Aeronautics Board. The main importance of the Biddle Report was the fact that it was the only published doctrine on the U.S. plan for postwar civil aviation.* The report declared that this country would not take advantage of

*There is an interesting story on the way the Justice Department got into the aviation picture. Attorney General Anthony Biddle was a close friend of the President. Roosevelt asked him for an opinion on the legal limitations involved in such a pow-wow as was about to take place at Chicago. It was expected that the report to the President would also expose violations by air-line operators of the antitrust laws. When the report was published it was a dud, as far as the antitrust reaction was concerned. Thurman Arnold, then in charge of the antitrust division, is said to have prepared an elaborate case against certain aviation companies. When Biddle realized the significance of the Chicago meeting and the bad publicity that might follow in the wake of the Arnold charges, he ordered the trust charges quashed. The action led to the resignation of Arnold and a breach between the former friends. During the antitrust investigation of the air lines, so much material had been collected that an expurgated edition was made public.

superior resources to dominate world air routes. It made no claims to wartime bases constructed by our money on foreign soil. All it asked was that these bases be made available to all flag-line operators. The report was firm in its opposition to the type of restrictions the British favored as a means of protecting national interests. Finally, its statement on the means for working out an international agreement was surprisingly prophetic. It said:

It appears inevitable that with the development of international air commerce the time will come when an increasing number of decisions with respect to the industry will have to be taken by the interested governments jointly rather than by independent action. When that time comes, it will be necessary to create an international aviation authority operating under its own constitution and superior, within the area of delegated authority, to the aviation authorities of the several countries. In order to prepare for such an eventuality, early action to set up an international aviation authority should be taken so that the world may have ample experience with such intergovernmental action before it becomes necessary to delegate mandatory authority to an international body.[12]

If the Biddle Report carried little weight with our official planners at the time, at least it told the public how this country stood on aviation matters. It described the situation as the United States and Great Britain gathered their respective henchmen for the contest at Chicago in November, 1944. The negotiations were the first test of the peace. Many of the delegates appeared to realize that. The meeting would determine whether nations could settle their trade differences amicably around a table, or whether the rivals would disperse to don their trade war paint. They knew that if they could solve trade problems solutions to other problems would also be found. The responsibilities of the delegates were very great during those terrible war days of 1944.

REFERENCES

1. *Hansard,* Lords, Fifth Series, Vol. 127, especially the speeches of Lords Londonderry and Semphill, pp. 479 ff, 495. See also Lord Beaverbrook's report to the House of Lords on October 20, 1943, in which he mentions

the agreement between President Roosevelt and Prime Minister Churchill, "subject to certain conditions." See also paragraph two of the memorandum cited in note 3.

2. "Declaration of Principles, known as the Atlantic Charter, by the President of the United States of America, and the Prime Minister of the United Kingdom, August 14, 1941," U.S. Statutes at Large, 5:1603.

3. From the private diary of A. A. Berle, Jr.

4. *Ibid.*

5. From the original memorandum, in Roosevelt's own handwriting, now in Berle's private files.

6. Memorandum to the State Department from C. D. Howe, dated December 18, 1943.

7. *Hansard,* Lords, Vol. 131, May 10, 1944, p. 694.

8. *Ibid.*

9. Text of a message in the private files of former Assistant Secretary of State A. A. Berle, Jr., dated August 29, 1944.

10. Air Ministry, *International Air Transport* (Cmd. 6561), London, October, 1944.

11. *Ibid.*

12. *International Air Transport Policy,* "Letter from the Attorney General of the United States," (79th Congress, 1st Session, House Document No. 142, 1945).

A NOTE ON SOURCES

Most of the information for this chapter was obtained from interviews. Of particular value was the diary of A. A. Berle, Jr., a journal telling the day-by-day development of U.S. aviation policy while Berle was in the key aviation post. Excellent material was also furnished by L. Welch Pogue, then chairman of the Civil Aeronautics Board. Irston Barnes and Arne Wiprud, who helped write the Biddle Report, were helpful in describing the background of that document. The Biddle Report is listed as *International Air Transport Policy,* "Letter from the Attorney General of the United States," Seventy-ninth Congress, First Session, House Document No. 142, 1945. For the British version of the Anglo-American conference at London see Volume 131 of *Hansard,* House of Lords, especially the speeches under "Aviation" between May 10 and 12, 1944. Wayne Parrish, editor of *American Aviation,* who was in London at the time, also gave the author interesting comment on that meeting.

SHOOTING IT OUT AT CHICAGO

WELCOMING the representatives to
the International Civil Aviation Conference at Chicago on
November 1, 1944, Adolf A. Berle, Jr. sounded this keynote:

Even as late as 1919 it was the opinion of the powers assembled at
Paris — the United States among them — that aerial navigation was
not a subject pertaining to the peace conference.

This time we shall not make that mistake.

The air has been used as an instrument of aggression. It is now
being made a highway of liberation. It is our opportunity to make it
hereafter a servant of peoples.

In bidding you welcome, let our labors be lighted by vision and
made fruitful by insight.[1]

Whether or not the Chicago Conference was "made fruitful
by insight" depends somewhat upon the viewpoint of the critic.
Mr. Berle and Viscount Swinton, leaders of the U.S. and British
delegations respectively, might each have repeated at the end
of the meeting the words of the Irish farmer who was asked on
his return from the local fair if he had received a satisfactory
price for his pigs.

"Well-l," answered the yokel, "I didn't get what I expected
— but then, I didn't think I would." *

Those who expected the conference to settle all the problems
of postwar aviation were of course disappointed. In 1944 no
one was certain of the issues, let alone the answers to them.

*This is a favorite anecdote of the whimsical C. G. Grey, former editor
of the British publication, *The Aeroplane.*

Every nation had its own peculiar problems, and no one plan could solve them all. The only way out was by compromise. That meant that no delegate could go home completely satisfied. Nevertheless, in the history of commercial aviation, the Chicago Conference ranks as the most important meeting ever held. This was not entirely because of its accomplishments, although they were impressive enough. It was because of the conviction on all sides that a way must be found to open up world air routes at once — and a way was found.

Curiously, the British, who had forced us into the conference, later complained that they were not ready for the meeting. Certainly Viscount Swinton was not ready. Had he been a genius as a statesman he still could not have grasped the issues in the short interval between his appointment as the new Minister of Civil Aviation and his appearance at Chicago. And Lord Swinton was not a genius. But the United States was not ready, either. The Senate was buzzing like an overturned hive of bees because of the commitments already suggested by our representatives. The Senate never likes to have anyone else assume responsibilities for international negotiations. Also, it was an election year, and therefore a bad time for momentous undertakings in the United States. The aircraft industry, which had most to gain from international air commerce, was too preoccupied with war work to give the attention to the deliberations that might have been helpful. As one of our delegates put it: "The time was not right, and the personalities were wrong."

The clash of personalities was between Lord Swinton and Berle. The leader of the American delegation was aggressive, brilliant in his grasp of intricate problems, and leftish in his thinking on aviation. Personally affable and gracious, he had an official aloofness that at first made him unpopular with the press. He came to the conference with a decisive, complete plan. Not everyone approved of it. Certainly Senators Bailey and Brewster were not in favor of the course set by Berle. Pogue of the Civil Aeronautics Board, far to the left of the Senators, did not himself see eye to eye with the assistant secretary of state and delegation chairman, although the CAB head was more likely to side with him in a showdown.

In spite of all this antagonism, Berle did what he thought he was supposed to do. He had been in close contact with the "upper echelons" shaping the postwar policies of the two countries. He thought of himself as speaking for the President. A comparison of his statements at the conference and of the President's directive quoted in the previous chapter shows that he hewed pretty closely to the line. Unfortunately, his sureness was sometimes mistaken for arrogance. His colleagues even accused him of acting without their knowledge, as in the final drafting of the fifth freedom agreement at the end of the meeting. But at least he knew his own mind, which is more than can be said of some of our delegates. And eventually he won the respect of the very journalists who had first scorned him as a typical braintruster.[2]

Lord Swinton was the antithesis of the American leader. In the first place, he represented a much harder attitude on the part of the British ministry than had his predecessor. Michael Wright of the British Embassy in Washington had assured the State Department that there would be no change in British policy at Chicago, but there certainly was a change in the leaders who were to interpret that policy. Apparently Lord Beaverbrook had expected an easy triumph in his role as aviation leader. He had assumed that the empire would stand together and would thereby bring the Americans to terms. He found instead that each Commonwealth member had its own plans for postwar aviation. With a united front Lord Beaverbrook could have afforded a soft attitude toward America. The lack of unity lowered his prestige. Lord Swinton had been one of his severest critics, and the ascendancy of the Swinton faction was warning that there would be little more compromise on the part of the British.

As Sir Philip Cunliffe-Lister, Lord Swinton had had some experience in aviation matters when he succeeded Lord Londonderry as Air Minister in 1935. He made the mistake of accepting a peerage when he was most needed in Commons.

Later, he became resident commissioner in South Africa. He was known to have little regard for Americans. These sentiments were not often expressed, but they were known and the attitude of contempt was not conducive to the ball-bearing smoothness needed at the international aviation gathering.* Lord Swinton was even further to the right on aviation matters than Berle was to the left. Such stuffiness was particularly inappropriate at Chicago, where everything was new, and where new ideas should have been exchanged freely. And yet he was an able man. Churchill in his memoirs paid him high tribute. "Lord Swinton was a very keen and efficient Air Minister," he wrote, "and for a long time had great influence in the Cabinet in procuring the necessary facilities and funds [for building up the military air force]." [3]

Despite the difference in leadership, the two countries did make progress at the aviation meeting. The need for agreement was so great that minor misunderstandings could not spoil the show. Everyone could agree on a number of points. It was generally accepted that the obsolete Paris and Havana conventions must be replaced. Nor was there much objection to the suggestion that the world routes must be ready for commerce as soon as the pressure of war would permit. Most delegates were willing to submit to international regulation of aircraft safety, navigation, and aerology. The main points of difference were all economic in nature, but they were enough to keep the conference in continual turmoil.

Under these circumstances the delegates of fifty-two governments met in the cavernous Stevens Hotel to work out the first problem of the peace. If the public later became impatient at the sluggish pace of the United Nations deliberations, or the writing of the peace treaties, it could take heart from the fact that the first test of the peace at Chicago was also discouraging.

---

*A neutral observer who attended all the meetings at Chicago declares that Lord Swinton took much of the blame for the narrow British view from the shoulders of underlings. There appears to be little doubt that W. C. G. Cribbett, British adviser at the conference, was responsible for some of the anti-American front of the British delegation. Lord Swinton was the spokesman for his country, and must therefore bear the brunt of such criticism.

The bickering went on endlessly. Yet in spite of the many disappointments, the main problems were eventually worked out. Not until thirty-seven days after the first session did the delegates depart after reaching an agreement, and even then many of them left in a huff. Many believed they had wasted those thirty-seven days. In perspective, however, it appears that much was accomplished in a remarkably short time. And despite the angry speeches at the meeting, the world was a little nearer to the promised land of international peace. The significance was not so much that the meeting had resulted in establishing world routes for immediate use, but that the fifty-two nations could agree at all. Only six weeks before the opening of the conference Berle had mused:

> The clash of interest is less national than horizontal. Pan American Airways, the British Overseas Airways Corporation, the Foreign Office imperialists, and the protagonists of air cartels want the closed sector theory. Their motives differ. Pan American wants to bar British competition in its sector; and is met by BOAC which would like to bar American competition in other sectors. Both would like to exclude all of the smaller nations and advocate riding roughshod over their rights, just as in older days the British fleet rode roughshod over Norwegian and American colonial ships. The imperialist bloc would like to close off certain areas so that British influence alone shall prevail there. Thus, they would like to set up a Western European bloc excluding the United States, and a Near Eastern bloc (Egypt to India) excluding everybody. To permit this sort of thing to get a foothold on either theory simply means that the strong air powers will gather to themselves by persuasion or force adherents which will compose great air blocs; and these blocs will interrupt the world-wide and round-the-world traffic which air makes possible. The blocs will grind against each other at their periphery in any event; but they will be a perpetual and standing menace to the great world-wide air trade routes.[4]

These were some of the issues discussed at the Chicago conference. As leader of the U.S. delegation, Berle hammered down four main planks on the American platform: (1) establishment of a provisional program under which all delegates would request their respective governments to grant landing

and transit rights to commercial aircraft of all friendly nations;*
(2) the establishment of an Interim Council to act as a clearing
house and as an advisory body during the transitional period;
(3) an agreement of principles regarding a permanent international agency to be set up at the end of the transitional
period; and (4) a "convention," or set of international regulations governing safety, navigation, and other technical matters.

The American plan differed from the others as to the power
that was to be given the international organization. The
Interim Council, as Berle proposed it, could only offer recommendations for ratification by respective national governments.
For the critics who pointed out the historic weaknesses of world
groups lacking coercive power (the failure of the League was
still a bitter memory), the State Department had an answer.
The first international authority was to be only a "mockup"
or prototype, of the future aviation congress. It would gather,
classify, and correlate the mass of information still lacking. It
would test out ideas — the ineffectual rules, for example, that
looked good on paper but were utterly impracticable. The organization could help clear the air of distrust. Then, when
all the "bugs" had been worked out, a permanent authority,
with much broader powers might be established. It was too
early to delegate such powers, said the men who had worked
out the U.S. air commerce future. "It is EARLIER than you
think," the Biddle Report had warned, in explaining the danger
of too hasty decisions.

The most drastic counter to the U.S. plan was offered by Australia and New Zealand. These countries had long been expo-
nents of industrial socialization, and they now proposed to carry
this policy into international aviation. Their delegates were
pledged to demand not only international control of world airways, but outright operation of air lines and factories by the

_____

*This was interpreted as meaning that no friendly nation would prohibit
another from operating through the country, but it did not mean that any
nation could send all its air lines across the borders. In other words, the
intent was to prevent discrimination, but the suggestion was not offered as
a means of demanding uneconomic services.

state. With a United Nations securely established, there might have been more reason to consider this demand, but at that point (1944) the United Nations had yet to meet for the first time. What the Americans needed was a program that could be put into effect at once. The Australian–New Zealand proposal was therefore rejected within a week after the first meeting of the aviation conference at Chicago.

The British stood on the platform described in their White Paper of the previous month (the "first White Paper"). They did not go as far as the Australians and New Zealanders in advocating internationalization of the world air routes, but they did hope to see an authority with power to control rates, frequencies, and subsidies. Such an agency, they believed, would establish an "equilibrium" among the leading aviation powers.

There was logic in their demands. The British pointed out that our internal, or domestic, air lines carried eight or nine times as much traffic as the international routes, and that the world operations were therefore somewhat incidental in our aviation program. In Europe it was just the opposite. Internal air lines were pip-squeak in comparison with international operations. Most European air traffic was international. Indeed, international traffic was more important to such nations as Great Britain, France, and the Netherlands than domestic routes were to the Americans. World routes were the backbone of air traffic to those countries. That being the case, the Americans were being very greedy, the British argued. They were demanding a share of international traffic, which was the core of European air commerce, but they would not let Europeans share the rich U.S. domestic field. On that basis, it was argued, Americans who cried "selfish obstructionism," when Europeans merely tried to protect international aviation interests, were doing the same thing when they selfishly protected their own domestic airways. It was a case of the pot and the kettle.

The Canadians tried to be the peacemakers, but no one blessed them for it. It is true that they did offer effective compromises. Canada had a stake in the future air routes, because the main airway of the world cut across Canada, and many of

the strategic traffic centers in the United States would some day
be reached by way of Canada. The Canadians saw themselves
caught between the two greatest air powers. They were quick
to see the necessity of compromise, and they saw themselves as
especially fitted for the task. Canadians had close relations with
the Americans geographically, commercially, and financially.
They had strong cultural ties with Great Britain. Indeed, the
Canadians believed they were in a fine position to earn the
privileges that always go to the nation that can turn the balance
of power. They could tell Americans that it was the Canadians
who broke the "united front" of Commonwealth nations,
which Lord Beaverbrook had counted on to bring the United
States to terms. The Canadians could say honestly that they
had always kept Washington informed as to policy.

Actually, the Canadians and British were working together.
The Canadians had ambitious plans for world routes. The
United States was more of a threat than Great Britain. Canada,
therefore, began working with the mother country. They worried the United States like a brace of hounds at a stag. Each
used the other to maneuver the United States a little closer to
the British goal. According to a reliable but unofficial observer
at the conference, the British and Canadians at one time had
won about seven-eighths of their demands. Then they made
the mistake of pushing the U.S. delegation too far on traffic
restrictions. The reaction of our representatives was "to hell
with all this; we'll go back to where we stood before." Stokeley
Morgan, the secretary-general of the American delegation, made
an interesting comment when he looked over the manuscript
for this book. He wrote:

It is true that during the closed sessions of the British, American,
and Canadian delegates, during which the rest of the conference impatiently marked time and grew hotter and hotter under the collar,
we had discussions and reached tentative agreement on a great many
of the points at issue, but we always stressed the fact that this was all
tentative, subject to reconsideration (as it would have been), and we
were simply passing questions on to others, not considering them in any
way as closed issues. From start to finish it was understood that everything depended upon a final agreement on Fifth Freedom traffic and

minimum regulation. The final blowup was precipitated by what the American delegation interpreted as a backdown by the British on what we thought was a definite agreement of the day before, which led, to the "to hell with all this" attitude, which, as you justly say, terminated the tri-partite secret talks.[5]

It was probably a good thing that these secret meetings broke up as they did. If the British had been just a little more responsive, the United States might have been led to approve the complicated formulae which the British were insisting upon for control of traffic. Although such agreements might have made the conference outwardly a great success, U.S. air transportation might have run into staggering head winds as the navigators of our policy tried frantically to get us out of the mess.

For several weeks the seven hundred delegates, advisers, and technicians listened to the mass of conflicting testimony on why various proposals should or should not be accepted. For the most part, however, the great battles were fought, not in the general sessions, but by the traditional "fifteen men in a smoke-filled room." Berle and Lord Swinton had raised their rallying standards before the conference was even called to order. Indeed, one of the main activities at Chicago was lining up recruits for the respective camps.

Berle raised his battle flag over the doctrine of mutual, or "multilateral" agreements binding all signatory nations to the same terms. He demanded that such agreements include fifth-freedom commercial rights for air lines of all nations party to the multilateral pact. Viscount Swinton had different ideas. He did not budge from the stand he had taken in his October White Paper. He himself described the British policy in the simplest terms when he explained his views at Chicago: "We want to encourage enterprise and initiative," he said, "and the development and application of all that science, design, and craftsmanship and industry can give us. But we want to avoid disorderly competition with the waste of effort and money and loss of good will which such competition involves." [6]

To carry out this plan Lord Swinton believed it would be

necessary to impose certain traffic restrictions. His plan was to set traffic quotas for each operator, based on past records. He would have agreed to a "liberal margin" above future traffic estimates because he realized that good service would bring forth greater use of air transportation, but relatively each nation would have definite traffic limitations. The British could not understand why the Americans objected to that. U.S. air lines had carried a preponderant share of world air traffic, and on the basis of past performance and future probabilities, American operators were assured of first place in air transportation under the British plan.

The quota system appeared to be fair to the British because it fitted in exactly with their concept of air transportation. It did not fit in at all with the American plan of international air commerce. For example, the British proposed to set traffic quotas for passengers in terms of air-liner seats. That is, the U.S. would have been allotted so many seats per week between New York and London. Again, that would have worked well enough for the British, for they planned to use smaller planes. The Americans were already ordering the giant transports which they believed would help lower flight costs and fares. Under the British system the entire U.S. quota of traffic might be carried in one or two such aircraft. The British, operating smaller aircraft, would thus have an advantage. Small craft could be just as safe and fast as the super liners. Polls had indicated that mere size did not lure passengers into planes. Thus, under the quota system, the British with more frequent service might provide better transportation than the Americans. Nor would we be able to take full advantage of large plane economies, if traffic were to be limited.

Even so, the Americans at one point were willing to compromise on traffic restrictions. It was suggested that the world routes be marked off by division points. These points would be centers where traffic changes were likely to occur. When the load factor on any division during a given period exceeded 65 per cent, operators were to be allowed to schedule another flight over the route.* The catch to the American suggestion was that load factors were to be computed at division points. Thus, on the U.S.–India air route, London and Cairo might have been designated as division points between New York and Calcutta. If traffic exceeded the 65 per cent load factor between London–Cairo division, even though the Cairo–Calcutta divi- New York for Calcutta to take up the traffic increase on the London-Cairo division, even though the Cairo-Calcutta divi- sion showed no increase in traffic. The British insisted that it was unfair to increase plane frequencies over the whole route simply because one division could support more air transpor- tation. Their logic was all right, but apparently they did not realize that this plan had been offered by the Americans not because of its soundness, but only as a concession, or com- promise.

The British answered this proposal with a modification they called the "escalator clause" — dubbed by Mayor LaGuardia the "emasculator clause." It was the weirdest and most gro- tesque plan ever offered to international air-line operators. Only a person with a Rube Goldberg mind could have designed this pattern for air commerce. Nobody at the conference could figure it out. In brief, it would have permitted the scheduling of extra flights, as demanded by the Americans, but only after the load factor for the entire route exceeded 60 per cent. That was not difficult to follow, but the formula for determining quotas, if carried out, would have filled our mental institutions with air-line executives.

The complexity of the escalator clause can only be mentioned in these pages, but one example may show why our delegates threw up their hands in despair over British pedantry. If there were 150 passengers a day bound for London and 60 for Paris, the U.S. quota under the escalator clause would be 126 seats to London and 60 to Paris (60 per cent of the total traffic to both points). Assuming the U.S. carriers operated planes capa-

*The load factor is the ratio of filled seats to empty seats. A plane with 100 seats and 65 passengers aboard thus is said to have a load factor of 65.

ble of carrying 15 passengers across the Atlantic, and 30 from London to Paris on 12 schedules a day, the British would have allocated traffic by dividing the combined New York–London and New York–Paris seat quota by 12. This would give the U.S. carrier the right to sell 15 seats on the London section, but from London to Paris he had only five seats allowed (the daily quota of 60 seats divided by the number of planes per day — 12). The 12 planes out of New York would already have deposited 30 Paris-bound passengers in London — an average of 2.5 passengers per plane. These, plus the traffic picked up in London under the escalator provisions, would have given each 30-passenger U.S. plane operating between London and Paris 7.5 available seats. The only way to increase the passenger pay load was to decrease the London–Paris frequencies from 12 to 4, let us say. That would add 13 passengers to the 7.5 already bound for Paris. Nothing was said as to how half a passenger was to be shipped between the two points, for by the time the experts had reached that stage, they were as confused as the reader who has had the patience to follow along this far.

As in all such negotiations, the important issue was obscured by a screen of lacy talk. The British argued that they were merely trying to protect the air lines of the smaller nations against such monsters as the BOAConstrictor and the Pan American Airways octopus. They tried to sell the idea that the big trunk lines would take all the business between any two nearby points. On the contrary, the Americans answered, such restrictions would be most unfair to the small countries, since they could not afford to support world routes and were thus dependent on the trunk lines. By penalizing the trunk-line operators, small nations would be depriving themselves of the frequency and quality of service only the big carrier could provide. Small countries needed international air transportation desperately, but they could not afford to "escalate" their way around the world.

Fortunately for the United States, many of the delegates from the smaller nations were not impressed by British solicitude for them. A majority favored the American doctrine, or at least a modification of it. They believed that the trunk lines would bring in far more business than their local operators would forfeit to foreign enterprise. They were willing to develop their respective air systems as safe, efficient, but small feeder lines. Since they could provide far more complete and frequent service in their areas, they had little fear of losing much local traffic to the trunk lines.

This is enough to indicate the type of argument that could have been heard day after day at the Chicago conference. Broadly speaking, each skirmish was fought over the issue of competition versus protection. Three weeks after the conference had been called to order delegates were still as far apart ideologically as they had been on the first day. There were members of the U.S. group who were willing to pack up and go home. They believed they had already given away too much, and they were determined to make no more concessions. The British were also tired of the tussle. They were ready to forsake this chilly and alien city, where they were constantly held up as first-class examples of British stuffiness.

On November 22 the Chicago conference was nearly on the reefs. The ship was saved by three expert navigators. They were: Adolf Berle, calling the soundings from the chains but keeping well out of sight; bustling little Mayor LaGuardia; and H. J. Symington, head of Trans-Canada Air Lines. Canada and the United States had been playing footie during the general discussions, and on November 20 they had come to a tentative understanding. Both agreed to come out for multilateral pacts as a means of opening up international air commerce to all the nations willing to sign a common document. They had not worked out the details as to rates, frequencies, and subsidies, but at least they were making progress. When the agitation for adjournment began on the twenty-second, the representatives of Canada and the United States saw their chances of success glimmering. The mutineers insisting upon scuttling the conference were becoming more numerous every hour. Just at this point Symington asked for the floor at the general session. Speaking as one "who has sat between Britain and America" he pointed out that the differences between the two air powers had been exaggerated and that the bitter feeling between the two was concocted by lack of understanding. The discussions must continue, Symington insisted, "so that a real convention will emerge from this very wonderful conference. . . ." This was not the time to quit, he pleaded. "You have before you a document which deals with everything except just that thing [Freedom of the Air]. We have fought through all the technicalities of organization and sanctions . . . but, in spite of that, the vacant clauses in the agreement mean that we have to go now and get bilateral agreements. I submit . . . that this world expects more than this from this conference." [7]

Symington's remarks received the loudest acclaim of any speech up to that point. Mayor LaGuardia clinched the Symington pep talk two days later, and thereby rendered a great service to world aviation, for there was still a movement afoot to bolt the conference. On November 23 the little mayor was briefed by Berle, who urged LaGuardia to turn on the forensic heat. With his high-pitched voice, his exaggerated but expressive gestures, and his famous hyperbole, Mayor LaGuardia held the attention of the delegates until he had put his points across. He declared that the main purpose of the conference had been to make certain that international air commerce was given the green light in the immediate future. He pointed out that the delegates had not yet settled the issue and therefore had failed in their duties. They were told that they must not depart until they had discussed every possible solution to the problem of greater freedom in the air. "Otherwise," cried he, "all the meat is taken out of the convention, and all the rest is sauce." The mayor took violent issue with Lord Swinton, who was reported to be packing up after achieving a few minor objectives. How could anyone be so obstinate as to wreck such an important meeting just when it was on the verge of performing a momentous service for the world, asked LaGuardia? He was certain there could be some kind of compromise, even on such controversial matters as the escalator clause or multilateral agreements. Spurred by LaGuardia's obvious sincerity, the weary delegates rolled up their sleeves to "sweat out" the conference.

The LaGuardia speech coincided with the newspaper accounts of the British and American programs. Both factions stated that they were through with compromise and delay. The United States appeared to be insisting upon acceptance of Fifth Freedom rights through multilateral agreement, although, of course, the public could not have known of the split in the American delegation on that issue. The British were determined to force through restrictions on rates and frequencies. There appeared to be no possibility of breaking the old deadlock. Leaders of both factions were under fire from their respective governments. Editors were flaying them for their failures. Those who did not criticize believed for the most part that the conference had been a waste of time. "He was cabined, cribbed, and confined," one countrymen wrote of Lord Swinton, adding that the man had never had a chance anyway.

Berle had also run into a cold front. He had been the voice of President Roosevelt and Secretary of State Cordell Hull. As such, he was the natural target of all those antagonistic to the New Deal. Senators McCarran, Brewster, and Bailey charged that he was squandering America's bargaining power by his insistence upon multilateral agreements. Even the Civil Aeronautics Board members were lukewarm to the official platform laid down by Berle. Harllee Branch had gone so far as to call Hull to protest Berle's attempt to force through Fifth Freedom rights by multilateral agreement. He and his Board colleagues would have preferred to work by bilateral agreement, where the U.S. could bargain face to face. Pogue, chairman of the CAB, himself preferred the bilateral plan but refrained from public criticism for the sake of U.S. solidarity. It should also be remembered that both Berle's and Pogue's agencies were branches of the *executive* department of the Government. They were both pledged to carry out the policies of the Chief Executive, and the President had declared for the multilateral agreement. Only because of this had Berle retained the right to speak for the U.S. without more opposition.

Berle also had to buck outside opposition. The Pan American Airways group were outraged at the course the U.S. appeared to be taking. Pan American had a policy of its own. "Highest British sources" had confirmed reports current in the United States that the number one U.S. flag line had reached an understanding with BOAC. Apparently executives of the two rival air lines had in mind a cartel agreement for the control of international air transportation. The British, it was reported, had learned that General Critchley, representing BOAC, had gone to America to discuss the matter with Mr. Trippe. According to the British source, the two had agreed that either might later deny the existence of such an agreement. A State Department private memorandum described the arrangement as follows: Pan American was to have the bulk of the North Atlantic traffic. BOAC was to have almost all the European continental traffic, and Pan American Airways was to serve only gateways in that area. BOAC was to be permitted to operate limited services to South America, Pan American's special hunting preserve. In certain South American countries (apparently Argentina was one) where the British had special interests, the British were to be allowed to operate on a more ambitious scale for prestige purposes. On the other hand, Pan American was to advocate the use of Hawaii by a BOAC Pacific operation. This would enable the British to fill the gap between Australia and Canada. It would, in fact, have made BOAC a round-the-world empire route in cooperation with Australian and Canadian enterprises.

A substantial number of the British government aviation policy planners disagreed with this plan. They were mostly concerned with the highhanded way in which BOAC had ignored them, rather than with the terms suggested, but at any rate they had it in for General Critchley. Lord Beaverbrook found himself in a most embarrassing position. While representing British aviation policy, he was forced by the above circumstances to oppose the plans of his own operator, although theoretically BOAC was a national implement under government control. By the same token President Roosevelt found himself in conflict with the U.S. carrier that had done more

than any other to spread the fame of American aviation efficiency to all parts of the world. The British settled the matter
by eliminating Lord Beaverbrook and replacing him with Lord
Swinton, who was more sympathetic to the BOAC policy. On
the other hand, the President did not soften, and the policy-
makers continued to oppose the Pan American plan. Obviously, Pan American moguls had little love for the officials who
blocked the intercompany scheme.

As long as Cordell Hull was at the head of the State Department, Berle went on negotiating agreements that he believed
to be the mandate of his chief. About this time, however, Hull
was forced to retire because of ill health. The State Department for an interim period was under Edward Stettinius, Jr.,
Trippe's brother-in-law. During the most critical days of the
Chicago conference — indeed, only five days before its adjournment, it was announced from the White House that Berle
had resigned as assistant secretary of state. Not too much should
be made of this coincidence. It is usual for a new department
head to sweep out subordinates in order to replace them with
men he knows and trusts. The President usually does this upon
inauguration. The White House announcement was taken as
an indication that the resignation was not to be greeted with
suspicion. But one thing was certain — Berle was out. True,
he remained as leader of the aviation delegation, but the change
in his status might well have been taken by his adversaries as
a sign that Berle's views did not necessarily reflect the official
policy of the United States. If the resignation announcement
had not been a slap, why could it not have been delayed the
five days until the critical agreements were signed and the
delegates were homeward bound?

Those who were "in the know" at the time say that plans
had been made for Berle even before the Chicago conference
was called. Berle's superiors had waited as long as they could,
but when the meeting dragged on for more than a month they
had to act. The war was still on; there were momentous issues.
to decide, apart from aviation, and Berle's successor needed the
title and prestige to get on with his tasks.

Whatever the reason, Berle was through as our top aviation policy maker. His career had been brief but busy. Shortly thereafter he was appointed Ambassador to Brazil. He had an important mission because of the role of that country in a war of logistics, but the work that he had started in aviation was left for others to finish.

REFERENCES

1. "Address by Assistant Secretary Berle," *Department of State Bulletin,* Vol. XI, No. 280, November 5, 1944, p. 530.
2. This change in attitude is typified by an editorial entitled "Cheers for Berle," in *American Aviation,* December 15, 1944, p. 9. There were other paeans by the journalistic fraternity.
3. Winston S. Churchill, *The Gathering Storm* (Boston, 1948), p. 231.
4. Diary of A. A. Berle, Jr., dated September 16, 1944.
5. Undated memorandum from Stokeley Morgan's notes on the author's manuscript.
6. *Hansard,* Lords, January 16, 1945, Vol. 131, p. 691.
7. Eric Bramley, "Agreement on Air Convention Fading," *American Aviation,* December 1, 1944, pp. 19-21.

A NOTE ON SOURCES

British aviation policy during this period may be traced through the *Parliamentary Debates.* See especially *Hansard,* House of Lords, Vols. 125, 126, 130, and 131 under "Civil Aviation." Interesting comments on aviation progress appeared in the newspapers and trade journals. Particularly interesting were: Eric Bramley, "Conference Organized: Tackles Big Job," *American Aviation,* November 15, 1944, pp. 17, 19; the same, "Agreement of Air Convention Fading," *American Aviation,* December 1, 1944, pp. 19, 21; the same, "Five Documents Emerge from Conference," December 15, 1944, pp. 17, 20. An authoritative comment on the work of the delegates is Stokeley Morgan's "International Civil Aviation Conference at Chicago," in *Blueprint for World Civil Aviation,* Department of State Publication, Conference Series No. 70, Washington, 1945. Morgan was secretary-general of the U. S. delegation at Chicago. Another able commentator on the conference was John Parker Van Zandt, then connected with the Broookings Institution as an unofficial observer of the meetings. See his "Quiz on

Crucial Conference," in *American Aviation,* January 1, 1945, pp. 28-31. The *Department of State Bulletin,* Vol. XI, No. 280, November 5, 1944, contains addresses to the conference by President Roosevelt and Berle. Information for this chapter was also obtained from interviews with A. A. Berle, Jr., assistant secretary of state during this period; L. Welch Pogue, chairman of the Civil Aeronautics Board at the time; Harllee Branch, board member; John Parker Van Zandt; and Stokeley Morgan.

GIVE 'EM AIR

UNDER the closed-sky pattern by which nations had formerly restricted air commerce, the American air-line operator would be virtually a prisoner within his own boundaries. Thus, the development of U.S. world air routes was dependent in the final analysis upon agreements with our neighbors. It was the purpose of the Chicago aviation con-. ference not only to open up international air routes at once, but to facilitate commerce of the future. When the conference was adjourned on December 7, 1944, it had made long strides toward the goal. This was all the more remarkable because only five days previously the meeting had been for the second time threatened with dissolution before it accomplished anything.

On December 2 the U.S. and British delegations were prepared to give up the negotiations as hopeless. A few decisions had been made, but the critical problems of air commerce were still unsolved. Both delegations had decided to leave their troubles with an interim council. On the same day the U.S. representatives had been ready to present a document for a provisional advisory organization and to suggest adoption of the Five Freedoms Agreement. Had a conference vote on these issues been called, the meeting certainly would have broken up at that point. Just before this was about to happen, up spoke chesty little Mayor LaGuardia again. He made a strong plea for a workable compromise: "We have built the hangar," he cried in his squeaky voice, "we have all the navigation instruments; we've provided for the weather reports; but we still haven't the plane."

Just because the United States and Great Britain could not agree on the controversial Five Freedoms document was no reason for scuttling the whole conference, he argued. Could not the two leading air powers agree on at least some of the freedoms included in that document? The mayor was given an immediate response. As though by prearrangement, the Netherlands delegation moved that the first two freedoms — the right to cross the skies of foreign lands and the right to alight for noncommercial purposes — should be written as a separate document to be known as the Two Freedoms, or Transit Agreement. There was an enthusiastic support of this proposal, and it was soon clear that the compromise reached had saved the day.

The Transit Agreement did not appear to be much in the way of progress, after more than five weeks of bickering. Many operators wondered what had been gained if they were still forbidden to pick up and to discharge traffic in countries bound by the Two Freedoms clause. But the agreement turned out to be a long stride toward the goal of the Merchant Airman. For one thing, the document made possible further negotiations with individual nations for more liberal contracts. Such agreements would have been useless, had aircraft been prevented from reaching countries offering the extra privileges. Furthermore, it might very well open the eyes of the people in the more restrictive countries when they saw valuable traffic en route to the airports of the more liberal nations. Stokeley Morgan, secretary-general of the U.S. delegation at Chicago, made an interesting comment on this point. Said he:

As you very justly bring out, the suggestion that at least two freedoms be granted was the turning point of the conference. If my memory serves, it was Lord Swinton who, perhaps resignedly and perhaps inadvertently, made the statement in one of the committee meetings that while Britain still must insist on her general policy with regard to commercial traffic, she would have no objection to granting the first two freedoms without any strings attached. This was seized upon by the Netherlands delegate, who proposed the formal resolution which later became the Air Transport Agreement. [Mr. Morgan probably means the Transit Agreement.] I suspect this was inspired by Mr. Berle's instantaneous recognition that a break had occurred and quick move to capitalize on it. Canada at this point felt that she had definitely been sold down the river by the mother country, and Symington was practically livid because of course Canada's main bargaining position was the withholding of transit privileges. Nobody was much interested in Fifth Freedom traffic in and out of Canada. However, after a night's reflection Symington said that Canada would go along and that settled it.

On the Five Freedoms agreement [right to pick up and to discharge traffic bound for other foreign countries] of course there was no such break or no such acceptance. It was a last desperate effort by Mr. Berle to line up states that were willing to sign up. We, of course, hoped for more than did sign up, because, as you point out, the Two Freedoms agreement enabled us to obtain access to the states which would offer us the Five Freedoms agreement. Even so, we recognized that for the most part we were going to have to fall back on bilateral agreements, and we began then and there during the last days of the conference our bilateral negotiations with the Swedes and Irish; agreements which were polished off and signed within a few weeks of the adjournment of the conference. We felt that the bilateral agreement with Ireland plus the Two Freedoms agreement guaranteed our ability to cross the Atlantic and to get into Europe. The one thing that disturbed us was Newfoundland, where Swinton claimed that Britain's signature of the Two Freedoms agreement did not apply. But after a few months we were notified that we had the Two Freedoms in Newfoundland.[1]

Thus, the acceptance of the Transit Agreement was as important a step in the progress of freedom of the air as Lord Stowell's decision had been in establishing freedom of the seas back in 1817.* Berle himself believed this to be so. As he told the departing delegates at Chicago:

When we met, the air of every country was closed to every other country. Every plane which passed its own national border was as-

_____

*The Two Freedoms Agreement had an important modification inserted at the last moment at the insistence of Cuba, backed by the United States for political reasons. This was the right of small countries to require reasonable service from the air lines using the territory for non-traffic purposes.

sumed to be an enemy. Little burrows had been cut through air frontiers by private concessions granted as favors to private companies or occasionally to favorite governments. These special privileges — for that is what they were — had begun to be the foundation of companies not unlike the imperialist trading companies of the sixteenth and seventeenth centuries. There was serious danger that the air of the world would become an instrument by which the few would exploit the many. The air, which is God's gift to everyone, was in danger of becoming a method of levying tribute on the masses of the world. In this situation there was danger that the historic pattern would repeat itself; that trading concessions would mix with political concessions and diplomatic intrigue; and that these in turn would lead in future decades to wars. This was the early history of the seas. . . .

I believe it will be found that without having to undergo two centuries of war and terror, we have begun to lay a foundation for freedom under law in air transport. . . . The day of secret diplomacy in the air is past. . . . We met in the seventeenth century. We close in the twentieth century in the air. We met in an era of diplomatic intrigue and private monopolistic privilege. We close in an era of open covenants and equal opportunity and status.[2]

The acceptance of the Transit Agreement broke the log jam that had blocked the conference for so many weeks, and in the last five days many important measures were approved. When the conference was adjourned on December 7, 1944 (the anniversary of our entry into the war) it had produced six important documents — five of them drawn up as appendices to the final act of the conference and usually considered separately.*

The most important of the documents was the International Convention on Civil Aviation, which included clauses on air transport, air navigation, and the technical phases of commercial aviation. It provided for the establishment of an International Civil Aviation Organization (ICAO) comprising both a council and an assembly. All states signing the document

*Appendix I was the Interim Agreement on International Civil Aviation. Appendix II was the Convention on International Civil Aviation. Appendix III was called the International Air Services Transit Agreement. Appendix IV was the International Air Transport Agreement. Appendix V was a tentative set of twelve technical annexes, to be made later a part of the Convention. The sixth document, contained in Recommendation VIII of the Final Act, is the Standard Form of Agreement for Provisional Air Routes.

were to be represented in the assembly. The council was to be made up of representatives from twenty-one states elected on the basis of their importance to air transportation, their contributions to air navigation, or their geographical position. Most of the fifty-four nations represented at the conference were in favor of the document. By December 7, when the delegates departed for home, signatures on behalf of thirty-seven states had been fixed to the Convention. Ratification by the home governments was relatively slow, however, as had been anticipated at the conference. Six months after the Chicago meeting only the Polish government-in-exile had deposited its "instrument of ratification" with the United States Government, as provided in the Convention. There was no reason for alarm over this slowness because there was a three-year maximum period for ratification under the terms of the Interim Agreement.[3] President Roosevelt transmitted the Convention to the United States Senate on March 12, 1945. Shortly after, representatives of the State, War, Navy, and Commerce Departments and the Civil Aeronautics Board appeared before a subcommittee of the Senate Foreign Relations Committee to endorse the Convention.

Meanwhile, progress continued under the Interim Agreement on International Civil Aviation. It was believed that many months would pass before the necessary twenty-six signatures of ratification were obtained for the Convention, but adoption of the Interim Agreement was possible under a much simpler process. The Interim Agreement contained many of the basic provisions of the Convention, but it was more limited in scope and was less detailed than the permanent document. It provided for the establishment of a Provisional International Civil Aviation Organization (PICAO), with an interim assembly and an interim council. As predicted, there was almost no opposition to the measure. Within a year every nation represented at Chicago, except Yugoslavia, had signed the document. It was provided in the Agreement that each government would inform the United States at the earliest date whether the signatures affixed at Chicago were to be recognized as binding by the respective governments. The Agreement was to come into force when the twenty-sixth nation accepted the Chicago commitments. This process was speeded up by a provision stating that each state represented on the first Interim Council by an election held at the Chicago meeting had to accept the Agreement within six months after adjournment of the conference in order to retain its seat. Within that period all twenty council-member states had underwritten the Agreement. Actually, there were twenty-one seats on the council, but a vacancy was left for the Soviet Union, which did not join the organization. By June 6, 1945, the required twenty-six signatures had been obtained and PICAO was open for business. The Canadian Government then invited each of the twenty council-member states to designate representatives for the first meeting of the interim council at Montreal, beginning on August 15, 1945.

One of the most important steps taken after the adjournment at Chicago was the revision of Appendix V of the Convention. This was a set of twelve technical "annexes," sometimes called "the nuts and bolts" agreement. Slated to become a part of the Convention, the Appendix was a set of rules on such subjects as communications, traffic control practices, licensing, aerology reports, and navigation procedure. It was stipulated at Chicago that the annexes were not to be absolutely binding on member states, but it was hoped that the rules and regulations would eventually bring about a standardization that would be of great benefit in world air commerce. In the meantime, the annexes were to be studied more thoroughly. Any improvements or suggestions were to be submitted to the U.S. Government by May 1, 1945, so that PICAO could work them into final form. To facilitate this study, a number of "technical working groups" were organized to offer advice.

In addition to the progress on the technical annexes, another step forward was taken by a very competent group called the Canadian Preparatory Committee. It was made up of technical experts loaned by the Canadian armed forces and Government, and its purpose was to draw up the agenda for the opening sessions of the council.

After several days of preliminary discussions, representatives of nineteen of the twenty council-member states opened the first session of the interim council in Montreal on August 15, 1945.* The council held nine meetings. Dr. Edward P. Warner, the erudite member of the U.S. Civil Aeronautics Board, was elected president, and the council was divided into three committees to study specific problems of organization, personnel, and finance. Later a fourth committee on procedure was appointed. The proposals of these four *ad hoc,* or specific committees, were amended and adopted at later meetings of the council.

The main divisions of PICAO were the interim assembly, the interim council and its three main committees, and the secretariat. The latter, which was the permanent office force, was to be recruited on an international quota basis. Main duties of the assembly were to approve PICAO's budget; to refer problems to the council for consideration; and to decide upon matters referred to it by the council. Chief functions of the council were to submit budget estimates to the assembly; to carry out the assembly's directives; and to exercise the following powers: (a) to gather information from member states useful in passing on recommendations made by such states; (b) to register and make available for inspection all existing agreements relating to routes, services, landing rights, airport privileges, or concessions to which any member state, *or any air line of a member state* was a party; (c) to coordinate the work of the three main committees on Air Transport, Air Navigation, and the International Convention on Civil Aviation; (d) to consider the reports of the various working groups; (e) to submit an annual report to the assembly; (f) to act as a board of arbitration when differences between member states were called to its attention — decisions to be binding or advisory, according to prearrangement; (g) to study and report on traffic and operational problems.

Chief executive was to be the secretary-general who was re-

*Mexico was the member state not represented.

sponsible to the president as the representative of the council and who was to supervise the secretariat. Because he was a more permanent fixture than the president, he was destined to be one of the most important members of the new organization. The secretariat itself was divided into the air navigation bureau, the air transport bureau, and the bureau of administration. The first two were set up to provide working personnel for the air transport and air navigation committees of the council, while the bureau of administration was to service the entire PICAO organization on such matters as personnel, offices, publications, and library facilities.

There was no provision in either the permanent Convention or in the Interim Agreement for an outright grant of commercial rights. It had been impossible to reach such an agreement at Chicago. Instead, two optional documents were drafted. The first, officially called the International Air Services Transit Agreement, was better known as the Transit or Two Freedoms Agreement. Each nation accepting this document granted to other signatory nations the privilege of flying across its territory and the right to land for non-traffic purposes. The second document, written as the International Air Transport Agreement, was better known as the Transport, or Five Freedoms Agreement. It provided for a mutual interchange of traffic privileges, in addition to the concessions granted by the Transit document. It would have allowed signatory nations the right to permit international air lines to carry country-to-country traffic along its route. This was the document that caused so much heated discussion at Chicago. The United States at first favored this measure. On the whole, however, it was not widely accepted. A year after the Chicago conference only nine states had accepted the Five Freedoms Agreement, although some of them were of great strategic importance to the U.S. international air-transport program.*

Resolution VIII of the Final Act recommended a Form of

---

*The nine were: the United States, the Netherlands, Turkey, Liberia, Ethiopia, Afghanistan, China, El Salvador, and Paraguay.

Standard Agreement for Provisional Air Routes, which, it was hoped, would be used by all nations concluding bilateral agreements. This form was a recognition that certain nations would object to the Five Freedoms Agreement but would approve a standard bilateral agreement form that would do away with discrimination against less favored nations. Within a year after the Chicago conference the United States had concluded eight bilateral agreements, which, in general, followed the standard form prescribed at Chicago.* In each of these agreements full Five Freedoms rights were exchanged. In addition there was a special arrangement with Canada providing for four of the five freedoms, and for discharge and pickup of world traffic under certain limitations.

The above account of the accomplishments of the Chicago conference does not describe all the results of that important meeting. It does indicate the scope of the negotiations, however, and the results bore out Berle's valedictory to the delegates departing home to explain the conference to their respective governments. Berle had said: "Oppressing none, considering all, establishing law where we can, and taking common counsel where the law has yet to emerge through customs and experience; liberating the wings whose line goes out to the ends of the earth, we shall succeed if our decisions are informed by that honor, and vision, and common kindness, which now, and always, are the great content of wisdom." [4]

Berle assured the delegates that the United States was sincere in its stand at Chicago and that the country would not use its "temporary position of monopoly as a means of securing permanent advantage." As an earnest of this proposition, he promised to release transport planes to the air lines of member nations as soon as the military situation warranted. [5]

Was the Chicago conference as successful as Berle said it was? That was a matter of opinion. Certainly Berle and his

*The countries and the effective dates of the agreements were: Spain, December 2, 1944; Denmark, January 1, 1945; Sweden, January 1, 1945; Iceland, February 1, 1945; Ireland, February 17, 1945; Switzerland, August 3, 1945; Norway, October 15, 1945; Portugal, December 6, 1945.

proponents had reason to argue for the affirmative. In the midst of a weary war half a hundred nations had sent representatives to work out one of the vexatious problems of the peace. That in itself was a remarkable achievement. If the delegates had merely stated their respective policies on world air commerce the meeting would have justified the cost. But the conference had been much more than a clearinghouse for international air-transport problems. The documents drafted at the meeting were impressive accomplishments, especially in view of the rancor and suspicion beclouding the issues at Chicago. True, there were gaps in the Chicago story. Not all the important countries were represented. As long as Russia remained aloof there could be no actual world agreement. Another fault was the lack of agreement on basic policies. This was indicated by the fact that all the documents were not approved. And on the Five Freedoms Agreement there was hostility between two rival camps.

Critics of the Chicago conference were likely to base their appraisals of the results upon this failure to "put over" the Five Freedoms Agreement — for it did ultimately die from lack of attention. If it were true that this document was the core of the conference, then the Chicago meeting might indeed be called a failure. Others said that the prime objective of the conference was to open up the world routes immediately. If that was the issue, then the meeting was a success. Those who cried "failure" could not have realized the restrictive nature of international air transport in the years before Chicago. Those who cried "success" did not foresee the misunderstandings that were to follow the meeting. All these factors must be considered in evaluating the results of the meeting. For it is all too clear that our aviation leaders were divided in their opinions. Said Senator Bailey, chairman of the powerful senate committee on aviation matters:

What happened [at Chicago] was that we negotiated and had conferences and studied for many days. We appeared to get nowhere, and in the last three or four days, Mr. Berle, having his reputation at stake in the State Department, and the head of the delegation, seeing that the thing was coming to an end; that Canada had pulled out, Great Britain had pulled out, and Russia had pulled out before she started in . . . Mr. Berle threw things together and tried to work out something in the last two or three days.

What he worked out is what we have, and Mr. Berle was trying to save as much as he could from what I considered to be right much of a wreck.

That is my interpretation of Chicago.[6]

The editor of one of the leading aviation trade journals has also described the Chicago meetings as "an awful mess." Had the United States simply assumed that world routes were to be opened immediately after the war, no issues would have been raised, he believes. According to this critic, the United States brought trouble on itself by making such a fuss at Chicago. He illustrates his point by citing the Dutch and Scandinavian operators, who moved out along the international air routes quietly and made rapid progress with little or no opposition. Whether these nations could have succeeded had they been more serious rivals of the British and Americans, the editor cannot say. At least, he says, we could have tried the quiet approach first.

One member of the Chicago delegation declares that more would have been accomplished at Chicago had the U.S. representatives acted as a unit. He blames Berle for taking over too much responsibility. According to his story, the American delegates did not know half the time what the chairman was going to bring up for discussion the next day. On the way to Chicago, says this critic, Warner of the Civil Aeronautics Board, was the only member of that body who saw a copy of the keynote speech that Berle was going to make the next day. Even L. Welch Pogue, chairman of the CAB and vice-chairman of the U.S. delegation, was kept in the dark about this important statement. This was all the more strange because the CAB at that time was deeply involved in international negotiations and had every reason to be kept informed as to U.S. aviation policy as developed at Chicago. At that very moment the CAB experts were working on bilateral aviation agreements with Eire and Spain — strategic gateways to all Europe — while at the same time Mr. Berle was advocating such negotiation by multilateral agreement. When these CAB officials discovered that their bilateral approach was being circumvented at Chicago without even an attempt to give their side a hearing, some of them were so furious that they have not forgiven Berle to this day.

On the other hand, there were staunch defenders of the meeting's results. John Parker Van Zandt, then connected with the Brookings Institution, and a student of aviation problems since his World War I flying days, has called the Chicago conference "a remarkable success when balanced up." [7] Van Zandt was a critical observer at the meeting and was permitted to attend many of the sessions at which policy was discussed. The intangible results were far more significant than the documents that were drafted at Chicago, he believes. He admits that the conference inevitably generated friction, as charged by other critics, but declares that the meetings provided the first openings in the international barriers to world air commerce.

British opinion was also divided. Lord Swinton was mildly optimistic in public. In his report to the Government, as published in the *Parliamentary Debates,* he approved highly of the technical agreements made at Chicago.[8] True, they had presented no serious objection ("Everybody is against bad weather," Mayor LaGuardia had pointed out in espousing these annexes), but the standardization of regulations had indeed been a valuable contribution. On other matters Lord Swinton was less enthusiastic but still tolerant. There had been bitter disagreement, he admitted to the House of Lords, but the bickering had been overemphasized in the press. He did not deny that little had been accomplished in the field of economic measures, however. That was a disappointment, he conceded, but at least he had stood fast to the principles of his October White Paper. He had won his point on multilateral fifth-freedom agreements and had indicated that Great Britain would never acquiesce on this point without some kind of control over "wasteful competition." Conversations on this point had been "very frank," he told the House of Lords (an understatement that his peers understood full well), but the U.S. had been obstinate in its demands for dangerous unlimited competition. Lord Swinton defended the "escalator plan," saying that once the formula had been worked out, operations would have been entirely feasible.

"Such is the story," the Viscount told the Lords. "If we did not convert all our tries, we certainly scored some goals." [9]

The Lords appeared to have been satisfied by the Swinton report. The House of Commons was more critical of British representation at Chicago. It was a little jealous, apparently, because aviation had been represented by the upper body. Even so, resentment was directed more at the United States then at Lord Swinton. The right Honorable Clement Richard Attlee, then deputy prime minister, complained that "to an observer on this side of the Atlantic that great country [the U.S.] does not seem to be able to make up its mind whether it is going to run by itself, or in harmony with the rest of the world. . . . It seems to be dominated by a conflict of ambitions — wanting to run the world, yet wanting to be isolationist and to run itself." [10]

Yet the future prime minister was ready to admit that the Chicago conference was a meeting of great significance.

"It was more like a war," an unnamed speaker from the floor shouted back at him.

But if Lord Swinton more or less reassured Parliament, he failed to win over the press to acceptance of Conference results. Said the *Daily Herald,* the mouthpiece of the Labor party that opposed such leaders as Lord Swinton, "We have witnessed the melancholy failure of the Civil Aviation Conference in Chicago — boycotted by Russia, approached by Britain with worthy but timid proposals for world control, and finally wrecked by American delegates' devotion to the fetish of unrestricted commercial competition. Fullest collaboration between all nations in the economic field must be written off for the present so far as civil aviation is concerned." [11]

The *Daily Mail,* owned by Lord Rothermere, once the head

of Imperial Airways, had followed developments at Chicago through the eyes of Don Iddon, one of the ablest correspondents in this country. *The Mail* declared the conference was a failure because of the lack of a concerted plan for the entire British Commonwealth. Divergent views were all very well in preliminary stages, the correspondent stated, but empire interests should have come first at Chicago. E. Colston Shepherd, commentator for the British national radio system, admitted the conference had been beneficial as a means of narrowing the issues, but he was of the opinion that Chicago had resulted only in "an amicable agreement to disagree." [12] The semiofficial *Times* maintained that British delegates had been correct in standing firm, but the paper declared that little had been accomplished at the aviation meeting. The British had not dispelled U.S. suspicion that the empire was like a player with poor cards trying to offset its handicap by tightening up the rules, said "The Thunderer." The *Times* was echoed by Lord Brabazon. "Poor Swinton," he mourned, "took on this complicated business . . . with poor munitions." [13]

Editors of the *Aeroplane* were even more depressed. Chicago, they intoned, "was a pathetic reward for sacrifices men [had been] . . . asked to take in war." [14]

The influential journal predicted for commercial air transportation only a continuation of the old game of tedious negotiations. "Air transport has been described as international dynamite," said the editors. "Britain tried to render the explosive harmless," but the United States had made the attempt futile. Britain had challenged the American postwar promise of cooperation in world affairs, and the challenge had not been accepted, said the magazine.

On the whole, the press indicated that the meeting was a failure; that Lord Swinton had been "cabined, cribbed, and confined"; and that the United States was internationally too immature to assume world leadership on anything as controversial as world air routes.

The trouble with all these comments was that they lacked perspective. When the Chicago meeting broke up in December, 1944, it appeared that Great Britain and the United States could never reach an understanding on international air transport. Delegates scuttled home to win allies for their respective campaigns to foist an aviation policy on the world. Soon the frantic rivalry began to infect our relations on other matters. To make it worse, spokesmen at Chicago appeared to have been repudiated, so that no one knew where the two great air powers stood. Adolf Berle, who had been the featured attraction for a short but exciting period, dropped into aeronautical limbo after his appointment as Ambassador to Brazil. Lord Swinton was soon displaced as the champion of British civil aviation when the Labor Party won a bloodless revolution a few months later. Immediately after the Chicago adjournment, the aviation picture was not bright. So much more could have been accomplished!

And yet a year later that pessimistic evaluation would have required modification. By that time PICAO had begun to exert a slow but healthy influence. Planes actually began to fly under the terms of the Transit Agreement, long before the war was over.* A new spirit of cooperation, fostered at PICAO's headquarters in Montreal, began to be felt.

By this time, the aviation spotlight was directed on the U.S. Congress. The Senate Foreign Relations Committee had become very suspicious of the manner in which the important aviation documents had been negotiated at Chicago. The orthodox way of becoming party to an international agreement is by treaty. Another method, just as binding, is known as the

---

*The earliest use of the new agreement was said to have been made by Trans-Canada Air Lines (TCA). TCA's route from Toronto to Winnipeg normally crossed Georgian Bay and followed the north shore of Lake Superior. It was prevented by the old international restrictions from veering south over U. S. territory when weather was bad. Under the new Transit Agreement the alternate course was permissible. In emergency, TCA could schedule its flights by way of Windsor, Milwaukee, and St. Paul-Minneapolis. This was along an airway providing the best facilities known. TCA was thus able to complete more of its flights. Of coure the Canadians could not discharge or pick up traffic along the U. S. airway, but even so, the route was a great boon to our neighboring air line.

"executive agreement." This gives the president power to sign international contracts without consent of the Senate. When speed, safety, or secrecy are essential to public welfare, the executive agreement has long been recognized. The Senate was suspicious that this method was being abused, however, in the case of the aviation negotiations.[15]

The investigation of executive agreements threatened to be embarrassing to the aviation planners. If all bilateral negotiations had to be submitted to the treaty process, aviation progress might be delayed indefinitely. Executive agreements made it possible for our aviation representatives to bargain with foreign diplomats. They knew just how far they could go in making commitments, and they could, in turn, give reasonable guarantees under the executive agreement system. If agreements had had to be by treaty, all such bargaining would have been subject to Senate review, and all commitments and promises would have been meaningless. This would have been a serious handicap when sharp bargaining and immediate action had to be taken to put our planes on the world routes at once.

The issue of executive agreements first came up when the documents signed by our delegates at Chicago were up for ratification. On December 20, 1944, Senator Arthur Vandenburg moved that no more action be taken on the Chicago documents until the appropriate committees had studied them. The resolution was passed. Hearings were called, but nothing tangible resulted, and the State Department began to get impatient. The United States had sponsored the Chicago meeting and had applied pressure for the adoption of the documents drafted there. One of these had to be ratified within six months, if the United States were to be named to the strategic Interim Council. And since the United States had pleaded with all the delegates for early ratification of the documents, the State Department was chagrined at the delay caused by the Senate committee.

Early in February the department announced that it was ready to go ahead on Documents One, Three, and Four. Document Two, providing for a permanent aviation organization was clearly a treaty matter. The department believed that the other documents might be concluded by executive agreement. Accordingly, Dean Acheson, then Assistant Secretary of State, went to his superior, Mr. Stettinius, to ask what his next step should be. Stettinius said it would be necessary to get a release from the promise made to the Senate at the time of the Vandenburg resolution — namely, that no action on the documents would be taken until the appropriate committees had studied them. Acheson thereupon made an appointment with Senator Tom Connally, chairman of the Senate Committee on Foreign Relations. He told the senator of the state department policy on aviation and declared that inaction would cause great embarrassment to his department. Senator Connally suggested that Acheson see Senator Bailey, who had been a delegate at Chicago and was chairman of the subcommittee on aviation. Senator Bailey agreed to call a meeting of his subcommittee, and there the matter was discussed at great length. At the end of the meeting Senator Bailey handed out a statement on aviation policy and asked his guests to take it home for study. Just as the meeting was adjourning, Acheson asked if there were any other reason for delay. Senator Bailey, believing the state department official referred to the meeting, not to the policy of the committee, replied, "None in the world." Through this innocent mistake, Acheson reported to Senator Connally that he had been given the go-signal on aviation matters. Senator Connally deferred to Senator Bailey on all aviation matters, and on the report that Senator Bailey had acquiesced to the state department request, the chairman of the Foreign Relations Committee released Acheson from the promise to take no action.[16] The State Department thereupon turned over Document Two to the Senate for ratification as a treaty and then went ahead on the conclusion of executive agreements on the three documents. This was a mistake. Neither Senator Bailey nor Senator Connally had intended to commit themselves to this extent.

There was consternation on all sides, then, when a state department press release announced the acceptance of the three

Chicago documents as executive agreements. At once Senator Wallace H. White of Maine demanded a meeting of the Foreign Relations Committee to investigate the matter. Hearings began on February 20, 1945. Called as a witness, Acheson insisted that the executive agreements were valid. He pointed out that if foreign carriers were permitted to engage in air commerce with this country under terms of the agreements, Congress could terminate the arrangement at any time. Thus, there was no reason for the senators to get excited about losing their power over foreign operators. On the other hand, to repudiate the state department agreements at this point would raise doubts on all future action taken by the U.S. Government on aviation matters, Acheson declared.

Senator White admitted that the misunderstanding had been innocent and that it was all very embarrissing. On the other hand, none of the measures were to become effective until twenty-six nations had approved, and at that time only three signatures had been affixed. Surely, said he, there was time for the Senate to consider the validity of executive agreements. Acheson denied this. He argued that the other nations were waiting to see what the United States was going to do, and that the leadership of this country was essential to the successful carrying out of the Chicago plans.

Apparently Acheson was convincing on that point, but Senator Brewster now attacked him from another quarter. How, he asked, could the State Department justify executive agreements under the terms of the Civil Aeronautics Act, which was the Magna Charta of civil aviation? Section 402 of that law specifically stated that no foreign carrier could serve this country without first obtaining a permit from the Civil Aeronautics Board. To win such a permit, a foreign operator had to file an application, posted in ample time for competitors to present possible objections. Hearings were to follow this step, and it was then up to the CAB to determine whether or not the applicant was "fit, willing, and able" to perform the required services. If the Board decided favorably, it could issue a permit at once, but this could be modified, suspended, or revoked at any time, after proper notice and hearing had been given.

By the terms of the Chicago documents, the State Department, not the CAB, would determine which applicants were to receive permits, it was charged. In at least one instance, that of the fifth-freedom document, signatory nations were to be granted concessions automatically. In that case, the documents appeared to be superior to the law — the Civil Aeronautics Act of 1938. If that were true, the executive agreements were illegal, the Brewster faction maintained.

Even the agile Acheson had trouble with that one, but he fought back valiantly. CAB permits, said he, were only one way of letting foreign operators into the country. The CAB permit method was useful, for example, when the applicant was not eligible under fifth-freedom terms. But the Civil Aeronautics Act did not prescribe CAB permits as the only way to gain access to our air gateways, said the Assistant Secretary of State. The Act provided that the State Department might sign agreements with foreign applicants *after consultation with the CAB*. In that event, said the spokesman, it was clear that the Board had to recognize such an agreement by granting a permit. Since the CAB had never officially denied the Chicago documents and had consulted with the State Department all along, the executive agreements were still within the law, said Acheson.

If that were the case, continued Senator Brewster, what was the point of issuing a permit at all, since the State Department had already told the foreign operator to come ahead? Pogue, as chairman of the CAB, answered that one. Even when permits were to be issued by the CAB under Section 402 of the Act it had been necessary to call in the State Department, he explained. Someone had to begin negotiations with the foreign governments, and that was a function of the State Department. Even under the old Air Commerce Act of 1926, the United States was permitted to issue permits to foreign operators *on a reciprocal basis only*. It was obvious that only the State Department could arrange such details. Therefore if the State Department completed negotiations, the CAB had to respect the understandings, said Pogue. There was plenty of precedent on that.

Then why did the CAB have to hold hearings before issuing a permit, asked the Senator? Because, said Mr. Pogue, the original negotiations were concerned with the granting of landing rights, but they had nothing to do with the fitness of the operator. In other words, the State Department gave permission to a foreign country allowing one of its operators to land in the United States, but the CAB could prescribe standards of operation. It could thus in effect decide which foreign air line was to be permitted to serve the United States, and if the new service were not in the public interest, it could deny a permit until the operator had proved his point.

"You might say 'What is the use of making the finding of public interest?'" Pogue testified. "Well, there are a good many things, of course, under the statute which have to be considered in granting a permit, besides the actual and fundamental right of entry. There may be questions about which airports they use and what points they serve and whether ownership of their lines complies with the . . . provisions in the basic agreement, and . . . terms, conditions, and limitations can be applied so long as they don't defeat the basic purposes [right of entry] of the agreement." [17]

In either case, said the CAB chairman, the President of the United States makes the final decision, since both the State Department and the CAB are his implements. The chief executive may ignore CAB recommendations, or he may modify, or accept them.*

Acheson and Pogue appear to have been very convincing, for although many members of the Foreign Relations Committee were sympathetic to the views of Senator Brewster, they must have admitted that executive agreements were necessary and legal. There is no doubt but that they would have preferred

*The President has, in fact, ignored or modified CAB recommendations. President Roosevelt granted American Airlines a route certificate to Mexico City over CAB objection during the war. President Truman modified Board recommendations in the Latin American Route Case after the war.

contract by treaty, but they were not prepared to block further progress in aviation. Senator Brewster did file an adverse report, which he says was quashed at the request of Acheson. At any rate, since the committee did not say "no," it was assumed by our policy makers that the United States would continue to move out along the high frontiers by executive agreement.

The next thing to decide was whether or not the United States would fight world rivals by means of a single company, or whether it would risk the hazards of competition.

REFERENCES

1. Letter from Stokeley Morgan, dated October 30, 1946.
2. Eric Bramley, "Five Documents Emerge from Conference," *American Aviation*, December 15, 1944, pp. 17, 20.
3. *International Civil Aviation Conference—Final Act and Related Documents*, State Department Publication, Conference Series No. 64, 1945. For a concise and accurate résumé of the conference results the author is indebted to Richard Kermit Waldo, Chief, Research Section, Aviation Division, Department of State. Much of the material in the first part of this chapter is based on his article, "Sequels to the Chicago Aviation Conference," in the Aviation Transport issue of *Law and Contemporary Problems*, School of Law, Duke University, Winter-Spring, 1946, pp. 609-628.
4. "Address of Adolf A. Berle, Jr., " as reported in *American Aviation*, November 15, 1944, pp. 17, 24, 26.
5. *Ibid.*
6. *Civil Aviation Agreements*, Hearings before the Committee on Commerce, U. S. Senate, 79th Congress, 2d Session, February 22, 1946, (from a rough draft of the hearing reports—no page numbers).
7. Interview with John Parker Van Zandt, August 12, 1946, Washington, D. C.
8. *Hansard*, Lords, Vol. 134, January 16, 1945, pp. 563 ff.
9. *Ibid.*
10. *Hansard*, Commons, Vol. 407, January 26, 1945, pp. 1151, ff.
11. December 12, 1944.
12. *International Aviation*, February 9, 1945, p. 164.
13. *Ibid.*, December 29, 1944, p. 119.
14. *Ibid.*

15. For a discussion of executive agreements see Arne C. Wiprud, "Some Aspects of Public International Air Law," *George Washington Law Review*, Vol. 13, April, 1945, pp. 247 ff.
16. Adequately covered in *Convention on International Civil Aviation*, Hearings before the Committee on Foreign Relations, United States Senate, 79th Congress, 1st Session on Executive A, Washington, 1945, pp. 100 ff.
17. *Ibid.*, 135.

A NOTE ON SOURCES

For source material on the Chicago conference, see *International Civil Aviation Conference—Final Act and Related Documents,* State Department Publication, Conference Series No. 64, Washington, 1945. A discussion of the conference is given in *Blueprint for World Civil Aviation,* Department of State Publication, Conference Series No. 70, Washington, 1945, which comprises reprints of four magazine articles by Adolf A. Berle, Jr., William A. M. Burden, Edward Warner, and Stokeley Morgan. One of the best summaries is by Richard Kermit Waldo, "Sequels to the Chicago Aviation Conference," in *Law and Contemporary Problems,* School of Law, Duke University, Winter-Spring, 1946. Other data used in this chapter are from "Chicago—A Lost Cause," *The Aeroplane* (London), December 22, 1944; *Convention on International Civil Aviation,* Hearings before the Committee on Foreign Relations, United States Senate, Seventy-ninth Congress, First Session on Executive A, 1945, especially pp. 186-196; "Message of the President" and "Addresses by Assistant Secretary of State Berle" in the *Department of State Bulletin,* Vol. XI, November 5, 1944. Chronological data were taken from unpublished "Minutes of the Proceedings," an undated transcript, not available now, used by courtesy of the Aviation Division of the State Department. The attack on executive agreements is discussed in the above-cited hearings, *Convention on International Civil Aviation,* especially pp. 49-54, 83-85, and 100-103. The attack is carried on in *Civil Aviation Agreements,* Hearings on S. 1814 before the Committee on Commerce, United States Senate, Seventy-ninth Congress, Second Session, Washington, 1946. For a summary of the dispute on S. 1814, see the *Congressional Record,* Senate, April 10, 1946, speech of Senator McCarran, pp. 3421 ff. Senator Brewster's resolution against executive agreements is given in *International Commercial Aviation,* United States Senate, Seventy-ninth Congress, Second Session, Senate Document No. 173, 1946. An academic discussion of executive agreements is given in Arne Wiprud's "Some Aspects of Public International Air Law," *George Washington Law Review,* Vol. 13, April, 1945, pp. 247 ff.; *Treaties and Executive Agreements,* an analysis prepared for the Senate Foreign Relations Committee by Henry S. Fraser and obtainable as Senate Document No. 224, Seventy-eighth Congress, Second Session, 1944; and Wallace McClure, *International Executive Agreements,* New York, 1941. Information for this chapter was also obtained from interviews with A. A. Berle, Jr., chairman of the U. S. delegation at Chicago; John Parker Van Zandt, then of the Brookings Institution, an unofficial observer of the aviation conference; Stokeley Morgan, secretary-general of the U. S. delegation; Joseph Walstrom, acting chief of the research section of the Aviation Division, Department of State; Wayne Parrish, editor of *American Aviation;* Senator Owen Brewster; Arne C. Wiprud; L. Welch Pogue, then chairman of the Civil Aeronautics Board; Peter Masefield, civil air attaché to the British Embassy, Washington; Harllee Branch and George P. Baker, serving at that time on the Civil Aeronautics Board.

THE ALL-AMERICAN FLAG LINE

CHICAGO gave us a departure point for the course set by this country on international aviation. Now the planners had to decide on the type of operation best fitted to our needs. Many have argued right up to the present time that American aviation should be concentrated under one organization in order to take full advantage of our resources and to meet foreign rivalry on even terms. Another group has stood for competition in world air commerce, believing it healthier for the industry and for the public. Before the United States could "move out along the world routes," as one authority put it, our representatives had to settle the issue of monopoly versus competition. This became the subject of great debate immediately after the Chicago conference.

Senator Brewster became the leading spokesman for the single company — he would not have called it monopoly — in world aviation. The Senator had been far more impressed by the failures than by the successes of the conference. Americans had come away from the meeting at Chicago after declaring an air war on Great Britain, he maintained. Adjournment at Chicago had been the signal for both great air powers to rush frantically about the world in search of allies for their respective causes, Senator Brewster believed. He was certain that if the United States was to keep its leadership in air commerce, it must take aggressive action against its rival. The Senator saw only two ways by which this country could develop as a commercial air power. The United States would either have to enter into some kind of working agreement — a cartel — with Great Britain, or it would have to begin a trade war, which, the Senator insisted might have "catastrophic consequences." He believed that at Chicago the dice had been loaded in favor of the trade war.

"Yes," agreed Senator Patrick McCarran, also a protagonist for the single U.S. flag line, "and in order to meet the very condition which you have set up correctly there, it is my judgment this government must put forward its strongest arm." [1] Senator McCarran believed he had provided the sinews for this "strongest arm." In both the Seventy-eighth and Seventy-ninth Congresses he had sponsored what he called "The All-American Flag Line Bills," officially called S.1790 and S.326. The latter measure was referred to the aviation subcommittee of the Senate Commerce Committee, and it was during the debate over S.326 that the spokesmen of both monopoly and competition argued their cases.

Senator McCarran proposed that all existing U.S. international air lines be dissolved. In their place would be a single air line in which the entire air-transport industry would have financial interest. This "community company," as the Senator preferred to call it, would remain a private enterprise, but it would be backed and guaranteed by the U.S. Government. It would thus have exclusive rights to air mail and other financial benefits. Investors would be protected by the Government itself, so that stock would literally be "as good as gold."

Others had already suggested this plan long before Senator McCarran's bills were up for hearings. It was Juan Trippe of Pan American Airways who had coined the phrase "community company." Over his signature in the 1943 annual report of his company Trippe had written:

Your Company's position has been that in international air transport, as in international telecommunications, our nation's best interest would be served by concentrating the effort of the United States behind a single American international operation, strong enough to compete on even terms with the great foreign flag air transport monopolies created by other principal trading nations. This operation would take the form of a community company in which all American transportation interests able to contribute would be permitted to participate under an organization plan approved by the Government. Your Company has considered that the policy of the Government on an issue of this importance must be determined, not by the interests of any company, or group of companies, but by what will be best for our country as a whole.

The legislative and executive departments of our Government have the final responsibility in this decision. Your Company has placed its knowledge and experience at their disposal.[2]

Actually, the community company was only the old chosen instrument in a new slip cover, but it looked appealing, and indeed Trippe did not understand why everyone should not be pleased with his clever needlework. Any carrier operating under a Civil Aeronautics Board license, except air lines entirely within Alaska, could buy Class A stock in the new corporation. Such subscribers had to put up a minimum of five million dollars, and no operator could buy more than fifty million dollars worth of stock. Senator McCarran did not foresee any difficulty in selling Class A stock because the investment would be guaranteed by the Government. That was just why he imposed a maximum stock limitation — to prevent any one company from making too much of a good thing out of a gilt-edged security. In many respects the bill was reminiscent of the measure sponsored by John C. Calhoun in 1816 for a second bank of the United States.

But many of the operators Trippe sought to benefit rebelled against joining a combine in which the Pan American interests would have the largest block of stock. These rebels banded together into an organization representing all but two of the domestic air lines of the United States.* They also had ideas as to how the postwar routes were to be organized. In May, 1943, the Civil Aeronautics Board sent out a questionnaire to all U.S. operators requesting an expression of views as to the

*At that time there were eighteen air lines within the United States operating under CAB licenses.

policy the Government should take on international air transport. All of the air lines except Pan American World Airways and United Air Lines favored competition on world routes. In July these operators organized the Airlines Committee For United States Air Policy, better known as the Seventeen Airlines Committee. Spokesman was a New York lawyer, Alexander B. Royce, who opened his war on the Trippe-McCarran-Brewster entente following a meeting of U.S. operators called by General Henry H. Arnold of the Army Air Forces.

Royce charged that the All-American Flag Line bill was nothing more than a sham to legalize Pan American's international monopoly. Pan American World Airways might disappear as a name, he admitted, but its stockholders would still have control over the new company because they would outnumber stockholders of any other company. There was no doubt in Royce's mind that Trippe and his lieutenants would still dominate the international air routes. Indeed, said Royce, he himself would vote for Trippe as head of such a company, if it were authorized, because Trippe had proved his ability to the world. But was the community company what this nation needed? Royce, speaking for the seventeen air lines, said "no." The domestic operators who had flown world routes successfully during the war were demanding a share of international air commerce of the future.

Royce pointed out that his clients had no intention of engaging in cutthroat competition or of glutting the world airways. As a matter of fact, only six of them had applied for Atlantic franchises, and these applicants were well aware that not more than two or three of them could win certificates. The domestic operators did believe that Pan American should have "potential competition, with its eye over its shoulder to see if anyone is coming." International aviation should be governed by the principle of regulated competition as specified in the Civil Aeronautics Act of 1938, Royce declared. The community company, he argued, was only a subterfuge. In reality, it was Pan American's bid for the chosen instrument in ocean air transport.

Senator McCarran strongly denied this accusation. Said he:

> If we are going to bandy the phrase "chosen instrument" back and
> forth, we should have a clear understanding of what we mean. . . .
> The bill does not propose a "chosen instrument" in the sense in which
> that phrase is most commonly accepted. It does not propose to take
> some existing air line and make it the favored company. The "chosen
> instrument" under this bill will not be an instrument picked from
> stock and given some sort of royal seal of approval; it will be an in-
> strument forged for the specific purpose for which it is to be used
> from all the best elements of the aviation industry of this nation.
> In this sense of the phrase, when we send a team of athletes to
> compete with foreign nations in the olympic games, that team is a
> "chosen instrument." We do not send to Europe the outstanding
> college track team of the nation. . . . We combine all the best talent
> and ability and skill into one team, and that team goes to the Olympic
> games to represent the United States of America.[3]

Webster's dictionary defines monopoly as "the exclusive control of the supply of any commodity or service in a given market, or popularly, such control as enables one to raise the price
above that fixed by free enterprise." By such definition, the
McCarran Bill was not a monopoly, said its sponsor. In meeting the competition of foreign carriers it in no sense controlled
a commodity or service. True, it might be the only U.S. flag
line (although nothing prevented an independent operator
from starting services, if he was willing to fly without Government aid), but even as a single line representing the United
States the community company could hardly be called a
monopoly under the definition, the Senator insisted. How
could it be a monopoly, with foreign competition and with
every air line in the country participating in its success? In
the Senator's opinion the All-American Flag Line was no more
a monopoly than were the hundreds of flourishing cooperatives
spread across the country.

In fact, said the sponsor of S.326, the community company
was far less monopolistic than was the system under which the
United States had developed its world routes up to 1945. Pan
American at that time was still the only holder of a permanent
international certificate. American Export Airlines had a tem-

porary permit, but it had been operating entirely by military contract. Under S.326 all international air commerce under the American flag would be shared not by one, or possibly two, but by twenty air lines. Instead of controlling 95 per cent of the transocean air operations, Pan American stockholders would be limited by law to a maximum 25 per cent share. That was assuming that Pan American would take its maximum quota of stock, amounting to fifty million dollars. On that basis the two biggest domestic operators, American Airlines and United Air Lines, would own 12½ and 11 per cent respectively. But these three largest stockholders combined would still control less than half the voting stock. How, then, could opponents of the bill cry "monopoly," Senator McCarran asked.

William L. Clayton, assistant secretary of state, tried to answer when called as a witness. Clayton argued that the right to carry on a business exclusively is a monopoly, regardless of the type of ownership. Comparing the All-American Flag Line with such accepted monopolies as the telephone system, the postal service, and certain public utilities was unfair, he objected. Monopoly, in his opinion, was permissible only where it could not be avoided. He believed such a policy not only unnecessary in air commerce but decidedly dangerous.

He explained himself as follows:

Between the two World Wars the movement throughout the world in the direction of restrictive practices in international economic affairs, such as trade discriminations of all kinds . . . was very strong. The policy of the State Department is opposed to all such restrictive practices, and we are trying to bring about by collaboration with other nations, a movement in the opposite direction. I believe that the adoption of a policy of turning over to one company a monopoly in international air transport service would be contrary to the policy that the Department of State has adopted in the international economic field, and I think . . . that if we should turn over the international aviation field to one company as a monopoly, that a cartel arrangement with other countries would be inevitable. . . . I do not think any such arrangements are in the national interest.[4]

Joseph C. Grew, acting secretary of state, saw a further danger. He voiced the thought that if we learned anything at all from the Europeans, it was that the chosen instrument policy led inevitably to state ownership. The regularity of the tendency, he declared, suggested that determination to accept or to reject the chosen instrument theory might well turn upon whether it was desired to accept or reject the probability of government ownership, or of government control amounting to the same thing.

But as Senator McCarran saw it, the "regulated competition" extolled by the domestic operators was no less monopolistic. It was a catch phrase, he charged, that meant nothing at all. Under "regulated competition" half a dozen air lines might be granted certificates over widely separated routes. That was not competition, the Senator insisted. That was *regional monopoly*. One might as well argue that the Southern Pacific and New York Central railroads were competitive, he continued, simply because there were two such transport systems in the same country.

In any case the argument was strictly academic, said Senator McCarran, because whatever name was used to designate his proposed company, it was, in his opinion, the only way to meet the competition of foreign, subsidized rivals. All European nations had learned from experience that the single company was the only logical implement of air commerce, the Senator declared. The British had started out with a competitive system, and it had been a miserable failure. So had the competitive operations of the French and Germans. On the other hand, the Dutch from the beginning had concentrated all their resources in one strong air line. Royal Dutch Airlines (KLM) had been one of the most successful carriers in the world — and still was. It was partly because the Dutch had been able to play off one British company against another that the British had been forced into merging all their air lines, first as Imperial Airways, then as British Overseas Airways Corporation. Eventually, every aviation power in the world had adopted monopoly in one form or another, except the United States. Even we had repudiated the chosen instrument more by word than by deed. From 1927 until 1939 Pan American had virtually been the chosen instrument of the United States on foreign routes, the Senator argued, and the system had served us well.

Was Senator McCarran correct in his assumptions? His facts were right, but his interpretations of them were open to question. True, European nations favored the chosen instruments, but these nations fell into three classifications. There were countries such as Nazi Germany, with basic political philosophies favoring state control. Such nations followed the chosen instrument policy not because of its proven superiority, but because it was part of a national trend. Other European countries had small homelands, with distant colonial interests. Such countries were Great Britain and the Netherlands. They did not have the traffic to support such long lines. Lastly, there were nations with limited resources, such as Italy, unable to support more than one aviation enterprise. The United States did not fit into any of these classifications.

William A. M. Burden, the ubiquitous assistant secretary of commerce, held that Senator McCarran's comparison of Pan American and European chosen instruments was highly inaccurate. Pan American's route certificates were of limited tenure, he pointed out, and the Government always had the right to withdraw them, or to add services from time to time if the company failed to measure up to standard. It was this fear of possible competition that kept Pan American Airways on its toes, said Mr. Burden. As for the European system — if it really were superior as Senator McCarran made out, why had these foreign air lines been out-performed in every instance in which they had been pitted against American operators? Not only had the privately owned American lines proved themselves superior, but they had become models for European rivals. Surely it would be a mistake to reverse this and make European lines our models. In the first place, European experiences were not comparable with ours. The French had been forced to merge their lines because of internal dissension and scandal. Monopoly was only an expedient with them. Great Britain had only been groping in the dark when it hit upon the chosen instrument. That was indicated by a look at the

British record. The British had shifted from competition to chosen instrument to regional monopoly and back to chosen instrument. As Burden spoke in the spring of 1945, the British were about to revert to a regional monopoly plan again. What lesson was there in all this for the American operator, Mr. Burden asked? Our own experiences, not the confusion of rivals, should be the basis for future aviation plans, he maintained.

Senator McCarran replied that history only proved the point that competition in international transportation was wasteful. He used as illustration the record of the U.S. Merchant Marine. The Senator showed that American clipper ships had once carried 90 per cent of the U.S. commerce with foreign countries. Relaxation of laws to permit greater privileges for foreign shipowners rapidly brought an end to the clipper era because the foreigner, with cheaper labor and lower costs, could offer lower shipping rates. As a result, American shippers were carrying only 66 per cent of the U.S. foreign traffic by 1860, Senator McCarran declared. By 1900 this share had dropped to nine per cent.

World War I gave the U.S. merchant navy a second chance. So many foreign ships had been sunk by enemy submarines that the United States came out of the war with the largest merchant fleet in the world. In 1922 American ships were carrying about 50 per cent of the U.S. foreign trade. Yet as soon as the Europeans rebuilt their shattered fleets, U.S. shipping at once began to slump. Americans just could not compete with foreign-subsidized, government-controlled merchant navies, the Senator argued. By 1939 only 15 per cent of our international trade was carried in ships of U.S. registry.

And these figures applied only to freight cargoes. The record on passenger traffic was even more discouraging. Americans, the greatest travelers in the world, bought 80 per cent of their passages on foreign packets. Had it not been for Government "blood transfusions," American merchant vessels might have disappeared entirely from the high seas.* In 1928 and again in

*Of course intercoastal and inland water shipping was not affected by this

1936 Congress passed laws to revitalize the dormant industry.
When World War II forced Americans to expand the merchant
fleet again, Congress wisely decided to abandon its old policy of
aiding competitive U.S. shippers. It centralized control of
shipping in the U.S. Maritime Commission, which, the Senator
explained, was the same type of organization he proposed for
the air lines. The commission controlled what amounted to a
"community company" made up of the "best elements" of the
shipping industry. It had operated successfully. Why could not
the same principle be applied to air transportation?

It was John E. Slater, executive vice-president of American
Export Airlines, who now carried the ball for his team. Slater
was qualified to answer the Senator, after a successful career in
the steamship business, and as the promoter of the only other
certified international air line at the time. Using the same figures Senator McCarran had quoted, Slater came to quite different conclusions.

Slater charged that McCarran had his facts right but that
he had not interpreted them correctly. He denied that the
record of the U.S. merchant navy justified repudiation of competitive American shipping lines. True, Slater admitted, in the
era of the clipper ship the *percentage* of U.S. commerce carried
in American vessels had been high. The *volume,* however, had
been low. In the 1820's each nation tried to keep its foreign
trade for the benefit of its own carriers. This was accomplished
by levying discriminating duties. The United States had been
no exception to this trend. Such a policy prevented foreign
shippers from carrying the bulk of U.S. foreign commerce. But
the same policy kept our merchantmen from entering world
markets which otherwise would have been available to them.
Therefore the volume of trade carried by American vessels had
been very small.

The Reciprocity Act of 1828 cost Americans a fat slice of
their commerce in U.S. goods, but it did open new ports to

---

rivalry. The United States insisted on protecting its own shippers engaged
in coastwise or inland waterway trade.

them. As competition became freer, the *proportion* of U.S. trade carried in American vessels declined. But the *volume* of trade carried by American merchantmen increased fourfold between 1830 and 1860.

From 1860 to World War I, the merchant marine did, indeed, decline steadily. But, added Slater, this was not a result of foreign rivalry. It was caused by this nation's complete preoccupation with internal expansion. U.S. capital was being invested in railroads and factories at the very time that the British were concentrating upon maritime development. Not until World War I was there any incentive to get back into the shipping business. We lost temporary ascendancy following the war not because U.S. businessmen were unable to compete with foreign rivals, but because the country had no policy. When the Merchant Marine Act of 1936 did provide the needed policy, the ailing industry began to recover, although Slater said that it was too soon to judge final results.

One other factor had not been brought out by Senator McCarran, Slater insisted. He said that the low over-all shipping percentage of American carriers just before World War II was a result of inroads made by foreign *tramp* vessels. Irrefutable figures proved that they had carried the bulk of foreign trade. They were thus engaged in the "most cutthroat game in the world." It should be noted, Slater explained, that the tramp-steamer business had nothing to do with the chosen instrument of foreign maritime nations, nor did it have anything to do with unfair competition by subsidized, government-controlled shipping companies.

In 1938 about 32 per cent of the total American foreign trade was carried in tramp vessels, mostly of Scandinavian or British registry. They were competing with their respective chosen instruments as aggressively as they were fighting U.S. independents. Tramp operators received no special benefits from their home governments. Yet here was a strange conclusion — the leading maritime nations owed their commanding positions not to their chosen-instrument shipping companies, but to their cutthroat, competitive tramp carriers. And what chance did we have against such ravenous wolves without a chosen instrument? A very good chance, Slater believed. Under the new merchant marine program the American shipper was able to own superior vessels for the first time since 1850. Fast, efficient vessels could more than counteract the wage differentials, he argued.

Perhaps the above comparison with marine transportation appears irrelevant at the present reading. It was a factor, however, in working out America's future in the air. Another factor was the effort to determine the amount of traffic that could be expected at the end of World War II. Sponsors of the All-American Flag Line asked how international air transport could survive under a competitive system if there were not enough traffic for more than one strong air line. All surveys had indicated that if the air commerce had to be divided among half a dozen operators, all would either starve from lack of revenue or have to ask for heavy subsidies from the Government. This was the point that worried William A. Patterson, president of United Air Lines, the one domestic operator siding with the McCarran–Brewster–Pan American bloc during the hearings on the community company.

Patterson was known to his colleagues as a very canny operator. Conservative in his views, he had proved time and again that the airman had to keep one foot on the ground, if he expected to survive in the air transport industry. The fact that United's chief denounced competition on world routes was enough to make rivals pause a moment in their wild grabbing for airway bargains. Patterson had a reputation for shrewd air-line management matched only by that of American Airlines' Cyrus R. Smith, or Pan American's Juan Trippe. And when General Arnold called the air-line operators together in the summer of 1944 to find out what routes they were eyeing, Patterson surprised everyone by announcing he had no interest in world routes. He had ordered an elaborate survey of postwar traffic, and his conclusion was that international air commerce was not worth the trouble. According to his calculations, twenty-three of the new aircraft on order could carry all the North Atlantic traffic through 1955.[5] If this traffic had to be split between seven or eight U.S. and foreign carriers, what was there in it for a company like United Air Lines, Mr. Patterson asked?

The Patterson Report was only one of many traffic surveys. All were discouraging as to the future of international air transportation. One of the most widely quoted reports was the one published by the Curtiss-Wright Corporation.[6] This company had produced the wartime Commando, or C-46, the largest twin-engined transport of the war period. Now the manufacturers wished to know whether or not they would be justified in retooling to make transports. Admitting that many of the factors in air transportation were unpredictable, the authors nevertheless looked at the postwar horizon and found it dark. They had found that only about one per cent of the people in the United States had ever traveled abroad. The entire annual international passenger traffic was only half as much as that between New York and Boston. And American operators were likely to get only a part of that. It was estimated that U.S. air carriers would transport about 50 per cent of the Atlantic traffic, 70 per cent of the Latin-American, and 60 per cent of the Pacific.

Juan Trippe, never one to sell aviation short, also agreed that many persons — notably his potential domestic air-line rivals — were too optimistic about the future of postwar international air transport. Trippe had collected a sheaf of graphs, charts, and tables, which, if laid end to end, would have reached this conclusion — that world air commerce was being vastly overrated. In 1941, said Trippe, U.S. international air carriers had accounted for only nine per cent of the total American traffic. According to the Curtiss-Wright figures, this traffic would be doubled by 1950. Even so, said Trippe, such traffic would be negligible, as compared with the domestic business.

Trippe was trying to refute the argument that the community company was too big an enterprise for any one operator. As he explained it, many of the domestic air lines were several times bigger than the international companies. It was therefore ridiculous to assert that the community company was too big to be efficient. People simply had the wrong idea about the magnitude of world air commerce, he declared. All the survey figures had been based on peak travel months. During the lean months eight planes could carry all the traffic allotted to U.S. operators, he argued. Even in peak months eleven planes would suffice for many years after the war.

Former Senator Josh Lee, the newest member of the CAB at that time, had little patience with this school of thought. Said he:

> They take a certain per cent of the passengers who before the war crossed the Atlantic by steamer first class, and a smaller per cent of those who travelled steerage — add them together, project them, and say, "This is the maximum number of passengers who can be expected to cross the Atlantic after the war." It would have been just as logical to have determined how many people crossed the American desert by stage coach, projected the figure, and announced, "This is the maximum number of passengers who may be expected to cross the United States by rail." [7]

Perhaps Lee was treating too lightly the careful estimates of Patterson, Warner, the Curtiss-Wright Corporation, the Civil Aeronautics Board, and Trippe, but as one editor said of the Board member's statement, "The man talks sense." [8] Major General Harold L. George of the Air Transport Command, thought so, at least. The ATC had taught General George some surprising lessons. One of them was that future air traffic would have little relation to past statistics. He told the Bailey Committee:

> I am completely out of agreement and not in harmony with any ideas that eight airplanes are going to be able to handle all the traffic across the North Atlantic. The ability of people to move from where they are to some place where they want to go, in the matter of hours and move at a tariff rate that they can meet out of their pocketbook is going to generate a great traffic potential. I would never leave home to go downtown to see a motion picture if I had to hitch up the horse to go, but I can get on a streetcar or in an automobile and I can

go to the theater with comparative ease. I am just one of many hundreds of thousands who do the same thing.

I think it is impossible to look into the foreseeable future and say what is going to be the traffic across the North Atlantic. You can take a man who has a two weeks vacation and if he can go to Europe or other parts of the world in a round trip of three days and can spend eleven days seeing the world — and that can be done with the budget he sets up — then that man is a potential passenger of the airplane.

The number of planes that are going to be engaged in overocean transportation in the not too distant future is something that will probably, in my opinion, stagger the imagination. I think it is going to be tremendous; I am sure it is going to be tremendous. Since we [ATC] have been operating, we have carried close to three million passengers. They are all air minded; everybody is air minded.[9]

General George was probably the world's foremost authority on international air transportation at that time. A late arrival in the business, he had developed the most extensive air-transport system the world had ever seen. By 1943 his Air Transport Command was carrying more passengers than all the rest of the world's air lines combined. In January, 1945, General George had disclosed that ATC planes were taking off for Europe every twenty-three minutes, and soon this was every nineteen minutes. Every ninety minutes another ATC plane started across the Pacific. In other words, this traffic amounted to an annual transportation of 1,500,000 passengers from Washington to London.

Most of the aviation people appeared to agree with the general. The Trippe-McCarran-Patterson clique was strong, and the industry listened with respect and interest as the group argued for a single U.S. air line for world routes. But the McCarran Bill was opposed not only by the seventeen domestic operators and American Export Airlines, but by virtually every Government agency. The Departments of State, War, Navy, Commerce, Justice, and the Post Office all issued strong statements opposing the bill. For the most part the aircraft industry also favored the competitive system, as did the trade press.

Labor was divided. The Railroad Brotherhoods sponsored S.326 and so did William Green of the American Federation

of Labor. On the other hand, the small but powerful Air Line
Pilots Association, an A.F. of L. affiliate, denounced the bill.
Wrote David L. Behncke, president of the pilots' association,
to Chairman Bailey of the Senate aviation subcommittee:

> Pan American Airways has been mentioned many times in these
> hearings. It has been held out as a model to show what can be done
> under a monopolistic setup. This company admits it is a monopoly;
> it has no qualms about such things. From our first-hand knowledge
> and contacts with Pan American Airways, we can state, unequivocaly,
> that as a result of the monopolistic position of this company on inter-
> national air-line aviation transportation prior to World War II, its
> labor policy was far from satisfactory and left much to be desired.
> This unsatisfactory employer-employee policy stems from its mon-
> opolistic tendency and position. Were it not for the existence of certain
> protective Federal statutes which Congress in its wisdom saw fit to
> enact in 1938, and prior thereto, the air-line pilots have every reason
> to believe that the standards, pay, and other working conditions on
> Pan American Airways, especially for the pilots, would be far lower
> than they are today. Pan American Airways had no competition —
> why should they desire to improve their employee's status?
> As the air line pilots view the single instrument proposal being
> sponsored by Pan American Airways, it is a bid to further secure and
> irrevocably establish this monopolistic international air line operating
> hypocrisy by Congressional action. . . .
> Our country's air-line pilots are overwhelmingly for the controlled
> competition method of developing and carrying on our international
> air-line activities much along the same lines as our vast domestic air-
> line network has been developed and operated so successfully for so
> many years.[10]

Richard Frankensteen, in charge of aviation matters for the
CIO, and James E. Nolan of the Air Line Mechanics Association echoed these sentiments. They did not believe the threat
of foreign labor was as serious as proponents of the bill had
made out. Ralph S. Damon, at that time with American Airlines, also expressed his views on the labor issue: "I think probably there has been more misinformation, supposition, and
fear on the matter of American costs versus foreign costs and
on the matter of costs of monopoly versus costs of regulated
competition than on almost any other part . . . of the discussion." [11]

Fear of lower labor standards in foreign countries was unfounded, Damon told the committee, because most of the wages in the aviation industry were paid to skilled workers. Such labor commanded almost as high a wage in England, or any other country, as in the United States, he declared.* Moreover, labor efficiency was a factor in measuring total labor costs. State Department researchers had found that it took more than 500 man-hours for British mechanics to complete a major overhaul on a Pratt and Whitney Twin-Row Wasp engine. The same work could be completed in the United States in from 225 to 350 hours. Since Pratt and Whitney engines were well known in Great Britain at the time, the comparison was considered to be a fair one. On this basis, the cost of an overhaul in Great Britain was $475, as compared with $247 to $385 in the United States. Thus, the 15 cents an hour differential paid U.S. mechanics did not put American air-line operators to any disadvantage — in fact, the reverse was true.

Damon also pointed out that on the world routes not all labor would be paid under the U.S. standard, since an air line would hire native workers wherever possible. Foreign air lines would have to pay higher wages for work done in this country. This would even up the wage differentials still more, he believed. "You can adjust the figures to suit," explained Damon, "but actually, to put a difficult case, it ends up as a difference in operating costs of about 5.9 per cent, and if our American ingenuity; if our higher utilization of equipment; if our desire to go out and get business; if the competitive spirit is retained, we should be able to more than use up that 5.9 per cent.†"

This was brave talk, but how much of it was sincere? Damon represented the domestic operators who were covetous of foreign routes. They stood for competition but whether they

*A State Department report described wages paid to aviation mechanics in Great Britain as averaging four shillings eight pence, or about 95 cents an hour. The same class of workers in the United States were then receiving $1.10 an hour for the same type of work.

†For arguments over the wage factor in international air transport, see the testimony of Ralph S. Damon in hearings on S. 326, *To Create the All-American Flag Line*, etc., pp 394-417.

stood for it because of principle or because of expedience is debatable. There was, for example, the case of Damon's own company, American Airlines. The company was one of the foremost opponents of the McCarran Bill. It fought determinedly for competition, as against the community company on international routes. And yet only the year before when an interloper had threatened to take traffic away from one of its domestic divisions, American Airlines had had nothing good to say about competition.[12] "Apparently," Senator Brewster commented, "it makes a difference whose ox is gored."

Whatever the motives, the Civil Aeronautics Board appeared to lean toward the arguments of the domestic operators. All during the hearings the CAB had been waiting impatiently to go ahead with plans for the development of the world routes. On June 14, 1944, it announced that it would receive applications for international route certificates from all interested promoters. That indicated that the CAB stood for competition, regardless of the debate in the Senate committee over the community company. Indeed, the Board would have acted much sooner, had it not been for the dillydallying senators. Chairman Bailey had asked that the CAB delay action until his committee had threshed out the issue of the community company. Some of the Board members were outraged at this request, because the CAB was empowered by law to develop aviation in the public interest, regardless of debates in Congress. Chairman Pogue of the CAB had pointed out to Senator Bailey that the Act of 1938 clearly prescribed regulated competition, and until that law was repealed, competition would be the policy of the CAB. That was on May 26, 1944. Three weeks later the CAB made the announcement about route applications.

Even so, the CAB moved slowly, hoping the senators would come to a conclusion about the monopoly-competition argument. Instead, the senators settled nothing. Up to the beginning of 1945 they were still fumbling the McCarran Bill. Chairman Bailey himself began to get restless, and he put pressure upon his committee members to reach a decision. That, of course, was just what some of them did not wish.

They hoped to stall off the CAB and all the potential rivals until monopoly won by default. On February 5, 1945, however, Senator Bailey finally got his subcommittee ready to issue a report. It favored the McCarran Bill. At the last minute this report was withdrawn, after Senators Bilbo, Overton, and Mead suddenly demanded a secret meeting at which confidential information, hitherto barred by war restrictions, was to be presented. On February 7, key officials from the State and Commerce Departments and from the CAB were called to an executive session of the subcommittee. Witnesses described the services then being performed by domestic operators on world routes. They also reported that General Arnold was definitely opposed to the community company, or to any other form of monopoly that might not make full use of air bases after the war. At the end of this meeting Senator Bilbo announced to the reporters that the monopoly report had been voted down by the subcommittee.

Apparently even Senator Bailey was convinced that the community company was a dead duck, at least for the time. Two days after the secret meeting he notified Pogue that as far as he was concerned there was no longer any reason for the CAB to delay opening up the world routes on a competitive basis. Thus the long debate ended with victory for competition. It was not a final victory, however. Up to the very moment this book was written the community company sentiment was being kept alive, and at least some of the early opponents of the Mc-Carran Bill were known to have changed their minds — even to the extent of suggesting a merger with Pan American.

In the summer of 1945 the United States took one more step into the air age when it decided upon its international air-transport policy. The selection of the air lines that could best serve the public was the next task. Anyone could see that it would take the wisdom of a Solomon to make the right decisions. And, curiously, it was a Solomon who brought the matter up for judgment — S. J. Solomon, president of little Northeast Airlines.

REFERENCES

1. *To Create the All-American Flag Line, Inc.,* Hearings before the Subcommittee on Aviation, Committee on Commerce, U. S. Senate, 79th Congress, 1st Session, on S. 326, Washington, 1945, pp. 49 ff.
2. Signed editorial of Juan Trippe in *Wings over the World,* annual report for 1943 of Pan American World Airways, pp. 3-4.
3. *To Create the All-American Flag Line, Inc., Hearings,* p. 28.
4. *Ibid.,* 190.
5. W. A. Patterson, *Some Views on Post War Air Transportation,* (pamphlet) United Air Lines, Chicago, 1944.
6. Bernard A. McDonald and John L. Drew, *Air Transportation in the Immediate Post War Period,* Curtiss-Wright Corporation, Airplane Division, Buffalo, March, 1944.
7. Editorial, "The Man Talks Sense," *American Aviation,* March 15, 1945, p. 9.
8. *Ibid.*
9. *To Create the All-American Flag Line, Inc.,* Hearings, p. 274.
10. *Ibid.,* 538.
11. *Ibid.,* 394.
12. *CAB Reports,* Vol. 4, p. 689, Docket No. 13–401–13–1.

A NOTE ON SOURCES

For postwar traffic estimates used in the debate on the community company, see W. A. Patterson's *Some Views on Post War Air Transportation,* a privately published company pamphlet put out by United Air Lines, 1944, and also his "International Trans-Ocean Air Transportation and The Domestic Airlines," an open letter addressed to the Civil Aeronautics Board, dated September 30, 1943, from CAB files; Bernard A. McDonald and John L. Drew, *Air Transportation in the Immediate Post War Period,* Curtiss-Wright Corporation, Airplane Division, Buffalo, March, 1944; *Civil Aviation and the National Economy,* Department of Commerce, Washington, September, 1945. Source of information on community company issues in this chapter is from *To Create the All-American Flag Line, Inc.,* Hearings before the Subcommittee on Aviation, Committee on Commerce, United States Senate, Seventy-ninth Congress, First Session, on S.326, Washington, 1945. A sidelight on the government policy regarding monopoly and competition is given in the Report of the Attorney General on International Air Transport Policy (the "Biddle Report"), as submitted to Congress on February 28, 1945, Seventy-ninth Congress, First Session, House Document No. 142, pp. 32 ff., Washington, 1946. The arguments of the domestic operators are given in digest form in "Worldwide Airlanes for United States Airlines: Competition vs. Monopoly," a brochure distributed by the Airlines Committee for the United States Air Policy (The Seventeen Airlines Committee), New York, September, 1944; and "Historic Battle on Freedom of the Air Gets under Way," in *Air Transportation,* August, 1943. Information for this chapter was also obtained from interviews with Joseph E. Casey, successor to Royce as chairman of the Seventeen Airlines Committee and general counsel for TWA; John Stuart, aviation columnist of the New York Times; and L. Welch Pogue, chairman of the CAB.

NORTH ATLANTIC TEMPEST

ON MARCH 16, 1943, Samuel Joseph Solomon arrived in Washington to see what could be done about getting a new route for his company. The Civil Aeronautics Board had turned down all applications during the war, but Solomon wondered if the Board would not at least file his petition for future consideration. Northeast Airlines was the smallest domestic carrier in the business, but under its aggressive president it was ready to embark on an ambitious program of expansion. What its backers sought was a route certificate for air service to England, France, the Scandinavian countries, and Russia.

Northeast Airlines had done a whale of a job during the war for such a small fry.* It was one of the first domestic carriers to begin cargo service across the Atlantic. It was awarded one

---

*Northeast Airlines had been born as Boston–Maine Airways. It was originally under contract to Pan American Airways, from which it leased all its equipment. This arrangement was terminated in 1932 when the Boston & Maine and the Maine Central railroads took over control. In 1940 the little air line was reorganized as Northeast Airlines. It operated out of Boston to nearby New England and Canadian points. The company had the distinction of being not only the first domestic air line to request an international route, but also the operator with the oldest application on file with the Civil Aeronautics Board—a plea for an extension from Boston to New York paralleling a route of American Airlines. It failed to win the international route, but in 1944 it was granted the intercity route, although it was not until May of 1945 that it was able to obtain the equipment for inaugurating service.

of the first contracts to supply air transportation for the Army. It conducted one of the first civilian schools for training transport crews, and it provided shops for maintaining all types of civilian and military transports. With that record, Northeast executives believed they had justification for continuing a transocean service in peacetime. The company was one of the leaders in the movement to open up international routes to the domestic operators. Solomon was a moving spirit in the Seventeen Airlines Committee — the group that fought monopoly and the community company so successfully. It was only appropriate that he and his company should be the first to demand an international route. As luck would have it, Solomon ended up with nothing to show for his efforts, but that does not detract from his place in aviation history.

When the CAB announced on June 14, 1944, that it would accept applications for world routes, it designated specific areas for U.S. exploitation. Calcutta was to be the division point between the Atlantic and Pacific operations. These two areas were then split into five subdivisions. Each was to be considered separately in awarding route applications. The subsequent hearings, named after the regions under consideration, were called the North Atlantic, South Atlantic, North Pacific, Central Pacific, and South Pacific cases. Since the North Atlantic case was by far the most significant, the Board gave this hearing priority on its docket.

Eleven operators were ready to bid on North Atlantic routes. There were also a number of "interveners" — individuals and organizations with special interests in the case. Included in this group were the Port of New York Authority; the Greater Miami Port Authority; the Commonwealth of Massachusetts; the City of Norfolk; the Baltimore Aviation Commission; the City of Philadelphia; and the National Federation of American Shipping, which did not see why steamship interests were being snubbed by the Board.

Pan American World Airways, which had continued to plug for the McCarran All-American Flag Line Bill, suggested an easy way of avoiding all the litigation that was clearly indicated.

Pan American held the only permanent certificate for Atlantic routes. Pan American Airways stood for the community company, but if that plan was turned down, the only alternative, said company attorneys, was to issue one, and only one, other permanent certificate — to American Export Airlines. Amex had been operating all this time as a contract carrier for the armed forces. It held only a temporary certificate — which Pan American had done everything possible to have terminated. With the threat of more serious rivalry, however, Pan American was willing to give grudging consent to the award of a permanent Amex certificate. The suggestion met with a cool response.

By this time the CAB had far more complicated matters to consider. Its problem was to achieve a nice balance between competition and uneconomical operation. The selection of a carrier "fit, willing, and able" (as the Act of 1938 put it) would have been no problem at all. Most of the applications probably could have provided ocean air transport. The question the Board had to decide was how best to allocate routes. That involved the number of certificates to be awarded; the traffic needed to support such air lines; the designation of airports; and the selection of operators who could present the strongest front against foreign rivals.

Two companies were certain to win franchises in the North Atlantic area. Pan American Airways was in by priority and by experience. American Export Airlines could hardly be denied its application after its harrowing struggle to develop as an international air carrier. But the award of a certificate to Amex involved an even further threat to Pan American. It may be recalled that the CAB had interpreted a court dictum as specifying that Amex must be split apart from its steamship host before it was eligible as a U.S. certified carrier. Pan American, which had virtually forced this decision, now found that what appeared to have been a clever maneuver to block a rival actually was a bad blunder. The only way Amex could settle its financial difficulties was to allow another company to buy up stock. Since surface transportation systems were prevented from trespassing on the high frontier, the only organization permitted to buy into the aviation business was another air line. But only a prosperous, and therefore powerful, air line could have afforded to buy into Amex. And that is exactly what happened. Had Pan American not insisted upon the diverting of steamship control, it would have been faced by an air line of limited resources (lacking steamship-company support) and confined to a definite area. The CAB would not have approved of a Pan American–Amex merger at that time, and even if it had, Amex executives were too resentful of Pan American to have agreed. So Amex merged with a powerful domestic operator and Pan American World Airways discovered that its obstruction of Amex had boomeranged.

Except for Pan American, only two air lines were capable of taking over the Amex operation. One was Trans-World Airline (the name given to the international operations of Transcontinental and Western Air, Incorporated, a domestic company) and the other was American Airlines. TWA planners believed they had a good enough case for world operation without tying themselves up in a merger with Amex. American Airlines, on the other hand, was willing to take over the responsibility. Ralph S. Damon of American and John E. Slater of Amex were good friends and were able to work out merger details satisfactorily. American Airlines, biggest and most prosperous of the U.S. carriers, was financially able to consummate the arrangement, and the CAB approved. The merger would insure strong competition to Pan American and would provide the type of operation that could meet all foreign rivalry. The advantage to American Airlines was that the merger would automatically make it an international operator, since it was assumed that acquisition of Amex would include the valuable route certificate to which the company was entitled, as almost everyone agreed. On the other hand, it was hardly fair to make American Airlines an international operator by such indirect means at the expense of its domestic rival, TWA, which had equally good reasons for requesting a franchise.

None of this made any sense to the Pan American people.

Henry J. Friendly, counsel for the company, argued that the certification of a second or third carrier was utterly unsound. In the first place, said he, those who favored the plan apparently were failing to take into account the very practical problem of obtaining operating rights in foreign countries. All the applicants blandly assumed that such rights would be granted upon request. In reality, many of the points and route sections specified in the CAB announcement of June, 1944, were certain to be sealed off from U.S. penetration. The experience of Pan American in other areas, and the attitudes of delegates at the Chicago conference had verified Friendly's thesis only too clearly. Russia, for example, had no intention of allowing American operators into its traffic centers. The Soviet satellites could be expected to follow a similar program of isolationism. Other nations, notably the United Kingdom and France, had refused to sign the Transport (Five Freedoms) Agreement at Chicago, so that no operator could be certain of enjoying the necessary commercial privileges in those countries. On the other hand, as the spokesman pointed out, Pan American World Airways did have a private agreement dating from 1939 which gave that air line a limited, but certain, franchise to operate to British and French gateways. Why not work with a sure thing, Friendly asked? Why set up operations that were unworkable when the nation had at hand an air line that was ready to offer immediate service? Accompanying the CAB announcement there had been a plea by Chairman Pogue for the air-transport industry to "stop chewing on the fringes of present travel and make a bold new stroke to serve air transportation to the common man." That was just what Pan American was willing and able to do — at once, Friendly declared. It was the one company ready to supply such service, but it was being delayed by all the talk about a second, third, or fourth carrier. Of course the rivals charged Pan American with selfish motives, but, Trippe explained to the Board, his company had a definite policy in answer to such accusations.

"It is to assume our national responsibility as a private enterprise, and to offer the most value to the most people," the head

of Pan American testified.[1] "That isn't as obvious at is sounds.
Because air transport does have a choice — the very clear choice
— of becoming a luxury service to carry the well-to-do at high
prices — or to carry the average man at what he can afford to
pay. Pan American has chosen the latter course."

Pan American could provide this cheap service only if it
could use the giant aircraft it had already ordered, argued its
spokesmen. The big planes would help to reduce operating
costs, but, on the other hand they must be flown on schedules
frequent enough to meet the convenience of the public. Nor
could such planes be offered as a means of cheap transportation
unless they were well filled. Pan American exhibits demonstrated this point. The company was already looking beyond
the Constellation, then believed to be the last word in transport
aircraft design. The "Connie" had become a standard for cost
analysis, and many of the exhibits in the CAB hearing were
based upon operation of this type of plane. Pan American
analysts estimated the operating costs of the Connie at 16.9
cents a ton-mile (a ton carried one mile is a "ton-mile"). That
was believed to be a remarkably low figure. But the planes Pan
American had on order should reduce the above costs to 13.7
cents and eventually to 10.9 a ton-mile, it was believed. If
given a free hand, Pan American planners were certain they
could sell fares from New York to London for about $148 one
way, as compared with the $300 tariffs charged by steamships
of the *Queen Mary* class.* All this depended upon the use
of the largest and most efficient equipment. If traffic were to
be diluted by a number of competitive air lines, the common
man would, in the end, pay more, not less, for his air travel,
it was argued.

If the U.S. policy on international air commerce was to
recognize competition, then one other company, specifically
American Export Airlines, was sufficient to provide the "yardstick of efficiency" demanded by the Pan American opponents,

*An ambition that was never achieved, because of forces beyond the con-
trol of the company.

the company counsel insisted. Surely, there was no need for three, four, or five such yardsticks. And in the allocation of routes, Pan American should be given its choice, because of its pioneering efforts, the spokesmen held. He demanded that Pan American be granted an exclusive Great Circle route from New York to London; another from New York to Paris; a third to Marseille via London; an extension of the Paris route to Cairo, Basra, Karachi, and Calcutta; and branch lines to Scandinavia and the USSR.

To all of this the Pan American opponents replied with a faint curl of the upper lip. They pointed out that every time Pan American monopoly was threatened the company pulled out all the stops in playing its old tune about the common man. Had Pan American's record in Latin America shown any concern over the fares the common man had to pay for travel in that area, they asked? On the contrary, Pan American, as a monopoly, had squeezed out every penny the traffic would bear, as made public in the Latin American Rate Case, cried the Pan American rivals.[2] Furthermore, all the talk about the advantages of planes still in the drawing-board stage was just a smoke screen, it was charged.

To get fares down to 3.5 cents a mile, as proposed in Pan American exhibits, it would be necessary to operate two hundred-passenger aircraft at a very high load factor, witnesses in the hearing testified. Such planes were not available, and probably would not be in operation until long after the postwar air transportation policy had been decided. Even if they were available immediately, such planes might not be the most efficient means of air transportation, it was held. At the current stage of development only a few airports in the world were capable of taking such enormous craft. Granting that New York and London might provide such facilities and that the big planes would be confined to that route for the time being, it was still debatable whether such service was what the public needed. More frequent schedules by smaller planes reaching European centers with ordinary airports might provide a more convenient service than could infrequent flights of super planes to one or two "gateways." Nor were savings anywhere nearly so great with bigger aircraft as Pan American witnesses had testified, the sponsors of competition maintained. Economies promised by Pan American would apply only if all passengers left together for a common destination. True, the cost to the air line might be less under such ideal conditions, but if passengers had to wait around for the big planes to fill up, and if they had to pay another fare in London or Paris to reach their respective destinations, there was no actual saving to the public. Furthermore, the big planes were economical to operate only under ideal conditions. If there was sufficient traffic to support the operation of such aircraft on frequent schedules, costs might indeed go down. In slack seasons, or during emergency, the big ships would be liabilities. If a company carried two hundred passengers in five forty-seat planes, it had only to drop one or two flights when traffic decreased temporarily. The big ship would either have to fly partially empty under the same circumstances, or it would have to reduce flight frequencies in order to fill its seats. In either case the public would suffer, if too much dependence was placed upon the economies of big-ship operation. Of course, these critics declared, they were not averse to using the larger aircraft when conditions warranted, but the point was that such equipment was not the whole answer to the problem.[3]

There was another major problem the CAB had to solve. That was the right of Pan American to tap new centers of traffic within the country. If the domestic operators were to be permitted to make international flights, would it not be fair to let our international air line reach inland — a privilege specifically forbidden since the days of Walter Folger Brown. If the answer to that were "yes," would the invasion by an aggressive company not upset the delicate balance of the domestic air-line system achieved after so many years of trial and study?

Spokesmen for the two biggest domestic applicants, American Airlines and TWA did not like to admit that they might have an advantage over Pan American under their proposed operation of world routes. If they could provide "one-carrier service" between major U.S. traffic centers and the United States and European cities, there was no doubt that they enjoyed certain advantages. Obviously, a passenger would prefer to travel by one route from Los Angeles or St. Louis to London or Paris. The air line could work out the most convenient schedules with a minimum amount of change. That was much easier than traveling to New York for passage on a Pan American clipper. The convenience of the one-carrier service offered a reason for Chairman Pogue of the CAB to advocate operation of international routes by domestic air lines. These companies had excellent traffic promotion facilities in every important American city. They could generate the traffic that the country would need under the competitive system to stand up against foreign chosen instruments. Sponsors of this plan explained that the one-carrier service would not seriously harm Pan American because it was certain to receive a quota of international traffic from all the other domestic operators who did not fly world routes. United Air Lines was not applying for an Atlantic route. Presumably, traffic along the United route would arrive in New York for transfer to Pan American planes. United could hardly be expected to turn over such traffic to the international operator that was also its rival on the domestic airways.

Pan American operators would not admit this argument. Depending upon exclusively domestic air lines for international traffic did not offer any assurance of fair competition to the one-carrier service, they grumbled. Suppose, they said, that American Airlines offered one-carrier service to Europe and discovered that United and Capital Air Lines were routing all international traffic by way of Pan American World Airways. Both United and Capital served common terminals off the American Airlines domestic route. If American believed that either one of these companies was sending too much traffic by way of Pan American, it could retaliate by routing all incoming traffic over the more friendly connecting line. The only fair solution was to let Pan American compete with domestic rivals (if the CAB insisted upon competition) by granting certificates for domestic routes.

This argument gave the smaller domestic air lines their big chance to present their cases. One of the most effective proponents of the small independent operators was C. Bedell Monro, then president of Capital Airlines.* Monro believed that the designation of his company as an international carrier would provide the answer to many problems confronting the CAB. Let Pan American remain an exclusive international carrier and let TWA and American Airlines stick to their special fields as successful domestic operators, advised the Capital Airlines chief. Any change in that arrangement was certain to wreck the domestic air-lines system, he believed. Capital Airlines could provide all the advantages mentioned by the TWA and American spokesmen, Monro declared. He was probably correct in that. His company had been flying to all parts of the world as a contract operator for the armed forces. Capital, or PCA, as it was called then, was noted as an efficient wartime operator.

The beauty of the plan described by the air-line president was that as an international operator, Capital would do the least harm to the domestic and international companies already certificated. Although Capital was a regional rather than a transcontinental company, it reached major cities in the most important industrial area of the United States. Surveys had shown that 78.2 per cent of the foreign-born population of the country lived east of the Mississippi — the very section reached by Capital Airlines. This was the section from which most of the postwar Atlantic traffic could be expected to flow. Even before the war it had accounted for 80.4 per cent of the annual passports for Europe. Thus, the air line could promise one-

*Capital Airlines was the old Pennsylvania-Central Airlines (PCA). When the company began to extend its routes throughout the Great Lakes region the old name became inappropriate. Wisely, the company educated the public slowly to its new title, Capital Airlines. It began by using the new name parenthetically. Later, the old name was played down by advertising the company as "PCA-Capital Airlines." Eventually the company dropped the old name completely.

carrier service for the most important traffic pool; it was assured of a comfortable backlog of traffic; and it would keep the domestic and international giants from tearing into each other.

Other independents agreed with Monro's general thesis, but some of them believed the Capital plan did not go far enough. True, Capital was not a trunk line, but it was certainly on a par with the transcontinentals as a major carrier. It had an important function to perform in the domestic system without adding new burdens. And it was so bound up with the domestic system that there would have been no advantage in certificating Capital in place of TWA, American, or any other trunk air line.

Two applicants believed they had special reasons for taking over the new international routes. One was U.S. Midnight Sun Airlines. The other was Trans Ocean Airlines (TOA). Why not, they asked, give international routes to operators who would concentrate on promoting foreign traffic in and out of domestic population centers? Such air lines would not interfere with the excellent existing domestic air-line pattern, yet they would provide Pan American with the competition demanded by the various government agencies, including the CAB.

The key figure in Midnight Sun was Thor Solberg, who had made the first flight from the United States to Norway in a Loening air yacht back in 1935. In 1945, when he was fifty-two years old, he could boast of being one of the few old timers who had made money out of flight training. He had a thriving business teaching students to fly and had proved that he had a sound business sense. His assistant was Frederick C. Mechier, a former member of the Swedish Air Corps and later an air-line pilot for the well-known A.B. Aerotransport company of his native land. Solberg believed his company could provide the experience, pilots, and equipment (wartime surplus) needed for successful operation of international routes.

TOA had similar qualifications. It was a company of former ferry pilots who had flown the Atlantic so many times that they had lost count. One of these veterans was Thomas G. Smith, who had been flying since 1925. Smith had organized the Trans-Ocean Pilots Association as the agency through which the non-military ferry pilots could negotiate with various governments over wages, flying conditions, and policy. The group was so successful that Smith did not see why they could not continue after the war as a tight little air-line company. Many of the pilots were independently wealthy or had salted away their ferry earnings until they had accumulated sizable cash reserves. They were good flyers who were interested in aviation for its own sake, rather than for sheer profit, but they were mature men, for the most part, and their enthusiasm was tempered by hardheadedness.

To these eager beavers TWA and American Airlines proponents replied that it took more than planes and pilots to build an air line. Just as important as the men and equipment was organization. The two big domestic operators not only were ready with planes, men, and financial resources, but they had developed over a long period of time an elaborate system of maintenance, sales promotion, and traffic research. If the United States was to maintain its lead over European rivals, argued TWA and American officials, the best way was to use the skill and organization of a rich and experienced operator. Both companies could claim fitness on such a basis. TWA boasted that it had crossed the North Atlantic more than any other private air line in the world. American had flown the route almost as frequently, in addition to flights in other areas. Under President Cyrus R. Smith and his staff, American Airlines had become the biggest and most prosperous U.S. operator. The prospect of Smith and Trippe facing each other in open competition for international traffic was enough to put the entire industry into a dither of excitement.

The CAB had to ponder all these factors in making the decision it announced on June 1, 1945. The results of the North Atlantic case hearings were as follows: American Export Airlines, as expected, won a certificate to operate from Chicago, Detroit, Washington, Philadelphia, New York, or Boston to the United Kingdom by way of Labrador, Greenland, Iceland, and

Eire. It could also serve northern Ireland (a concession that
was galling to Pan American, which by the terms of the same
decision was limited to specified points), the Netherlands, Denmark, Norway, Sweden, the Baltic States, Poland, Russia, and
"that portion of Germany which lies north of the fiftieth parallel" (including Bremen, Hamburg, Frankfurt, Leipzig, and
Berlin).[4]

Pan American's old certificate was amended so as to allow
the air line to pick up and discharge international traffic at the
same U.S. co-terminals as designated in the Amex franchise.
It was also authorized to carry passengers, mail, and express
beyond the United Kingdom (which it was currently serving
under its old unilateral contract) to Belgium and "that portion
of Germany south of the fiftieth parallel," including Munich,
Nürnberg, and Stuttgart. Under the new certificate Pan American was also to serve Czechoslovakia, Austria, Hungary, Yugoslavia, Rumania, Bulgaria, Turkey, Lebanon, Iraq, Iran, Afghanistan, and "intermediate points within that portion of
India north of the twentieth parallel," including Karachi,
Delhi, and Calcutta.[5]

TWA was granted the right to use the same U.S. ports of
entry mentioned in the Pan American and Amex certificates.
By the terms of the decision TWA could serve France (except
the city of Marseille, which was a Pan American gateway to
the country) Italy, Switzerland, Greece, Egypt, Palestine, Trans-
Jordan, Iraq, Saudi Arabia, Yemen, Oman, Ceylon, and "that
portion of India which lies south of the twentieth parallel,"
including Bombay. TWA also won an alternate route from
the United States to Portugal. Lisbon was to be the junction
for two branches. One cut across Spain to reach Italian traffic
centers; the second veered across North Africa to connect with
the main line at Cairo.

The new certificates were to be valid for seven years. The
Board believed that by 1952 it could revise its certificates if a
fair trial of the operations indicated the need for change. Answering the criticism of Pan American spokesmen, the Board
reported that in view of the unsettled conditions throughout

the world the single operation advocated by Pan American had much to recommend it. It was true that these conditions were harmful to competitive air commerce. Even so, the Board explained, there was every reason to establish a strong policy on competition, even though the routes might be vague and even though they might have to be revised drastically by 1952. Indeed, said the Board, this policy had to be established before the Government could go ahead with its foreign negotiations. Not until the State Department knew what lines had been authorized, and not until the department knew where they would operate, could it work out agreements on a diplomatic level. The Board declared that it had no intention of being reckless or wasteful in authorizing uneconomical enterprises, but on the other hand, it refused to be "ultraconservative or overcautious" at this critical phase of world aviation development.

In making the decision the Board had considered only two issues: (1) whether or not more than one carrier should operate over the North Atlantic; and (2) if so, whether or not the domestic operators should be permitted to engage in such competition. The first question has already been answered by the Board at the time of the American Export decision. Pan American in its brief had denied the justification of such a finding on the ground that the American Export case did not apply in 1945. In 1940, it was argued, there was very little foreign competition, whereas in 1945 there was not only strong rivalry for American patronage, but insufficient traffic to warrant two U.S. carriers. The Board held, however, that a decision in favor of Pan American would have been the same as an adoption of the chosen instrument operation. Pan American was the only applicant certified to operate in other international areas. The precedent set in the North Atlantic case would be called up when the other regional hearings were held, so that Pan American would likely as not end up with all the world routes. Lastly, the Board held, the North Atlantic was the only area where traffic was heavy enough to give competition a fair test. To have decided in favor of Pan American would have repudiated the advice of every government agency.

On the matter of international operation by domestic air carriers, the Board was equally specific. It admitted the precedent whereby domestic and international operations had been carefully segregated since 1927. But, said the Board report, conditions were different in 1945. Until the war most international operations had been conducted with flying boats. Such planes required special skills and were adapted for coastal bases. The use of land planes "transcends natural barriers," the report stated. By 1945 Detroit was just as logically a U.S. gateway as New York. Indeed, the Board wished to encourage the tearing down of artificial barriers. From this point of view, a domestic operator was just as well equipped for world service as was Pan American. On the other hand, Pan American could equalize any advantage of the domestic operators by its newly acquired right to fly from inland cities.

The Board had selected TWA and American Airlines as the domestic operators best fitted for international service because they represented the strongest and most aggressive organizations in their field. American Airlines ranked with the railroads as one of the fifteen biggest passenger carriers, and TWA was not far behind. Both companies had the necessary financial reserves for the long and expensive pioneering period — or so it was believed.

The choice of American Airlines as a certificated international carrier necessitated a supplemental decision by the Board. American Airlines was authorized to purchase sufficient stock from the parent steamship company to take over control of American Export Airlines. This transaction was completed on December 5, 1945. After that date Amex became the international section of the American Airlines System and henceforth was known as American Overseas Airlines (AOA).

Concurring in the decisions of the CAB were Chairman Pogue and members Edward P. Warner, Oswald Ryan, and Josh Lee. The fifth member, Harllee Branch, agreed on the competitive principle, but dissented on the allocation of routes. He believed it was a mistake to extend TWA's route from

Cairo to India, because that was a section with meager traffic possibilities, and even the few available travelers were more likely to "fly British." Pan American had been authorized to fly a parallel route to the north, through Lebanon — enough of an enterprise for the U.S. to support in that part of the world, Branch argued. He admitted that he might be pessimistic in his estimates, but if he was wrong, there would be plenty of time to correct the error after the seven-year period of trial had been concluded.

Pan American criticized every item of the decision. Its attorneys immediately filed a petition, as permitted in such cases, demanding a reargument, rehearing, and reconsideration. The company had abandoned the idea of the single company, however — at least for the time being. Its petition declared that the "CAB's mind is obviously made up." This time the Pan American attack took the form of a petty skirmish. The Board was accused of favoritism to TWA and American Airlines. The company pointed out that the decision "froze" Pan American to points specified in the old agreements negotiated years before by the company. On the other hand, it charged, the domestic interlopers were permitted to operate to any points within the enumerated regions. Pan American, the oldest and most experienced international carrier, had access to only 25 per cent of the potential traffic, Friendly maintained, whereas the newcomers had much more than a fair share allocated to them. In at least eight earlier decisions the Board had recognized the "grandfather" rights of carriers operating under previous agreements, yet in four of the countries reached by Pan American under the old contracts, a rival not only had been permitted to poach, but had actually been given more privileges than the original promoter, said the attorney. TWA, for example, was authorized to go anywhere in France, while Pan American was restricted to touching at Marseille, a city which few Americans ever visited directly. Pan American's route to Marseille was not even the shortest, the spokesman complained. By flying via TWA the U.S. tourist visiting Marseille could save 260 miles. In like manner, TWA was permitted to land anywhere in Ireland, whereas Pan American, which had been flying to that country since 1939, was restricted to Foynes or Rineanna (successor to Shannon as a terminal). American Airlines was authorized to serve any city in the United Kingdom; Pan American could touch only at London.

"Then," said the Pan American brief, "after practically throwing Pan American out of France and Eire for the benefit of TWA and placing it in an inferior position to American in the United Kingdom, the Board would exclude Pan American from all other major traffic areas and confer a monopoly of them on TWA and American." [6] It was denied access to Italy, one of the great tourist magnets for Americans; yet TWA was granted exclusive rights there. It was denied access to Egypt, another tourist mecca; and again TWA had an exclusive right. It was denied access to Scandinavia, Russia, and 75 per cent of Germany; American Airlines had all these areas to itself. It was denied access to four of the five greatest traffic centers of Europe — Paris, Rome, Berlin, and Moscow, while a fifth great center, London, had to be shared with American Airlines and British Overseas Airways Corporation.

Instead of these important traffic areas, Pan American was handed a route to the Middle East which it did not need. By no stretch of the imagination could this route across the Balkans be called an operation in the interests of "public convenience and necessity." It was an impossible route, the company spokesman declared, since the governments were all under the influence of Russia and hence sealed off from foreign commerce. Finally, the route to India — a route of very little profit possibility — had been made impossible by competition with TWA. Now neither company had a chance to operate economically over this barren land, and both would have to call for government subsidy of some kind, if the routes were to be maintained.

To this rebuttal the new international carriers made angry reply. As usual, they cried, Pan American was only roiling the water to confuse the issue. TWA spokesmen frankly accused Pan American of causing trouble so as to delay the beginning of route operation either until Congress passed laws more favorable to Pan American, or one of the rivals dropped out in despair. Pan American got much the best of the bargain in the CAB decision, TWA attorneys insisted. The share of traffic available to TWA amounted to only about 17 per cent of the U.S. total, it was stated. Pan American had lost nothing it had held before the decision; on the contrary, the new certificates authorized it to serve fifteen additional traffic-generating countries. It had access to ten cities of more than 750,000 inhabitants (London, Barcelona, Brussels, Marseille, Munich, Prague, Vienna, Budapest, Istanbul, and Calcutta), whereas TWA reached only five such centers (Paris, Madrid, Rome, Cairo, and Bombay). It was typical of Pan American, said the TWA defenders, to be satisfied with nothing less than everything.

Pan American was not even consistent, it was charged. The company had itself suggested that it operate to specific points as part of its gateway policy. In its brief of February 21, 1945, the company had stated that service to London (which it was awarded) would be adequate to maintain a flow of traffic. At one time Pan American had asked only three stops in all Central Europe. Similarly, Pan American complained because it was denied access to Saudi Arabia. Yet only three months before, when the situation was generally understood by all, it had ridiculed such service in oral arguments.

Eventually a partial compromise was worked out. In July, 1946, the CAB amended the Pan American certificate to include Dublin, Frankfurt, and Naples. Meantime, decision or no decision, Pan American kept right on fighting the competition issue. It had lost the round in the North Atlantic case, but as demonstrated in the American Export fight, a CAB decision did not always signify the end of the battle. The struggle was carried over into Congress, as in the American Export case. Here Pan American had more influence than it had had before the CAB.

The North Atlantic decision had ignored Baltimore as a U.S. co-terminal. The city had spent millions preparing a new airport, and as an intervener in the case, Baltimore threatened to make trouble. Senator Radcliffe of Maryland was furious when he heard the CAB announcement, and he got up a petition, which he called a "progress report to the president." Its gist was that the CAB had acted "recklessly." The report pointed out that the senate aviation subcommittee had been evenly divided on the community company issue as well as on the question of whether or not to let domestic operators fly the international routes. Senator Radcliffe got thirteen of his twenty committee members to sign the petition, including Senator Pepper, high up on the New Deal ladder. All this sputtering tended to delay opening of the new routes, which of course did not trouble Pan American at all.

Not long after this flurry had subsided, Senator McCarran reintroduced his S.326 for the creation of the All-American Flag Line. The first S.326 had been defeated in July, a day after the announcement of the North Atlantic decision. In the fall it reappeared with a few changes calculated to add to its popularity. The new bill provided for the participation in air commerce of Class I railroads and steamship lines. This was a bid for the support of these two experienced transportation systems, with their batteries of lobbyists and their hundreds of interested stockholders. The bill was reported out favorably in December of 1945 but was tabled until the next session.

The consensus is that the North Atlantic case established a definite policy that would be repudiated only with a breakdown of the competitive system. But the decision provided only U.S. authorization of American air carriers. None of the routes could be opened up until every country along the line had flashed its green light. Great Britain had the power to obstruct U.S. air expansion in many important areas. Unfortunately the relations between the United States and Great Britain on aviation matters had grown steadily worse since the Chicago conference. Not until the two leading powers came to a working agreement could the newly authorized routes be opened to U.S. air transports.

It was time for the diplomats to carry the ball again.

REFERENCES

1. *CAB, Docket No.* 855, original copy, (The North Atlantic Case), Exhibit PA-12.
2. *CAB Docket No.* 298, original copy, (The South American Rate Case).
3. These arguments are summed up in "Brief of TWA," *CAB Docket No.* 855, original copy.
4. *CAB Docket No.* 855, Final Decision.
5. *Ibid.*
6. These arguments are set forth in *CAB Docket No.* 2076, original copy, "Brief before the Examiner on Behalf of Pan American Airways, Inc." See especially pp. 19-22.

A NOTE ON SOURCES

The most complete single source of material on the North Atlantic case is the Civil Aeronautics Board, Original Docket No. 855, especially the following parts: "Brief of Pan American Airways," "Speech of Juan T. Trippe on Accepting the Medal of the National Institute of Social Sciences, May 19, 1943," as quoted in Exhibit PA-12. The report of the CAB and the final decision are also to be found in the same docket. The general policy of the CAB was described long before the final decision in a CBS broadcast by Pogue from Oklahoma City on November 17, 1944, and reprinted as a CAB undated press release. For the early agreements of Pan American Airways see *U.S. Statutes at Large*, 53:2422, State Department Executive Agreement Series No. 153. For data on the revised McCarran bill see S.326, Seventy-ninth Congress, First Session, U.S. Senate, December 3, 1945; also, Senate Report No. 805, Seventy-ninth Congress, First Session, Washington, 1945. A quick summary is given in "America's Future in International Aviation," a brochure published by the Airlines Committee for United States Air Policy (The Seventeen Airlines Committee), Washington, 1945.

BERMUDA HONEYMOON

ALL the table-thumping at Chicago about freedom of the air was just so much double talk. What the delegates actually had in mind was "freedom of the airports." For, no matter how free the air might be, it would be empty of transport planes unless landing fields were available all over the world. The right to land, not freedom of transit, was the important issue after the Chicago conference.

By the summer of 1945 American operators were poised for the take-off. The war was about over. More energy could now be devoted to planning and developing the new routes recently authorized. The U.S. air lines had the equipment, the men, and the experience to assume immediate leadership in the air. All that the airmen awaited was final clearance from the tower. Unfortunately the diplomatic weathermen in the State Department had reported a cold front in the region of Great Britain.

Delegates from both the United States and from Great Britain had gone home from Chicago determined to seek allies for their own air-commerce campaigns. The United States stood for competition and a minimum of restrictions. Great Britain stood for distribution of traffic by quota, or by such restrictions as regulation of fares, flight frequencies, and subsidies. Countries which had little chance of becoming important air powers, but which might gain by efficient air service, tended to side with the Americans. Nations with small air-transport industries that might be swallowed by too powerful rivals, came into the British camp. Each country had friends and effective weapons. Governments obligated to the British were scattered across the world and they set up ramparts against U.S. air-commerce penetration. On the other hand, the Americans had the support of the Latin Americans and the Chinese. U.S. rivals could be checkmated in the Pacific area by denying them the use of the essential Hawaiian base. Thus, throughout the world both countries worked frantically to win friends so as to block the aspirations of rivals.

Egypt and the Arab states provide case histories of how this warfare was conducted. These countries lay athwart the proposed Pan American and TWA routes. It was essential that the United States win landing rights in these countries before the world airways could be opened up, yet both areas were within spheres of British influence. For a time U.S. diplomats appeared to be making headway. The Egyptians were cordial to the suggestion that Cairo might become an aerial crossroads, if the great TWA enterprise were allowed to make it a division point on its world route. The Egyptians knew from war experience what American enterprise could accomplish, and at first they met all our representatives with the red carpet.

Then the British agents began to get results. They told officials that the Americans would ruin such local air lines as Egypt's little Misr Airwork, known to airmen as "Misery." Originally operated by British promoters, Misery had been designed as a feeder service for Imperial Airways. It served the Nile valley and extended north into the Levant. The U.S. minister at Cairo had been telling the same officials at Cairo that TWA was not a threat. Misr Airwork, it was pointed out, could never be a world-wide operator. As a feeder to the TWA trunk line it would reap a rich tourist harvest, however.

What the British had in mind was to make Cairo an exclusive base for BOAC. As the junction point for the various African routes, Cairo was essential for a British air-line monopoly. Since the British still wielded great influence in Egypt, they might well have succeeded, had the United States not had a few good

cards left to play. Payne Field, just outside Cairo, had been
built and equipped by the U.S. Government. It was now offered to the Egyptians, together with all the thousands of
dollars worth of equipment stored in its hangars, as the price
for opening up Cairo as a base not just for Americans, but for
any authorized air line. The Egyptians knew a bargain when
they saw one, and things began to pick up a little for the
American representatives on the spot. Then a new British mission arrived at Cairo, and the Egyptians began to play footie
with both suitors. Eventually the Americans won their point,
but not until after weeks of diplomatic palaver, during which
the U.S. minister was heard to cry despairingly on one occas-
sion that Payne Field had certainly lived up to its name.

The same sort of international horse trading went on in
the Near East, where Pan American World Airways was trying
to burst through to the Orient. Again, sympathetic officials
turned against the Americans after British representatives went
to work on them. Requests by the Americans for airports were
answered by the assertion that all available fields were needed
by the British Royal Air Force. A curious twist in world affairs
also resulted in an unfavorable reaction to Americans in the
Arab states. By denying Jewish immigration to Palestine, the
British won support from the Arabs. This was not the purpose
of the British, perhaps, but it is what happened. On the other
hand, the Arabs, who had once welcomed Americans as the
bringers of money and technical assistance for local air lines,
broke off negotiations just after the United States had taken
up the Zionist cause.

In Argentina, Mexico, and the Antipodes the story was repeated. Wherever the Americans met the British they ran into
trouble. If the British had any influence in these spheres, the
Americans usually came out second best. Every trick was used
to cut down American advantage. Even currency became a
weapon of the British. Non-priority British travelers were allowed to depart from the homeland with only $400 of foreign
exchange, unless they remained in the sterling areas. Plane
fares were exempt from this limitation if the traveler "flew

British," but fares on U.S. planes were deducted from the allowance. This effectively kept British passengers out of American planes. It was a legitimate regulation, no doubt, but it did not lessen the growing ill will between the two countries.

Americans also got in a few punches. China was as close to the Americans as Egypt was to the British — much closer, in fact. For a long time British transports had been taking off from Chinese airports immediately after filing flight plans. This was a violation of the Chinese law requiring seventy-two hours' notice of flight plans. It was one of those laws that was utterly ignored, as so many were in China in all the chaos there. Sometimes British pilots did not bother to file at all, and nobody appeared to care. But when the British began to prod Americans in other parts of the world, British pilots began to have trouble in China. In 1945 the British put in a request for the termination of the seventy-two hour flight plan rule, since it was never enforced anyway. Instead of acceding to the request, the Chinese threatened to ground all British planes and crews failing to heed the law. Yet for some strange reason the same crackdown did not apply to the Americans. It was all very obviously part of the world sparring match between the two nations.

In the meantime, the British had girded up their loins at home for the coming struggle for airways. On March 13, 1945, the Government announced (in the so-called "Winster White Paper," after the air minister) the reorganization of the international air-transport system. British routes were to be divided amongst three companies. One was to be the government-controlled BOAC, which was to operate the Commonwealth routes to India, Australia, and South Africa, as well as the old routes to the United States, Canada, and the Far East. A new company was organized to operate internal services. It was set up as a community company, owned partly by the British railroads, travel agencies, "short sea" (ferry) lines, and the prewar domestic aviation companies. A third company under the control of the government-dominated BOAC and the five major steamship lines was to develop a South American service. These lines were thus regional monopolies, regulated directly or indirectly by the government. The plan was severely criticized by the opposition parties, but when the Labor Government came to power in the summer of 1945, the air-transport policy was taken over intact. Indeed, the civil aviation program offered one of the first tests of British socialism.

Another agency also began to work to the advantage of the British. This was the International Air Transport Association, better known as IATA, the successor to an organization of similar name. It was not an official agency, in the sense that it could hand out orders through government bureaus, but it had great influence with all international air-line operators. IATA was a voluntary organization of representatives from all the air-transport systems. Its purpose was to stabilize air transportation on world routes. Some critics accused it of being nothing less than a cartel, a word in ill repute in the United States.

IATA was organized in Havana at a three-day conference of air-line operators in April, 1945. Representatives of forty-one air lines from twenty-five nations signed the original articles. Soon the organization was so powerful that no operator could flout it with impunity. Headquarters were moved to Montreal, adjacent to PICAO, with which it had close, although unofficial, affiliations. The Civil Aeronautics Board had some difficulty clarifying its relationship with the new international body. At one time the British demanded of the CAB that some kind of rate and frequency control be imposed upon American operators. The Board replied that of course it had no such power. Under the Act of 1938, the CAB could regulate rates and frequencies of domestic operators, but it was specifically denied the same control over international operations. The authors of the law had feared that if the CAB had the power to regulate international air lines in this manner, other nations would thereby have an excuse to pass retaliatory measures. The British recognized this point, but they insisted the Board had sufficient power (through designation of routes, regulation of mail pay, and so on) to curb cutthroat competition if it cared to. The Civil Aeronautics Board did not concede the point.

An easier way was to regulate by means of IATA. Sir William Hildred, who had resigned as director-general of British civil aviation to become chairman of IATA, believed that the world's air-line operators could work out a solution on a voluntary basis. All that the British asked was some kind of agreement to limit rates and frequencies. They were willing to accept almost any reasonable figures, so long as the Americans came around to voluntary self-regulation by IATA as a curb on uneconomic competition. Had this been conceded, IATA would indeed have become an international aviation cartel, as charged. There were, however, two bylaws in the association's charter that took most of the sting out of such an accusation. In the first place, all IATA agreements had to be unanimous. Any operator who suspected that his rivals were ganging up on him could thus block action by IATA. Secondly, all decisions could be repudiated by the respective governments. And in any case, decisions were binding for only one year.

The British pinned their faith on IATA. They were so certain IATA would function as a protector of rates and frequencies that they virtually ceased further agitation for other forms of restriction for the time being. One small, vociferous faction still insisted that IATA would not be effective against the Americans, however. This group clamored for government control and regulation as the only safeguard from competitive abuses. When an American operator suddenly announced that he would not recognize IATA agreements, this group of British diehards cried, "I told you so." Sir William's prestige fell rapidly, since he had been the rock of IATA.

The American rebellion started late in 1945. An announcement by Pan American Airways in October that the company planned to reduce the fare from New York to London from $375 to $275 only confirmed the fears of the British faction opposed to Sir William. A canvas of other nations convinced the leaders of this group that Europe was solidly behind the British stand for international restriction. The cutthroat reduction in fare by the Americans was just what this faction had predicted all along. It was the very action that would wreck the international economic structure, it was held. True, the charge did not apply to all American operators. Some were charging up to $570 for the trip because they had agreed to maintain rates at a high level until conditions warranted lower rates. Indeed, it was through this understanding with the more amiable American operators that Sir William had lulled the air ministry into believing rates were safe in the hands of an unofficial agency, such as IATA. Pan American's rebellion now threatened the very life of the organization.

At once the British dropped their gloves and reached for the pile of rocks always at hand to throw at the rowdy Americans. The British had a way to stop tough customers, like Mr. Trippe, with or without IATA. Great Britain and the United States had not yet ratified any agreement on flight frequencies. Up to the time of Trippe's announcement Pan American and American Overseas had operated five flights a week each to London. But this was simply by sufferance in the absence of any formal contract between the two countries. The British could break that agreement on a moment's notice. They could not shut out Pan American Airways entirely because of the old prewar agreement allowing two flights a week, but they could certainly cancel three of the five flights.

The British hoped to beat some sense into the rebellious U.S. operator by allowing its competitor, American Overseas Airways, to continue on a five-a-week schedule. They were blocked by the CAB, which refused to let AOA be a party to such foreign manipulation. Besides, there was every reason to believe that the British were bluffing — that their attempted crackdown on Pan American was actually a maneuver to swap more frequencies for higher rates.

But Trippe may have been bluffing, too. The $275 proposed by Pan American might have caused heavy financial loss to the company. One official of the company has denied this. He declared in an interview that Pan American could have made money at this rate. On the other hand, when the CAB asked for operating figures from all the international air lines some

time after the Pan American announcement, none of the operators, including Pan American, could convince the Board that
any such reliable figures were available. Not one of them had
a reasonable basis for determining what a proper fare should be.
It was just possible that Pan American had deliberately set its
proposed fare so low that denial by the CAB would be certain.
Trippe might very easily have lost his shirt if the tariff schedule
had been permitted. But knowing that the rate would be
upped, he could safely propose it, and when it was denied he
could say, "See — this is how your vaunted competitive system
works. We establish a fare that the ordinary traveler can afford — a fare still higher than that asked by other American
operators during the route hearings, incidentally — and what
happens? The rivals who boasted that they would bring lower
fares to the public, but who accepted protection under the
IATA cartel, have ganged up on Pan American World Airways
and have actually forced that company to raise fares. With the
chosen instrument or community company we might have told
IATA to go to hell. Under this system we are helpless. When
are our policy-makers going to see the light?"

Had the other European nations not backed up the British,
Pan American might have gotten away with its low fare, if
the move had been seriously intended. Pan American planes
had only to bypass the British Isles — which was possible — and
to make Belgium or Holland the European terminal. A local
air line might then have whisked passengers to London with a
minimum of inconvenience and extra expense, and the British
would probably have given up the fight in short order. But the
Belgians and Dutch, like the British, looked upon aviation not
so much as a business or private enterprise, but as an instrument of national policy, and they stood squarely behind the
British.

On November 30 Pan American gave in to the demands of
its opponents. It was less a surrender than a truce, however.
The company filed for the standard $375 rate, with the under-
standing that as long as that rate was effective, it was to get
half the London frequencies (AOA taking the other half) *plus*

the two to which it was entitled under the old unilateral agreement. Both the CAB and the State Department objected to this arrangement. They asked, instead, that the British allot the United States ten more temporary frequencies a week to London. These were to be distributed as the CAB saw fit and used as a very effective weapon against rebellious American operators. The British allotted the frequencies, and over the anguished cries of the Pan American crowd, the Board divided them equally. Pan American was right back where it had started before its revolt, except that now the company was more unpopular than ever in Government and industry circles. The little flurry had cleared one point, however. When quiet had once more descended over the North Atlantic, the CAB informed the British that although the Board could not officially agree to restrictive measures it was now ready to "study the situation." That was interpreted by the British as meaning that the Board was willing to reconsider some kind of control over rates, which had been exactly counter to U.S. policy up to that point.

The British had saved face in all this skirmishing. Sir William Hildred of IATA had insisted that the London–New York rates be set "by agreement." He was much more concerned with the principle of the agreement than with the rate agreed upon, apparently believing that it would indicate that the operators were at least willing to penalize unfair competition. With Pan American back on the reservation, Sir William once again could report to his Government that operators were abiding by an "agreed rate," as demanded by the air ministry. True, Pan American officials stated in a news release that they still opposed "cartelization," but Sir William chose to believe that, technically, at least, all operators were once more members of the happy IATA family.

This was the situation a year after the Chicago conference. All over the world British and American operators snarled at each other. The two governments worked to keep foreign rivals from their spheres of influence. Wherever one country had friends in power, the other was driven from the air. Great Bri-

tain and the United States were like rival gangsters. Each had
its "mob" and its respective "patch," where it was unsafe for
others to venture.

It was under such tension that the representatives of the two
countries met at Bermuda in January and February of 1946.
Not much was expected of the meeting but the leaders knew
that an effort must be made to settle the quarrel before it began to widen the breach between the two old allies. Both
nations had caught each other in some rather shady undertakings in the attempts to gain supporters. Haggling over civil aviation was damaging to the solidarity of the Western nations at
the very time when it was most essential that the democracies
present a united front. That was the reason for calling the Bermuda meeting, but the chances of any reasonable conclusions
looked slim.

However, the conference was a whopping success. By a document signed February 11, 1946, the two air powers began a new
phase of friendly development. Terms of the agreement were
mutually beneficial, but the meeting went far beyond the document itself in cementing a friendship that never should have
started to come apart. It was this understanding reached at Bermuda, rather than the words on paper, that made the meeting
significant.

In air commerce matters the United States and Great Britain
had fallen out frequently. After each misunderstanding, however, the two nations had been forced to make concessions to
each other out of sheer necessity. The rivals emerged from
each squabble with much friendlier regard for each other — for
a period at least. This improved relationship was slow in progress and subject to lapses, but the trend was encouraging.
After the early conferences between President Roosevelt and
Prime Minister Churchill there had been an agreement as to
wartime roles in aviation. It was a happy solution to a problem.
As the war sputtered to a close, however, relations between the
two countries deteriorated. Legislative leaders in both countries were fearful of the pending civilian rivalry and began to
impose pressures for discriminatory regulation. Feeling ran so

high that eventually the two governments had to face it. The London conference was an attempt to resolve the differences. Although nothing was accomplished of a practical nature, airmen at least heard each other out. When the bickering started again, the Chicago conference was called. Many difficult problems were settled at this meeting, but immediately afterward, the quarreling appeared to be more bitter than ever. It was necessary to call the Bermuda conference as an attempt to prevent a serious breach between the two allies. After Bermuda it was all sweetness and light between the two nations. But it should be pointed out that Bermuda was only a stage. Later there were other meetings — at Rio and London — at which time peace was restored again. There will probably be many other such meetings of necessity in the future. To many, this erratic course was an indication of international confusion. Yet every meeting served a useful purpose. The United States and Great Britain were like two drunks helping each other back to their walk-up apartment, climbing a few steps, wrangling on the landing, wobbling up another flight, fighting again noisily, to the annoyance of the neighbors, but slowly nearing the peacefulness of their destination.

Subtle influence no doubt affected the Bermuda reconciliation. Great Britain was trying at the time to obtain a huge American loan and was meeting stiff opposition from a group fearful of perfidious Albion. The loan request was humiliating to the British and they were eager to get it off the front pages. At about the same time Russia began throwing its weight around and the British realized that as a European bulwark against Communism they needed the full support of the United States. Finally, British airmen had learned that although they could delay U.S. plans indefinitely they could not deny this country forever. They, too, hoped to fly extensive world routes — with planes that must be furnished for a time by the Americans.

But the Americans had also learned a few lessons since bidding the British a cold farewell at Chicago. If Russia drove the British to us, it was also driving us to the British. Great

Britain was our outer bastion against Communism. We had also discovered that the development of world routes called for some kind of compromise in our earlier demands for unlimited competition. It was at Bermuda, for example, that we officially gave up the fight for fifth-freedom agreements.* After the meeting the policy of the United States was to obtain fifth-freedom concessions by a pattern of bilateral agreements, to be obtained in most cases in exchange for some kind of economic restriction. Blanket, or multilateral agreements ceased to be an issue.

Much of the success of the Bermuda conference depended upon the men who represented the respective governments. Here, again, something had been learned since the Chicago days. The British were careful to select spokesmen who could face new ideas without rancor. The U.S. delegation was much more unified than it had been at Chicago. George P. Baker, former CAB member, headed the U.S. delegation. He was then chief of the state department section concerned with transport and communications problems. Other representatives were Chairman Pogue of the CAB, Oswald Ryan and Harllee Branch, Board members. Experts from U.S. air lines were also invited to attend the meetings unofficially and to offer advice.

Both the British and Americans believed they had outsmarted each other at Bermuda. Baker had come to Bermuda prepared to make certain compromises in rate regulations. Peter Masefield, one of the British delegates, has said that the British also arrived on the island ready to give up cherished demands in exchange for limited frequencies. It was evident that the British had been frightened by the recent IATA revolt of Pan American Airways. Perhaps this situation was known to the insiders in both countries, but there is something humorous about both delegations congratulating themselves afterward on their shrewdness when actually each was doing what the other side desired. On this point Stokeley Morgan, one of our rep-

*This hot potato had been dropped by the United States months before and had long been recognized as a dead issue, but the Bermuda meeting endorsed our unofficial actions.

resentatives at Bermuda, has made the following comment:

Your statement that each side had decided to make concessions but that the other side was not aware of it, is not strictly accurate. A little history may help. During the few months before the Bermuda Conference the State Department had been urgently pressing the British for this meeting. It had been subtly pointed out the bad effect it would have on the British loan negotiations if a strong effort to reach some agreement were not made before the loan came up for debate in the Senate. It was no secret that the airlines lobby would work against the British loan if our aviation interests continued to be ignored.

During this period I had many talks with Peter Masefield, who was urging his government to meet our wishes. He said that his people were very much afraid they would go to Bermuda and find us in exactly the same mind as at Chicago. In that case, the conference would be a complete flop, with great resulting loss of face to the British. I was able to assure Masefield that our people were definitely of a mind to make some concessions — that they would not find us of the same opinions as at Chicago — and that there was a good chance that a conference would be successful. Masefield, through personal letters to Hildred and others in London, convinced them that I knew what I was talking about. They decided to try the experiment. Baker is quite right, however, in saying that we did not give out the fact that we were going to change our position on rates. That would have affected our bargaining power. If the British had known they were going to get their own way on rates, they would have been twice as tough on frequencies.[1]

Some of the provisions of the Bermuda document were: (1) seven routes for the British (three straight across North America) and thirteen for the United States; (2) the right of IATA to set rates (much to the surprise and pleasure of the British), subject, of course, to government approval; (3) reciprocal fifth-freedom rights, with some minor limitations; (4) unlimited frequencies, to be determined by the respective governments; (5) an "understanding" (actually an agreement to agree) on the use of bases leased by the United States from Great Britain.[2] In this exchange of privileges the United States won fifth-freedom traffic rights and the extra frequencies so long demanded. The British won a U.S. commitment against cutthroat competition. It appeared to be a reasonable compromise.

True, the British were awarded only about half as many

world routes as the United States obtained under the terms of
the agreement. That was of no great significance, because the
British routes were all top quality airways. Permission by the
U.S. for the British to operate from London to San Francisco
by way of New York made it possible for BOAC to ring the
world with air transportation. Of course no cabotage rights
were involved. That is, the British could not pick up passengers in New York bound for San Francisco; but they could take
on traffic headed for Australia or New Zealand. And it was
stipulated that BOAC could use the vital Hawaiian base for
commercial purposes — a concession that was to bring denunciation in the U.S. Senate.*

Another British route was to turn south at New York to
reach New Orleans. This was to be a junction for two branches;
one to Mexico City and the other to Cuba, Jamaica, across to
Panama and the west coast of South America. This was an invasion of Pan American Airways' special preserve and the agreement was at once attacked by that company. The British were
also entitled under the Bermuda document to extend their old
Bermuda route from the east coast of the United States on up to
Montreal by way of the government-operated airways. Since
this would drain traffic from the Pan American's Bermuda operation, there was no enthusiasm for this agreement on the
part of the pioneer American flag line.

On the other hand, the United States won some worth-while
privileges, too. American operators were granted the right to
operate the routes designated in the North Atlantic decision.
Routes allocated at that time were meaningless, of course, until
the foreign countries involved granted permission. In fact, we
won more concessions at Bermuda than we had requested
under the North Atlantic decision. Not only did the British
grant fifth-freedom privileges for the North Atlantic routes,
but they extended those rights to regions the CAB had not
mentioned in its June decision. The British were willing after

*Bermuda agreements established only the *rights* of the respective foreign
operators. It did not follow that the British would activate all the routes
designated.

the Bermuda meeting to let Pan American World Airways and TWA operate beyond Calcutta and Bombay, where they had been temporarily halted under the terms of the North Atlantic decision. The extensions made it possible for the U.S. operators to push on to Burma, Indo-China, and China, where connections could be made with the Pacific operations. The British were even willing to open up Singapore — heretofore a citadel of British commercial aviation interests. These were useful links in U.S. round-the-world air service, but the British drove a hard bargain for them.

The British had insisted all along that traffic rates must be set by international "consultation." That was the main purpose of IATA — to bring together all international operators in order to prescribe rates. The danger was that the British might have enough influence to offset American attempts to lower fares. At Bermuda the United States agreed to approve the IATA rate conference machinery for one year, subject to disapproval by the CAB. At the same time the Board was to request permission from Congress for the right to set international rates for its own carriers, heretofore prohibited by the Aeronautics Act of 1938. Until such permission was granted, it was agreed that British and Americans would hold meetings whenever rates became an issue. If the governments failed to reach an agreement, the party objecting could "take steps" to prevent the inauguration or continuation of service. The dispute was to be submitted to PICAO upon application of either party, and when that organization reached a decision both governments were to "use their best efforts" to put such rates into effect. The clause was full of loopholes and certainly justified close scrutiny by the legislators who feared that U.S. representatives had been exploited by the British.

If, for example, the U.S. carriers agreed to the IATA rates and then found that the CAB disapproved of the agreement, would they be violating the antitrust laws?* What about our traditional opposition to cartels? Would not adherence to the

---

*The answer is "no." IATA participation was specifically privileged under the Sherman Act.

IATA agreements take control from the CAB? True, IATA was not a cartel in the sense that its decisions were binding for more than a year, but if "protracted" disputes were to be settled by PICAO arbitration, where the United States was likely to be outvoted, the question of whether or not IATA was a cartel was merely academic. At least that is how CAB member Josh Lee saw the situation when his organization was called upon to approve the Bermuda document. His views were summed up in the minority report of the Board. The majority report had stated: "We cannot accept without proof the proposition that the present resolution, which establishes the only presently available machinery whereby the United States Government through the Board can share and have a voice in the regulations of the rates of our international air carriers, is inconsistent with the policy of controlled competition which the Civil Aeronautics Act contemplates." [3]

Lee maintained that the control of rates by IATA was "the antithesis of a competitive system, since competition by consent is not competition." He argued very persuasively on this point. His colleagues held that competition did exist. Equipment, service, efficiency, and promotion were factors as important in competition as rates, and over them IATA had no control, it was pointed out. Even so, it did appear that the British had made a good bargain.

Americans apparently did not win much when they traded frequencies for rate control, either. A clause in the Bermuda document stipulated that the number of planes flown by each operator was to depend on the available traffic. Airlines were bound not to "overpromote" uneconomical traffic, despite the exchange of fifth-freedom privileges. The British insisted upon machinery for control of such "overpromotion." This was accomplished by the so-called "change of gauge" clause. When a big trans-Atlantic plane reached a European gateway, it might happen that half its passengers would disembark, leaving seats available for fifth-freedom traffic to other points along the world route. But if passage was not engaged, it would have been expensive to operate the trans-Atlantic type ship half empty the rest of the way, and so it was agreed that smaller equipment might be used instead. That was the "change of gauge." The Americans believed the change was optional, for economy. The British insisted that the rule had to be followed. It was, in fact, just another way of keeping Americans from developing traffic. Instead of holding down the number of flights, the British would accomplish the same result by holding down the number of available seats.[4] This was the source of much irritation at the end of the Bermuda honeymoon.

Both governments took the broad view on the use of military bases for civil air transport. The "heads of agreement" clause provided no specific solution to the problem but it did indicate that both governments were willing to be reasonable in working out disposition of these essential airports.

Finally, to appease those who suspected that the United States had been sold a bill of goods at Bermuda, it was provided that the document could be repudiated by either country within twelve months of notifying PICAO. Having attached this safety valve to the machinery, the delegates packed up and flew home. The next task was to sell the agreement to the respective governments.

Was it a good agreement? Baker and Pogue believed that it was. Some of the other delegates were not so certain. The Pan American observers called in for advice were opposed to the terms. So were Senators Brewster and McCarran, legislative leaders for aviation matters. True, they said, Great Britain and the United States had come to terms at last. They were willing to open up air lanes to each other. But, complained Senator Brewster, the United States had come out very definitely second best. Whereas by the agreement the British had increased their route mileage from 29,000 to 109,000 miles, the United States had gained only 57,000 miles. He declared that this was unfair to the country that was to provide most of the international air traffic.

Pogue replied that such figures were unimportant. Passenger-miles, not route-miles, measured the effectiveness of air routes, he insisted, and on that basis the United States would be the gainer. Indeed, one of the aims of the conference had been to *reduce* U.S. mileage in some cases. If, by agreement, we had won a direct route that offered more traffic and less costly operation, the loss of mileage should not be criticised. Actually, there was no reason why the United States should have more route-miles than Great Britain had. The British had many unprofitable areas to serve, said Pogue. The United States could confine operations to the most profitable routes. In any event, if the U.S. expected to extend its air frontiers, it had to grant concessions to other nations, he declared.

On the whole, the consensus in both countries appeared to be that the Bermuda agreement was a good document. The two great air powers had made an amicable adjustment of their differences. They had agreed to keep each other informed of developments in civil aviation. Both the CAB and the Air Ministry were to maintain attachés at each other's capitals. In many cases these agents might smooth out disputes before they became serious.

It appeared at the time that all had gone smoothly at Bermuda. Such was not the case. There was strenuous debate up to the end. On the last day, when Sir William Self, leader of the British delegation, received final instructions from London, there was still doubt whether the two nations could reach an agreement. The triumph came in the overriding of the obstacles and misunderstandings. Delegates returned home with almost none of the bitterness that had characterized the Chicago conference. They had acquired a new respect for each other.

Indirect results of the Bermuda meeting were as important as the direct results. At the end of 1945 the French had made a tentative agreement with this country regarding air rights, but operations had been conducted on a month-to-month basis. The French apparently were waiting to see what the British would do. Immediately after the close of the Bermuda deliberations France and the United States signed a bilateral agreement patterned on the Bermuda document. It was signed March 27, 1946. By its terms the United States won concessions on eight routes.

Some members of the British Commonwealth refused to follow the lead of the mother country. Australia, New Zealand, India, and South Africa were slow in exchanging the same privileges provided by the British and Americans in 1946. Yet in spite of these pockets of resistance, the United States was steadily pushing back the high frontier, and Bermuda was a memorable date in this conquest.

REFERENCES

1. From a memorandum written by Stokeley Morgan, dated October 30, 1946, and modified with his approval during subsequent interviews.
2. *U. S. Statutes at Large,* Vol. 60, Part 2, p. 1512, *Treaties and International Acts,* Series 1507, Final Act of the Civil Aviation Conference Held at Bermuda, January 15 to February 11, 1946. See also *Department of State Bulletin,* Vol. 14, April 7, 1946, p. 584.
3. Statement of Josh Lee, *Civil Aviation Agreements,* Hearings on S.1814 before the Committee on Commerce, U. S. Senate, 79th Congress, 1st Session, Washington, 1946. Also available in *CAB Reports,* Vol. 6, p. 644, Agreement No. 493.
4. British Embassy, "United Kingdom Proposals for Working Principles for the Framing of a Multilateral Agreement," Washington, D. C., no date. The principles enunciated in this informal proposal were similar to those offered by the British at Bermuda, an official told the author.

A NOTE ON SOURCES

Most of the information for this chapter was obtained from interviews. Among those who discussed the Bermuda conference were L. Welch Pogue, chairman of the Civil Aeronautics Board at the time; George P. Baker, former CAB member, then head of the Office of Transport and Communications, State Department; Peter Masefield, civil air attaché for the Air Ministry at the British Embassy in Washington; Stokeley W. Morgan, a U. S. representative at Bermuda; and Harllee Branch, CAB member. A discussion of the Bermuda issue appears in *Civil Aviation Agreements,* Hearings on S.1814 before the Committee on Commerce, United States, Seventy-ninth Congress, Second Session, Washington, 1946. See also "Agreement Between the United States and Great Britain Relating to Air Transportation,"

Congressional Record, Senate, April 10, 1946, pp. 3421-3428. Criticism of the Bermuda document is summarized in *International Commercial Aviation,* Resolution of the Committee on Commerce, United States Senate, with an accompanying report, relative to the so-called Bermuda Agreement between the United States and the United Kingdom regarding international commercial aviation, Senate Document No. 173, Seventy-ninth Congress, Second Session, Washington, 1946. The CAB press release of May 8, 1946, and the CAB *Foreign Air News Digest,* Vol. IV, No. 87, July 1, 1946, pp. 653 ff., give information about rate matters.

NO MORE OCEANS TO CROSS

U NFORTUNATELY, the progress in international understanding was not duplicated at home. A storm was brewing in Congress on the issue of executive agreements. There had been a mild disturbance in the Capitol after the Chicago conference, but after the Bermuda meeting the turbulence threatened to be devastating. The Bermuda document was a more effective instrument than the Chicago agreements had been, and that in itself was enough to bring on the banshees. Not only did the new contract open up the United States to our most dangerous rival, but it committed our own operators to the rate-fixing manipulations of IATA.

First warning of trouble came when Senator McCarran introduced a bill, S.1814, proposing that all international agreements of the Bermuda type must be made — "if at all" — by treaty rather than by executive agreement. Hearings on this bill were held before the Senate Committee on Commerce in the spring of 1946, immediately after the Bermuda conference. When the hearings were over, the committee submitted a report in April 1946, accompanied by a resolution — both written by Senator Brewster. His resolution condemned executive agreements and suggested:

> . . . any executive agreement which purports to grant to any foreign country the right to have an air line or air lines nominated by it to operate to or from United States territory without public hearing in advance and the determination of public interest by the Civil Aero-

nautics Board called for under section 402 of the Civil Aeronautics Act, is inconsistent not only with the Constitution, but with the letter and spirit of said Act, and therefore illegal and void; and that any and all proceedings thereunder should be forthwith terminated by appropriate notice to the governments concerned.[1]

The Senator had many allies in his efforts to make "totally inoperative" all executive agreements since the Chicago conference. Labor, including the railroad brotherhoods and the potent little Air Line Pilots Association, was on his side. Executive agreements did not give labor a chance to insist upon "safeguards," it was held. The steamship companies, which were again clamoring to be let into the aviation field, also preferred treaties to agreements. Debate over treaties would give them a chance to present the steamship operators' views on international air commerce. Lastly, there were those who objected to giving the chief executive the power of making agreements. Some of these critics were politically prejudiced about anything a Democratic president might do, but others sincerely believed that executive agreements were a usurpation of senate prerogative.

Nevertheless, it now appears that if S.1814, the McCarran bill, had been passed, international air commerce would have been right back at its 1939 status, as far as the United States was concerned. That was pointed out by men high in the counsels of a state. In a letter to Senator Bailey, chairman of the subcommittee which heard the aviation witnesses, Secretary of State Byrnes explained that despite the persuasive arguments in favor of the treaty method he believed legislation restricting negotiations by the executive method would be illegal. There were occasions, he said, when executive agreements *had* to be made in the best interests of the nation. "For the Congress to attempt by legislation to prescribe in blanket fashion which particular constitutional procedure should be followed in relation to any one or all types of foreign arrangements could only result in very adverse consequences to the conduct of our foreign relations," the Secretary of State declared.

Senator Bailey had to admit, in all fairness, that there was truth in Byrnes' assertion. Senator Bailey's solution was to define the difference between treaty and executive agreement and then let the Senate decide whether the Bermuda document was, or was not, a treaty. Secretary of Commerce Wallace also spoke against arbitrary prohibition of executive agreements. In a letter to Chairman Bailey dated April 10, 1946, Wallace admitted that treaties were theoretically to be preferred. Because of the "fluid situation" of international aviation in the postwar period, he favored the use of executive agreements. He said they were a "quick, efficient, flexible procedure" for accomplishing the purposes of our merchant airmen.

In any case, the Bermuda Agreement was allowed to stand. In a memorandum of June 18, 1946, Attorney General Tom Clark held that the contract was valid. Protest began to die down. Even before this date the Civil Aeronautics Board was ready to designate carriers for the other world routes outlined in the CAB announcement of June 14, 1944. For more than a year the Board had been collecting information and hearing testimony on other routes, but it had delayed its decision until the Bermuda Agreement was accepted. The operators were getting impatient. The war was over and U.S. airmen wished to take advantage of their favorable status. It could take as much as three years to start up a new service, after permission for it had been granted, and the promoters could not make plans until they knew which routes they would win.

On May 17, 1946, the CAB published its findings on Docket No. 525, known as the Latin American Route Case. Next to the North Atlantic decision, it was the most important announcement of the Board since the beginning of the war. To Pan American Airways it appeared to be an unreasonable verdict — harder to take, in many respects, than the North Atlantic decision. In the North Atlantic Pan American had asked for special consideration because of its pioneering, but the company soon realized that it would have to share the air lanes to Europe. Latin America was different. That was Pan American's citadel. The company had developed that region's

aviation resources, and by itself, or with close affiliates, had won
a monopoly of U.S. air services throughout the Good Neigh-
borhood. To be told that this preserve must be shared with
rivals — air lines that had never penetrated the area before —
was galling. Small wonder that the company took the decision
in bad grace. Characteristically, Pan American settled down
to a long siege.

The Latin-American case was as involved as the North Atlantic hearing. There were four thousand pages of testimony.
Exhibits filled twenty-nine volumes the size of the New York
telephone directory. Pan American's briefs alone, with peti-
tions and answers, weighed more than thirty pounds. When the
decision was announced, it should have been a momentous
event, after all the debate that preceded it. Instead, it was
virtually ignored by the press. Only one Washington daily
carried the story. A few days before, the Washington papers
had given page-one prominence to an accident near Richmond,
Virginia, involving an obscure, nonscheduled operator. As
usual, the press thought of commercial aviation in terms of
sudden death. Yet the Latin-American Route Case was a story
that went far beyond the little public of air-line people. Thousands of ordinary persons were part of the story, as stockholders
in the various air lines included in the case. Politics, government policy, and diplomacy also figured in the decision.

One newsworthy angle of the case was that President Truman had drastically modified the route pattern recommended
by the Civil Aeronautics Board. Such action on the part of the
chief executive was neither unprecedented nor beyond his
powers, but the fact that he had ignored the suggestions of his
own Board after the CAB had worked seventeen months on the
case should have given the editors something to talk about.
The President's most surprising move was to give two routes
to operators who had not applied for them. Less surprising was
his treatment of Pan American Airways, although he was more
ruthless with the pioneer air line than even its opponents had
predicted.

Eleven applications had been filed for collective action under

Docket No. 525. The CAB had concluded that no more competition was desirable on the Bermuda, or on some of the South American, airways. The President disagreed. With the advice of experts from the State, War, Commerce, and Navy Departments, he had decided that public interest would be better served if additional carriers were assigned to these routes. Truman thereupon overruled four of the CAB recommendations and went so far as to name the carriers who were to fly the new airways—a decision that had no precedent, although apparently it was legal.

The route from the United States to Argentina by way of Mexico City, Rio, and Buenos Aires was awarded to a booming domestic operator who up to that time had developed only a regional air-line system. He was a wealthy Oklahoma insurance man, Thomas E. Braniff, who had become a legendary figure in the Southwest. Braniff had muscled into commercial aviation by acquiring (against his better judgment) a pipsqueak air line managed by his younger brother, Paul. That was in 1928. A year later, much to Tom Braniff's relief, the Braniffs sold out to a now-forgotten enterprise known as Universal Aviation Corporation. Universal eventually was swallowed by the parent company of American Airlines. In 1930 the Braniffs started up another route when mail pay on a north-south route offered an incentive. They failed to get the mail contract, but they stayed in business anyway, with Tom in charge. Under his able management Braniff Air Lines (The Bee-Line) was expanded until it reached "from the great lakes to the gulf."[2] At the Mexican border Braniff connected with a subsidiary, Aerovías Braniff, which operated in direct competition with Compañía Mexicana de Aviación, S. A. (CMA), a Pan American affiliate. At once the two foreign rivals began feuding. Occasionally these brushes flared into violence. Because of the bitter feeling and because Pan American officials resented what they believed to be poaching on their Mexican skyway, Trippe and his minions were incensed when they learned that Braniff was to be a rival in the coveted South American area.

Pan American might not have had to face this new rival if it had patched up an older quarrel in time. It will be remembered that W. R. Grace and Company shared ownership with Pan American of a west-coast air line called Pan American Grace, or Panagra. The Grace interests hoped to connect the line to a United States gateway, but since Pan American owned a half interest in the line and had no intention of letting Panagra tap territory already served by Pan American, the Panagra extension never materialized. Had this been accomplished, Braniff might never have been designated as a second South American carrier because Panagra could have provided the desired competition. Apparently the President was persuaded that the Pan American–Grace and Company feud was undermining U. S. prestige in the Andes countries. There was danger that the aggressive British might take advantage of the situation. The best defense against such foreign infiltration appeared to be the certification of an aggressive U. S. competitor for Panagra and for Pan American.

Nearly as painful to Pan American officials was the certification of a U. S. rival for the Bermuda traffic. Colonial Airlines was designated as the new Atlantic carrier. Colonial had been operating between New York and Montreal. With Pan American and BOAC providing adequate service to the British resort island, there did not appear to be any good reason for authorizing another carrier. Diplomatic expediency was probably the answer. Colonial Airlines was operated according to the terms of a U.S.–Canadian permanent agreement signed in February, 1945. Canadians had demanded a service to Bermuda by way of New York, and if Colonial had not been designated for this purpose, Canadians could have carried out the terms of the bilateral document, which gave them the right to select their own air line for such service. The only odd part of the Colonial announcement was that the air line won a certificate for a direct route from both New York and from Washington, although no one had asked for the service out of the national capital. True, Colonial had applied for a route from Norfolk to Bermuda, but the officials had never presumed that the CAB would listen to a plea for a capital route. The CAB turned down the New York application, but made Washington, instead of Norfolk, the U. S. terminus — which made everything all right with the Colonial people because of the heavy potential traffic between Washington and Bermuda. Then the President reversed the New York decision of the CAB and made Colonial a direct competitor of Pan American out of New York.

The only substantial prize Pan American drew from the grab bag was the coveted direct route from New York to San Juan, Puerto Rico. Traffic predictions between these points were encouraging. The direct route to San Juan was a short cut on the Rio airway, which was another inducement for South American traffic to "fly Pan American" out of New York. But joy over this decision was dampened by an order of the President. Mr. Truman again ignored the recommendations of the CAB by authorizing additional service to San Juan out of Miami. The President even named the carrier—Eastern Air Lines.

Again the aviation industry blinked, because Eastern had no wish to take over the route. The company's vice-president and its director of research, Paul Brattain and Hugh Knowlton, had investigated the possibilities of Caribbean routes in 1944 and had come to the conclusion that development was not worth the cost. They had discovered that most of the traffic to San Juan originated in the Atlantic states. Passengers were almost certain to fly the New York–San Juan route, which was 597 miles shorter than the New York–Miami–San Juan airway. That was why Eastern, known as one of the most efficient air lines in the business, had shown little interest in the Latin-American Route Case.

Eastern Air Lines won another Caribbean route that angered the Pan American people. It was certificated to fly beyond its domestic terminus at New Orleans to Mexico City by way of Yucatan. Both Eastern and Pan American bid for this route. The water airway by-passed the old Pan American route through Texas and Mexico and threatened to drain traffic away from the older route. New York was the heaviest passenger pool for the area, and Eastern now provided the shortest way to Central America. On the other hand, Pan American was compensated in part by winning permission to carry passengers between its old gateway at Brownsville, Texas, and Houston, by way of Corpus Christi. That gave it two more traffic centers to serve. Such traffic was confined to passengers traveling to and from points outside the United States, but it did give Pan American a little more chance against its two rivals in the area—Braniff and American Airlines.

American Airlines had been operating to Mexico City during the war on a temporary certificate awarded by President Roosevelt in the early days of the war. Three of the five CAB members had opposed the route certification but the President believed he had special reasons for his action, as over-all head of all executive branches. American Airlines developed a Y-shaped route into Mexico. The main line was from Mexico City to Monterrey, Mexico, where the route was split. One fork terminated at El Paso and the other at San Antonio. In the Latin-American decision, the air line won a permanent certificate for this route—a prediction of Pan American interveners at the time of the Roosevelt decision that was borne out.

Two small air lines also won impressive international routes by the decision. Chicago and Southern Air Lines, Incorporated, was primarily a regional carrier operating up and down the Mississippi valley. Under the terms of the Latin-American decision it was authorized to fly from its U. S. co-terminals at Houston and New Orleans to Cuba, from which two branches were to extend across the Caribbean. One route cut across the island chain to Haiti, the Dominican Republic, and Puerto Rico. The other division was a long over-water route to Caracas, Venezuela, by way of Jamaica and the Dutch metropolis of Curaçao on the Venezuelan coast. The routes threatened to strain the resources of the little company, but a 1943 refinancing program had been encouraging, and the company had a reputation as an efficient operator. (It had the highest equipment-utilization quotient—up to thirteen hours a day per plane —of any U. S. carrier at the time.)[3]

The other small air line to become an international operator was National Airlines, second smallest (after Northeast) domestic air carrier. National was granted access to Havana. The decision made it possible to extend the company's Florida operations so as to tap the rich Cuban tourist market, but the little line had to share mail, cargo, and passenger traffic with Pan American, Braniff, and Chicago and Southern which also served Havana, directly or indirectly.

The decision that Pan American officials appeared to resent most was the award of a Los Angeles–Mexico City direct-route certificate to Western Air Lines, another regional operator. The certification of American Airlines' Mexican routes made it possible for passengers to reach the Mexican capital by way of El Paso, but Pan American spokesmen argued that as the original Mexican carrier, their company should have the direct route between the two cities. Pan American's subsidiary, Compañía Mexicana de Aviación (CMA) was already operating over the route under a foreign permit for the U. S. section granted by the CAB in 1941.

There was a good reason for Pan American's insistence upon the right to fly this route. Surveys had shown that there were more long-distance telephone calls from Mexico City to Los Angeles than to any other U. S. city. That indicated strong "community of interest." California ranked just under Texas in the number of tourist cards issued for Mexican travel. Pan American attorneys told the Board they believed the company would carry one hundred passengers a day each way between the two centers. This was indeed a worth-while operation, and the Board apparently believed that the estimate was a conservative one. To lose this lucrative business to Western Air Lines, a small domestic operator with no international experience beyond its war record, was galling to the pioneer Mexican carrier. The Board was willing to recognize Pan American claims, but the President went over his advisers in awarding the route to a competitor.

Was Pan American Airways being punished for its antagonism to government aviation policy? There were many who saw

the Latin-American decision as an example of administration
vindictiveness. Even the trade press, which often criticised Pan
American, conceded that Trippe and his henchmen had been
soundly slapped.[4]

Although Pan American officials maintain that the company has no political policy, it has been under fire more than
once during the Democratic administration. Postmaster General James A. Farley made it his special target just after the
New Deal was launched, and although the company emerged
from the air-mail scandals unscathed, it was severely repri-
manded at the time. Pan American had fought most of the
international aviation measures sponsored by such administration agencies as the CAB, State Department, and Commerce
Department. It had done what it could to scuttle American
Export Airlines as a competitor, even after the CAB had designated Amex as a second international carrier. It had opposed
administration doctrine and policy at Chicago and Bermuda.
It backed up such men as Senators Brewster, McCarran, and
Bailey, who attacked the aviation course taken by the United
States. It stood for monopoly against overwhelming support
of competition. One of its vice-presidents was Samuel F. Pryor,
a Republican wheel and a leading Connecticut politician.
Pryor had helped elect Mrs. Clare Booth Luce to Congress,
where she had become one of the administration's most pub-
licized aviation critics.

Others said Pan American was being punished for alleged
greediness. In 1942 charges of this nature had been argued
before the CAB by Samuel E. Gates, representing the public
(a "public counsel" is provided for most CAB hearings). In
both the Latin-American rate case and in the Amex-TACA
merger petition Gates had pointed out the shortcomings of the
great U. S. air carrier.[5]

Or was Pan American Airways merely paying the penalty of
being too successful? Trippe had often outsmarted his competitors. Inevitably, they had ganged up on him. There were
others who had resented the shrewd tactics of the Pan American generals. The CAB could not forgive Pan American's

attempt to kill the Amex certificate in Congress after the Board had awarded the route. The Post Office Department had not forgotten Pan American's lobbying against mail appropriations for the second Atlantic operator. Steamship companies blamed Pan American for the decision forcing the separation of Amex from its parent company—a decision that appeared for a time at least to have closed the door on possible aviation enterprise sponsored by surface carriers. Domestic air-line officials recalled Pan American opposition to competition in the North Atlantic and All-American Flag Line hearings. Aircraft manufacturers remembered how Pan American had played one designer against another—ordering planes from Sikorsky, Martin, Boeing, and Lockheed before experimental costs could be written off by the unsuccessful bidders. Foreign companies declared that Pan American was out to wreck international aviation good will. The British were especially provoked. Pan American had nearly ended the truce between the United States and Great Britain, following Trippe's rate-cut announcement of 1945, it will be recalled. The CAB had also been embarrassed by that announcement. Yet when Pan American had been asked to supply figures to justify the proposed rate, it was unable to prove the point. That made some of the Board members even more furious.

These factors possibly had a bearing on the decision, but it is also possible that vindictiveness had very little to do with the decision. Pan American emerged at the end of the route decisions with some of the best territory in the world. The company couldn't be given *all* the best routes, for if competition were to be given a fair trial, the new operators had to be given a chance to fly profitably. This might have convinced more friends of Pan American, had the certificates been granted for a limited period, as they had been in the North Atlantic case. Latin-American certificates were permanent. No trial period was contemplated. On the other hand, the new operators would have been handicapped had they been awarded seven-year certificates. The North Atlantic was relatively new operating territory. Latin America had already been developed and the new carriers needed to plan long-range programs, if they hoped to compete successfully with established operators.

Granted that new carriers had to be designated, then, the CAB was still willing to concede special consideration to Pan American because of its early enterprise in air commerce. But, the Board insisted, the pioneering days were over. Public interest was the primary concern of the Board, not air-line promotion, and the public demanded cheaper, more efficient service. Competition, the Board held, had proved time and again that it served public interest better than could private monopoly.

It was aggravating for Pan American to have to share world routes, admittedly, but the Board was willing to compensate for the loss of that dominance by granting the company domestic concessions that it had never enjoyed before. In the Pan American annual report of 1945 stockholders were told that the company planned to demand the right to operate in the domestic sphere. Apparently the Board was not averse to this. Shortly after he resigned as chairman of the CAB, Pogue told the writer that he believed Pan American was entitled to routes across the United States as the price of giving up exclusive international areas. The Board had intimated a similar view in its Latin-American decision, for the summary of Docket No. 525 had declared that Pan American was "to conduct new and important operations" from points within the United States. No mention was made of point-to-point service within the United States, as demanded by Pan American, but even that was not beyond the realm of possibility.

In any case, Board members insisted that there had been no discrimination against the pioneer carrier. Braniff, Pan American's feuding partner in Mexico, had not been selected as a rival South American operator just for the sake of chastising the original promoter. Pan American analysts had themselves predicted that outbound passengers to South America would exceed eight hundred a day. With reduced fares brought about by competition, even more passengers would be lured south, it was believed. Predictions for mail cargo were just as opti-

mistic. The Postmaster General's report for 1942 showed that
41 per cent of the Latin American mail originated in the New
York area. That was enough to provide a profitable load for
four or five planes of the DC-4 type. Surely, it would appear,
there was room for competition in the light of such figures.

Braniff was selected as the rival carrier not to punish Pan
American, but because it was the second choice. First choice
had been Eastern Air Lines. Eastern was the type of air line
the CAB approved for international operation. It had an excellent record and was second only to American Airlines as a
domestic revenue producer. Eastern served the two largest
Latin-American traffic pools — New York and Chicago. Much
of this traffic could have been funneled on through from
Eastern's New Orleans terminal. The company, however, was
not interested in the proposal.

Second choice as a Pan American rival might have been Panagra. With a U.S. gateway at New Orleans, Panagra could
have provided excellent service over its established system. But
as long as Pan American Airways controlled 50 per cent of
Panagra stock, it could block this competition between the
United States and South America. Later, Pan American and
W. R. Grace signed a truce and Panagra was given the green
light for a U. S.service, but by that time another rival had
muscled in on the area.

Braniff was the only other possible choice. It tapped the
Chicago area, next to New York the most promising traffic res-
ervoir for a Latin-American service. Only Pogue favored giving
Braniff a certificate to fly all the way to Buenos Aires, however. One other member was willing to let Braniff fly as far
as Lima, Peru. There were only four members of the Board
then—Warner having left to take charge of PICAO—and the
other two opposed the selection. President Truman followed
Pogue's advice. Braniff accordingly won the right to fly over
two routes, one from San Antonio and Laredo to Mexico City
via Monterrey, and the other from Houston to Buenos Aires
via Havana, Balboa, Bogotá, Quito, Lima, La Paz, and Asunción. A branch from Asunción reached up to Sao Paulo and

Rio. This made a regional air line into a great international network overnight, but it could hardly be said that the scheme was developed out of sheer meanness to Pan American.

Pan American executives were not mollified by such explanations. They had maintained all along that Latin-American traffic would not sustain the competition outlined in the route applications. Strong foreign operators, certain to be given U. S. landing privileges, were ready to drain away much of the traffic counted upon by the optimistic applicants, it was pointed out. KLM, the Royal Dutch Airlines, had already mapped out an ambitious postwar program in the area. So had TACA (Transportes Aéreos Centro Americanos), the bustling little contract air line in Central America operated by an aggressive New Zealander, Lowell Yerex. The Brazilians, Venezuelans, and Colombians also were ready to start air-transport enterprises. Any traffic they left would be gobbled up by the scores of U. S. nonscheduled operators who were already eying international air commerce.

Pan American Airways could do more than complain about treatment by the CAB. The Board had only certified Braniff as an accredited U. S. carrier. The franchise did not guarantee the new operator access to airports on the proposed routes, however. That was a matter for the individual governments to decide, and here Pan American had a chance to even up the score. As a veteran air-line operator, Pan American wielded great influence in Latin America. Braniff was thwarted time and again in its efforts to push through the new route. U. S. representatives sent to Mexico to negotiate endorsement of the U. S. certificates were amazed at the opposition they met. Mexican authorities refused to grant operation rights to Braniff, except upon reciprocal terms. The fine hand of the British could be detected in the way the Mexicans steered the negotiations, but there was no doubt in Tom Braniff's mind as to the real cause of the delay. Said he: "The conference between Mexico and the United States failed because Pan American World Airways accomplished with the assistance of its Mexican satellite, CMA, what it had failed to accomplish in the United States, namely, perpetuation as a monopoly." [6]

Inevitably, the Pan American–Braniff issue became a political hot potato in Mexico. It was soon apparent that it would take U. S. official pressure and blandishment to overcome Latin-American opposition. And while the Government worked away at opening up routes for new Latin-American carriers, the CAB had gone quietly ahead with plans for the development of air routes in other parts of the world. The new air-transport systems were described in the announcements of the Pacific Route Case and South Atlantic Route Case decisions.

The Pacific case was officially designated as CAB Docket No. 547. The decision was made on June 20, 1946, and was approved by the President on August 1. In effect, it established two round-the-world services. Northwest Airlines won the Great-Circle route to the Orient, where it connected with the TWA route awarded in the North Atlantic decision. Together the two companies could carry passengers and cargo around the world. The other route went to Pan American World Airways.

Northwest Airlines had operated for years as the second largest regional air line in the country. Until 1944 the Northwest route stretched from Chicago across the northern tier of states to the Pacific Northwest. In December of that year the CAB gave the company a route extension to New York, thereby making Northwest the fourth transcontinental domestic carrier. During the war it developed a service across Canada to Alaska. The operation gave it valuable experience in cold-weather flying. Northwest had a fine safety record, despite rugged operating conditions, and this no doubt was a factor in its successful bid for an international route.

As a result of Pacific decision, Northwest Airlines more than tripled its route mileage. According to the terms of the certificate, it was authorized to fly from New York, Chicago, and Seattle to Anchorage, Alaska. From the Alaskan base the route followed the Aleutian and Kuril chain of islands to Japan. Tokyo was the junction of two Asiatic branches. One cut across the Sea of Japan to Harbin, Mukden, and Peiping before zigzagging down the coast to Shanghai. The other branch reached Shanghai by way of Korea. From the Chinese metropolis the route continued to the Asiatic terminus at Manila. As in the North Atlantic decision, certificates were issued for a seven-year period.

The second trans-Pacific route was awarded to Pan American Airways, which was no surprise. Pan American was authorized to fly from both San Francisco and Los Angeles to Hawaii. Here, one route turned off for Noumea, from which two antennae reached out for Australia and New Zealand. Another branch out of Hawaii followed the old 1935 airway to Manila via Midway, Wake, and Guam islands. At Manila there was a junction with two route extensions linking the Pacific routes with airways awarded under the North Atlantic decision. One of these branches reached Hong Kong, the gateway to the continental system of China National Aviation Corporation, a Pan American affiliate. The other division crossed the South China Sea to Saigon, Rangoon, and Calcutta (terminus of the route designated in the North Atlantic decision).

Pan American also won access to Japan over two branch routes. One was the inter-Asia airway reaching up from Java via Singapore, Hong Kong, and Shanghai. The other was an off-line service from Midway on the main Pacific route. Since Tokyo was the plum of the Pacific area, and could undoubtedly support more service than Northwest alone could provide, it would appear that Pan American had no cause for complaint. But if one consults the globe instead of the usual Mercator map projection, it will be seen that the Northwest route was much the shorter airway to Japan and the Philippines. In fact, it was 650 miles shorter to Manila by the northern route than it was by the Pan American air track far to the south—which must be seen on the globe to be believed.

True, the northern route passed through some of the worst flying country in the world. Many passengers would thus prefer the longer, but sunnier, Pan American service. That was a compensating feature that the Board took into consideration in allocating Pacific airways. Furthermore, Pan American

was given the two most important traffic centers on the west
coast—San Francisco and Los Angeles—cities that Northwest
Airlines could not tap.   On the other hand, Northwest had
access to the centers in the east, not reached by Pan American,
and these cities had close business relations with the Orient.
Whether the sunny southern route would turn out to be an
advantage for Pan American was problematical. Certainly cargo
and mail would have no preference for the longer route just
because it was pleasanter.   And it was doubtful whether passengers would, either, once they were educated to the fact that
terrain was of little consequence in air transportation.

Could the Orient support that much air traffic?   Members
of the Civil Aeronautics Board were aware that conditions in
Japan and China were too unstable to allow irrevocable decisions.   But if some degree of peace was achieved in those war-
torn areas, there was every possibility of developing a sound
air commerce.   Maintenance of large occupation forces, the
establishment of U. S. Pacific bases, and the rehabilitation of
China were expected to stimulate air transportation immediately after the war.   Peacetime trade was then counted upon to
support air commerce.   China and Japan accounted for about
25 per cent of the world's population.   This market had long
been neglected by Americans, but even before the war there
had been significant increase in trade between the hemispheres.
In 1898 our Oriental trade amounted to only one hundred and
fifty million dollars a year, as compared with a European commerce in excess of one and a quarter billion.   In the interven-
ing forty years trade with Europe had increased to about two
billion dollars a year, but U. S. trade with Asia had increased
tenfold.[7]   Asiatic commerce might have increased even more
during this period had there been better communication and
transportation between the two areas.   Cable service was costly
and inadequate.   It took about two weeks to reach Asiatic gateways, even by the fastest steamship, and the trip was too expensive for the casual businessman.   Lastly, the Japanese had
captured a large part of the Asiatic market because of their
proximity, aggressiveness, and abundance of cheap labor.

Many of these conditions were changed by war. Air transportation made it possible to send communications to the Orient quickly and cheaply. A businessman could arrive in Shanghai from most American centers in about the time it formerly took him to cross the continent by train. And with the collapse of Japan, American merchants could compete favorably for Asiatic trade.

It was a market worth exploiting. Even before the war Asia had attracted more tourists than had South America. Various applicants in the Pacific hearing had tried to estimate future traffic. The discrepancy in their figures indicated that they were all merely guessing, but the fact that there was general agreement on postwar increase in Asiatic travel and commerce was significant.

The CAB was unanimous in its stand for competition in the Pacific area, and there was no disagreement on the selection of Northwest Airlines as the second carrier. The only difference of opinion was on the way the routes should be laid out. Board member Harllee Branch declared it was utter nonsense to extend TWA from India to meet the Northwest operation at Shanghai so as to provide round-the-world competition for Pan American Airways. He was certain there was not enough future business to justify such a "thin" route for TWA. It will be recalled that Branch had objected in the North Atlantic decision to extending TWA beyond Cairo for the same reason. The mistake was being compounded in the Pacific case, Branch contended. He believed Pan American could supply all the service required.*

Board member Josh Lee also dissented from the majority point of view, but for different reasons. He believed that the Board should have designated even more routes. The demand for international air transportation, especially in the Asiatic theater, was debatable, he admitted. It was very possible that the majority estimate was on the conservative side. If so, it would be a mistake to let other flag lines absorb this new busi-

*Mail and cargo, not passengers, provided the reason for wanting a second world route, however.

ness just when Americans were most able to compete successfully. If, on the other hand, estimates were high, the correction
could be made when the certificates expired in seven years. The
risk was not great for such a wealthy nation, and the rewards
were worth the chance, said he.

Lee wasted no sympathy on Pan American Airways for the
breaking up of its Pacific air transportation monopoly. He
would even have denied the company's application for Shanghai and Tokyo routes, and he believed the balance of competition in the area had been destroyed by granting the Pan
American request to tap these points. He summarized his
objections as follows:

> Pan American, as the result of the route extensions authorized
> to it by the majority opinion, will have a virtual monopoly in
> Australasia, the Indies, and Southwest Asia. In addition, it will
> serve the Philippine Islands, and through its connection with its
> subsidiary, CNAC, at Hongkong, it will have reasonably direct access
> to the traffic generated in China. When it is realized that historically
> approximately *three fourths* of the trans-Pacific traffic has moved to
> and from these areas, it becomes apparent immediately that the com-
> petitive position occupied by Pan American is already as powerful
> as the public convenience and necessity will permit. If Pan American
> is authorized to add to its traffic potential and traffic generated in
> Japan and, in addition, to make a second connection with CNAC at
> Shanghai, the position of Pan American in the Orient will become so
> overpowering that it is difficult to see how any other American service
> can ever offer really effective competition. The only advantage which
> Pan American's competitors would have would be the traffic delivered
> to them through their connection with TWA at Shanghai. Obviously,
> this one factor would not be sufficient to place them in a satisfactory
> competitive position.[8]

The Pacific decision had hardly been announced when Pan
American was dealt another jarring left jab. Early in July the
Hawaiian case was reviewed by the President as a separate part
of the Pacific route hearings and United Air Lines was awarded
a certificate to fly from San Francisco to the island territory.
Since the operation was entirely within the jurisdiction of the
United States and therefore required no foreign negotiation,

United's certificate gave it immediate access to a promising market. Although the U. S.–Hawaiian route might have been considered as only a section of the much longer trans-Pacific airway, it did merit special study. There was no doubt that travel to and from Hawaii would be greater than traffic to and from any other point in the area. The islands had close ties with the mainland. Tourists might very well flock to the ideal resort land, if they could avoid the long sea voyage. Therefore, the designation of another important carrier to serve this market had the special consideration of the CAB.

United Air Lines up to that point had shown no interest in international operations, beyond affiliation with a small Mexican air line. It had a great deal of experience in ocean flying, however, as a wartime contract carrier for the armed forces. Yet United was the logical choice as a competitive carrier serving Hawaii, and apparently its antipathy to ocean routes did not extend to "overseas" flying ("overseas" in the airman's parlance meaning operations to U. S. territories beyond our national boundaries). United flew the "main line" from New York to San Francisco, tapping major population centers along the way. It was a wealthy, reliable company, headed by one of the ablest administrators in the industry. The Hawaiian route was actually only an extension of the old route and required no extensive preparations.

The decision on the Hawaiian route was not clear-cut, however. Pogue had announced his intention of resigning from the CAB and did not wish to make his wishes binding on remaining members. His successor, James M. Landis, did not believe himself well enough informed on the issue to cast a vote. Clarence M. Young, another new Board member, likewise hesitated to give an opinion.

The original plan had been to designate both Los Angeles and San Francisco as co-terminals for the second Hawaiian service. It was agreed that United would fly out of San Francisco, but the Board could not decide upon the service out of Los Angeles. Pogue and Branch believed that United should be given both routes. Ryan and Lee urged that Hawaiian Airlines, the only inter-island carrier, be awarded the Los Angeles section. To give Landis and Young a chance to participate in the case and perhaps to break the deadlock, the Board agreed to put up the Los Angeles branch of the route for reargument. But whatever the outcome, United was certain of one section. In any case, Pan American Airways could look forward to stiff competition on this leg of its Pacific operations. The company which had pioneered the Pacific route could scarcely be blamed for being disgruntled over the decision forcing it to share its most promising market in that area.*

Pan American Airways came out supreme in only one of the great route cases. In the South Atlantic decision the company was awarded all the routes. This was a rather left-handed gift, however, because few other top operators had any interest in the routes, and Pan American itself was not too enthusiastic about the operations. The case involved routes to South Africa, with which the United States had little relation, or "community of interest," as the phrasing in the hearings described it.[9] Capital Airlines (Pennsylvania-Central) had eyed one section of the route when the New York–San Juan airway was up for decision, but when Pan American won that certificate, the Capital people cooled to the idea of operating the long, "thin" airway to an area with little potential traffic.

Two routes were awarded. One was from the United States by way of the Azores and the west coast of Africa to Dakar, Monrovia, Accra, and Leopoldville, with co-terminals at Johannesburg and Capetown. This route might produce some profit and Pan American continued to apply for it. But the other route was mostly a water haul and showed little promise of attracting traffic. It was a continuation of the New York–San Juan route to Natal, on the bulge of Brazil.† From Natal

_____

*CAB Docket No. 2537 et al., original copy. Also in CAB Reports, Vol. 9, pp. 414-439. United never did get its Los Angeles route. In the reargument an entirely different carrier was selected to operate a route to Hawaii —and from entirely different terminals. Northwest Airlines was the winner of the certificate, operating from Seattle, Tacoma, and Portland. See "Hawaiian Service Goes to NWA," Aviation Week, August 9, 1948, p. 39.

†Originally this was part of Pan American's main trunk line in South

the route plunged across the South Atlantic by way of Ascension Island to connect with the Azores–Accra–Leopoldville route at some unspecified point. Not much traffic could be expected over this alternate ocean route to Africa. There was even less "community of interest" between Africa and South America than there was between Africa and the United States. Even if there had been traffic, planes had to fly with such heavy fuel loads for the long water hop that pay load was necessarily insufficient to bring in much profit. Here was a clear case for government subsidy, indeed.

Pan American was handed this unwanted route because the CAB believed it was necessary to keep up South Atlantic air facilities. That could best be done, with the least amount of diplomatic wire-pulling, by a commercial operator. The Board was well aware that the Ascension route was unsound economically, but, it declared in its report, "under our Congressional mandate the national defense is an explicit objective to be attained in the establishment of an international route pattern." [10] Ordinarily the CAB had not been moved to act as an agency for the development of national defense, except in emergency. During the war the Board did spend time and energy in mobilizing the air lines to supplement military trans-

America. The Brazilian government had insisted in the early days that the internal routes be operated by nationalized subsidiaries. Main routes of foreign operators were to be confined to coastwise traffic. Pan American Airways was very desirous of developing a shorter route to Rio by way of the Barreiras Cutoff, cutting directly across the shoulder of Brazil from Belém, at the mouth of the Amazon waterway system, to the national capital. The company had the opportunity of carrying out this plan during the war, when the United States won concessions from Brazil during the emergency. When Pan American demanded a continuation of the cutoff division, the Brazilians reversed former policy. They argued that since the Americans were given the cutoff route, they no longer needed the coastal airway. And since the government-protected domestic lines had given up the internal operation, they should be compensated by having exclusive operating rights along the old Pan American coastal route, it was held. Under this arrangement, the route awarded to Pan American in the South Atlantic decision was actually an "off line" operation—far less valuable than it might have been in the old days when the U. S. flag line operated down the coast of South America.

portation, but the CAB has tried to avoid the mistakes of the
Europeans, who forced their commercial operators to adapt
themselves to military domination. The frank admission of the
CAB that in the Atlantic case, at least, economic factors were to
be subordinate to defense policy indicates the heavy pressure
that must have been applied by the military.

The announcement of the South Atlantic decision just about
completed the U. S. international airways system. It must be
borne in mind, of course, that the issuance of route certificates
was only one step in the development of international air commerce. It was still necessary to obtain landing rights, either by
negotiation, treaty, or agreement. This was a slow process, because one country might block operations on an otherwise
clear route. In most cases it took from two to four years to
develop full service, as authorized. Such areas as China, India,
and Indonesia were trouble spots and it might take years to
carry out route programs in those areas. It took more time
after permission had been granted to build up maintenance
depots, fuel dumps, and ground personnel. Many of the air
lines granted extensive international routes by the various
decisions were lacking in equipment. Equipment was very difficult to obtain after the war. Even the veteran operators, with
reasonably adequate equipment, could not begin operations
at once. Pan American planned to take at least two years to
get some of its new routes into operation, and that was an optimistic estimate in many cases—the South Atlantic, for example.

But at least the U. S. air lines could begin to plan for the
future. They knew where they stood in relation to each other.
The day was approaching when American transport planes
would begin to arrive at the goal set by Otto Praeger in 1919.
Praeger, who was in charge of the first U. S. air-mail operation,
had dreamed even then of a vast international network of commercial air lines. He envisioned America as the leader in this
world enterprise; serving to bring the world closer together by
means of cheap, fast, and efficient communications and transportation. Everyone at the time believed that Praeger would
never see that day. Sitting in his home in Washington, D. C.,

in the summer of 1946, Praeger must have gloated inwardly at the way his predictions had turned out.[11]

REFERENCES

1. *International Commercial Aviation,* Resolution of the Committee on Commerce, U. S. Senate, 79th Congress, 2d Session, Senate Document No. 173, Washington, 1946.
2. For more on the development of Braniff Air Lines see Henry Ladd Smith, *Airways: The History of Commercial Aviation in the United States,* New York, 1942.
3. *Airlines 1946,* Merrill Lynch, Pierce, Fenner & Beane, New York, 1946, p. 29.
4. See articles throughout *American Aviation,* June 1, 1946.
5. *CAB Docket No.* 491, original copy, (the Amex-TACA proposed merger); *CAB Docket No.* 298, original copy, (the Latin American Rate Case), the statement of Samuel Gates.
6. "Braniff Accuses PAA after Failure of Mexico Air Conference," *American Aviation,* August 15, 1946, p. 24.
7. *CAB Docket No.* 547, original copy, Decision of June 20, 1946, p. 5. Also in *CAB Reports,* Vol. 7, p. 213.
8. *CAB Docket No.* 547, original copy, "Josh Lee, Member, Concurring and Dissenting," p. 13. Also in *CAB Reports,* Vol. 7, p. 243 ff.
9. *CAB Docket No.* 1171, original copy, "Brief of Public Counsel Russell S. Bernhard."
10. CAB press release of August 16, 1946.
11. He died early in 1948.

A NOTE ON SOURCES

Most of the material for this chapter came from the voluminous hearings and reports of the Civil Aeronautics Board. See particularly Original Docket No. 525, the Latin American Case; Original Docket No. 547, the Pacific Route Case; and Original Docket No. 1171, the South Atlantic Case. *Airlines,* the annual reports of the firm of Merrill Lynch, Pierce, Fenner and Beane, supplied some of the statistical data.

THE SKYLINERS

AT THE end of the Napoleonic wars famous diplomats convened at the Congress of Vienna to write a new chapter in world history. Many books have been written about that meeting and about its political results. But while the diplomats debated at Vienna, obscure men were working away in grimy shops to find ways of making steam perform the labors of man. Today, more than a century later, who will say that Watt in Scotland, Trevithick in England, Woolf in Cornwall, Fulton in the United States, Sugnot in France, and countless followers elsewhere did not do more to change the course of history with their steamships, locomotives, and power plants than all the diplomats and ministers at Vienna in 1815?

In like manner, the engineer and designer have worked more or less obscurely in helping to develop air commerce. This book has been largely devoted to a discussion of those who made aviation policy. No one has had a more important part in this development than the designer. When he produces a plane that can be operated economically, he fosters air travel and influences national policy thereby. When he perfects craft that are reliable and easy to build, he gives the diplomat bargaining power in national demands for aviation recognition. In the long run, indeed, it is the designer and the engineeer who determine the future pattern of world air routes.

How the designer and builder affect air commerce may be seen in the record of British international air transport. In the early days the British were committed to the land plane—

the ungainly craft of the Hannibal type that was once a familiar sight on the Kangaroo route. The practicability of the flying boat made possible the "all-up" Empire Mail scheme. This changed not only policy, but routes as well. Seaplanes could not operate in certain areas formerly served by land planes, but on the other hand, they opened up markets hitherto inaccessible. In any case, the seaplane modified operating procedures and international negotiations.

The trend in the United States was just the opposite. We started out with flying boats because water provided the only practicable landing facility for long-range operations. That meant that the diplomats had to negotiate for bases such as the Azores and Bermuda. Planes had to be built to cope with rough water, primitive docking facilities, and icing conditions. These limiting factors affected pay load, so that rates had to be maintained at a high level, if profit was to be made without government subsidy. The switch to land planes brought about many changes. No longer were island bases so essential. The diplomats who had used air sovereignty as a kind of blackmail no longer could block expansion. The switch to land planes brought traffic closer to metropolitan destinations and made it possible to operate more economically. As a result, fares could be lowered whenever the operators agreed.

And all this time the designer and engineer kept working away, probably unaware of the roles they were playing. Certainly they had no intention of bringing about a revolution in commercial aviation. Of all men the designer and engineer are least interested in radical change. They prefer evolution—the slow process of refinement leading to perfection.

It will be recalled that it was the general adoption of the land plane that brought the U. S. domestic operator into the international picture. Hitherto most world-wide operations had been conducted with flying boats, and there was a recognized sphere for domestic and world promoters respectively. Flying boats usually were operated from coastal bases. They required personnel with special training. Government regulations also kept the two services entirely separate.

When land planes began to replace flying boats it made no

difference whether the home base was New York, Chicago, or St. Louis. With land planes the domestic operator could send traffic across oceans as easily as he transported people across mountains and deserts. The insistence of the domestic operator on being allowed to break out of the artificial boundary confines thereupon led to a change in U. S. aviation policy.

At this writing, the land plane is definitely dominant on international routes. That does not mean that the flying boat is doomed. Indeed, construction of such craft has never ceased. Where speed and passenger comfort are concerned, land planes may be preferred for a long time. For air cargo the seaplane may be the answer. True, the flying boat is not as aerodynamically efficient as the land plane, since it must be designed for both air and water. On the other hand, its aerodynamic qualities remain the same, regardless of size. The land plane may be cleaner in design, but as its size is increased, more and more space and pay load must be sacrificed for complicated landing gear. Somewhere along the line of development there comes a point where the aerodynamic advantage of the land plane may be canceled by the weight of its landing gear.

More than likely designers and engineers will continue to produce both types of equipment. Huge, high-speed, land planes will fly between specified points, like the crack ocean liners. These super planes may be confined to routes where airports are adequate and where traffic is sufficient to support them. But many countries, unable to justify the building of enormous airports, may be better served by flying boats. There are also operators who list speed as a minor consideration when ordering new equipment. Air-freight promoters, or organizers of world tours might well sacrifice speed for economy and pay load. Seaplanes might be the answer. Apparently there is no limit to the size of the flying boat. Howard Hughes' *Hercules,* granddaddy of all flying boats, weighs two hundred tons, has wings thirteen feet thick at the roots, uses an electronic, or "pneudyne," system of remote control to trim the control surfaces, and is powered by eight engines. True, the *Hercules* was designed to cruise at only 175 miles an hour—about one-third the speed of transports already on order by some air lines. But the Hughes flying boat is said to be capable of carrying four hundred soldiers fully equipped, and it can transport enormous cargoes to all parts of the world, according to the statements of its builders. (Although it had been tested on the water and had actually flown a short distance, it had not been put into operation at this writing.) Since the flying boat "carries its airport on its bottom" and can reach even the inaccessible points on the globe, it presents attractive possibilities.

Thus, the designer may offer the policy-makers another set of problems, since the cargo operator, who uses slower, more economical flying boats, may very well threaten the scheduled air line by draining away lucrative freight at lower rates. Regulations might then have to be negotiated. Perhaps new international routes would be planned. And again the diplomats would be called in.

The influence of plane design is apparent all through the negotiations described in the preceding chapters. The North Atlantic case demonstrates the point. All the applicants appearing before the CAB in that hearing presented elaborate exhibits to show what they would do if given the opportunity to fly world routes. In each instance, the plan was dependent upon equipment available. TWA, for example, presented three plans for service to Europe, Egypt, and India. Each plan was to be modified as the new planes appeared. TWA was ready to start out with five Boeing Stratoliners, the first high-altitude, pressurized aircraft—revolutionary in 1940, but obsolete by the end of the war. The company proposed charging fares of seven cents a mile at the beginning. With the Lockheed Constellations, the fare would be reduced to five and one-half cents a mile, and such planes would be flown from inland cities of the United States directly to European centers.*

*CAB Docket No. 855, Exhibit No. TWA-305-312. The 5.5 cent rate would have reduced the New York–London fare to about $263. This is $12 less than the fare Pan American World Airways actually tried to offer in December of 1945, at which time the pioneer air line was accused of "undercutting." At that time TWA, along with most other air lines, was charging $575 for the trip one way. It is interesting to point out here, then, that TWA

There is another way in which the designer has entered into the development of our international aviation policy. Nations have sought to restrict each other in fear that rivals will take business away with superior equipment. It will be recalled that the European nations, led by Great Britain, operated for the most part on the theory of confining air-line schedules to the traffic need. Thus, the British had tried consistently to get Americans to agree to the findings of IATA, which sought to stabilize fares and frequencies by voluntary agreements of the respective private operators. This was the British way of avoiding overexpansion, excessive subsidy, and the cutthroat competition that the country could ill afford. It was also Britain's way of protecting its aircraft industry by insuring more equitable distribution of traffic even though the public might prefer superior aircraft of another flag line.

The American system has been just the opposite. Most of our operators, if unrestricted, would start out with planes much bigger than current traffic warranted. Then these operators would set about promoting air travel until the big planes began to be filled regularly. But before that happened, they would already be calling upon the designer and builder to supply even larger and faster aircraft. When ready, the new planes would be offered to the public at reduced fares. This would call out even more traffic, and the process would be repeated until saturation was reached. Americans looked upon the British system as stuffy and unprogressive. The British called the Americans wasteful.

Americans have never been impressed by this charge. Our economic philosophy has always been based on waste. We have expended irreplaceable resources without thought of the final cost. Such wholesale exploitation has brought quick and fantastic profits. Our high standard of living is largely a result of this thoughtless expenditure of natural wealth. Vast areas have been denuded of forests, and the abundance of this "crop"

made no effort to defend the lower fare suggested by Pan American, even though the cut rate was higher than the fare suggested by TWA in the North Atlantic hearings.

has founded many of the largest fortunes in this country.

The Chinese, representing the other extreme, might have tried to conserve all this wealth. Not so the American. He goes right on "mining" his farm land, squandering his minerals, and leveling his trees. When they are gone he will turn to plastics, synthetic foods, and new sources of energy. His wastefulness drives him on. He will create immense wealth by using up resources recklessly. With this wealth he will buy the scientists and equipment to open the way for an even more lavish era. The American believes he has found the way to eat his cake and have it too.

This kind of thinking has held in aviation. The British believe we are utterly stupid. When they build a good plane they expect to use it like a steamship or a railroad car—to keep it in operation as long as it is safe and useful. Frequently in the past they have resented competition that has forced them to replace equipment before it has lived out its usefulness. One way to prevent such annoyance is to protect the industry by restrictive measures against foreign operators. If aggressive promoters are kept away from empire routes, then equipment can be kept running for years. It appears to be an economical pattern—but is it?

The wasteful American operator abandons his equipment long before it has served its purpose.* He demands bigger and faster planes because, under certain conditions, they mean cheaper operation. Cheaper operation spells lower fares and more traffic. But because the experimental cost of new planes is extensive and because the return on displaced aircraft is negligible, replacement is a drain upon air-line resources. The large, postwar planes cost as much as a whole fleet of prewar transports. And this cost must be written off in a limited time. Eventually this building boom must level off, as it did in the

---

*There are many exceptions, of course. The old workhorse of the airlines, the Douglas DC-3, continued to be depended upon fifteen years after it first appeared. Modified from time to time, it continued to give good service. But it should be noted that it remained in operation not because it was "protected," but because it was a splendid craft for certain purposes.

early thirties with the advent of the DC-3. Then the nation that has been plodding along trying to save money by using obsolete equipment will find that America has, by waste and expenditure, equipped itself with planes that can carry more passengers at far less cost than any rival can offer. If the rival then tries to even up the score by means of restrictive legislation, the greatest injury is to himself. For the big American plane with its lower fare and superior service can be like the fabulous goose of the golden eggs—the eggs in this case being tourist dollars. Meanwhile, our wasteful policy has taught us a great deal that can be applied to military as well as to civil aircraft. Expansion will have called the best brains into aviation. An army of flyers, administrators, and technicians will have been trained in the use of the most modern equipment. Thus, over a period of half a century our extravagance may very likely pay for itself many times over. The doctrine of progress by waste may be a dangerous one, but as long as it remains our policy, the designer and engineer will continue to wield enormous influence.

What the designer has accomplished in the last twenty years may be realized by a comparison of his products. In the early thirties it appeared that the Douglas DC-3 was about as efficient a plane as could be built, although there were larger and faster planes even then, it is true. The Fokker 32, a four-engined transport, was a giant of its day. So was the Russian version know as the Maxim Gorky (the Maximum Gawky, our airmen called it). These planes had the passenger capacity desired by the air-line operators, but they were inefficient and costly to operate. At that time the "square-cube" law, based on the ratio of weight to lift, limited transports to about 35,000 gross pounds. The DC-3 fitted nicely into this pattern.

Ten years later all the big companies were working with designs in which the square-cube law was ignored. By the end of the war some of these planes had even materialized. The Boeing C-97, a commercial version of the famous B-29, was designed to weigh 130,000 pounds and to carry 100 passengers. And this was one of the more modest of the modern aircraft.

The Lockheed Constitution, test-flown in the fall of 1946, weighed more than 180,000 pounds. Even this plane was puny in comparison with the proposed Consolidated-Vultee 200-passenger monster designed to be assisted off the ground by means of jet thrust. Henry Kaiser, miracle man of war ship-building, who liked to dabble with big things, discussed plans for an eighteen million dollar flying boat that was to weigh 425,000 pounds. Apparently there is no limit to the size of future aircraft.[1] Traffic, landing facilities, and financial resources are the only obstacles to such building.

Until the world was ready, air-line operators were content with intermediate aircraft. The standard equipment of the immediate postwar period was the Douglas DC-4 (known to the Army as the C-54). This was a sturdy, four-engined transport that normally hauled thirty-five to forty passengers on long journeys. The plane was a favorite with pilots because operation was as simple as that of the beloved old DC-3's, but the air lines had been slow to accept them when they first appeared in 1939. Indeed the prototype (the three-tailed model) was sold to the Japanese because of insufficient interest in the United States. The war proved the worth of the DC-4, however, and by 1946 this type of equipment (including an improved version, the DC-6) had relegated the familiar DC-3's to short-line and feeder operations.

Another great ship, especially adaptable to international use, appeared just before the war but was grabbed by the military authorities before it could be put to commercial use. This was the Constellation-type transport developed by Lockheed Aircraft Corporation with the advice of TWA and Pan American engineers. Capable of flying at well over 300 miles an hour with 50 passengers,, the Connie brought new standards of speed and economy to international operation. It was easy to fly. Passengers who had had the opportunity of riding in it at 20,000 feet in the pressurized cabin appreciated its "over-weather" characteristics.* The operator liked it because of its

*Only a few were privileged to enjoy high-altitude, pressurized flying, however. Military versions of the ship dispensed with such luxury travel.

flying efficiency. Connies were the last word in aerodynamic design. The dolphin-shaped fuselage had a curious curve that was, in reality, a carrying-out of the air-foil pattern that had amazed the profession when it appeared. Almost at once Constellations began setting new records. On April 17, 1944, a Connie established a transcontinental transport record when it landed at Washington national airport less than seven hours after leaving Burbank, California. Average speed was more than 340 miles an hour during that flight.* Thereafter the Connie broke records on almost every route where it was tried out.

As is usual when new equipment is first tried out in operation, there was trouble. Pilots complained that the Connie "ran hot," and some of them were afraid of it. There had been some narrow escapes. Over Connecticut a Europe-bound Constellation dropped an engine after catching fire. Had the accident occurred two hundred miles further along the route, all passengers might have been killed. Fortunately the pilot brought it down safely. Two other mishaps during test runs added to the apprehension. In July a Connie training crew was killed when the ship crashed near Reading, Pennsylvania. To forestall public reaction Civil Aeronautics Administrator T. J. Wright ordered all Connies grounded for thirty days.

The grounding of the Connies was a blow to the transport operators of the world and to a great aircraft company. Many of the leading air lines were committed to the use of Constellation equipment. The British were the hardest hit, because the Connie was about all they had for trans-Atlantic transport. Altogether, fifty-eight planes were grounded. Some critics said the Wright order was a blunder. But it did prove one thing— that safety was the first consideration in air-line operation. At least the grounding order helped to restore public confidence.

Fortunately, the Connie was too good a plane to stay down.

*Pilot and co-pilot on the transcontinental flight were Howard Hughes, the famous world flyer, and Jack Frye. Hughes was chairman of the board of TWA and Frye had not yet resigned as president of the air line. TWA and Pan American had a priority delivery on the Constellation because of their interest and aid in producing the ship.

It piled up nearly two million passenger miles during the war without injury to passenger or crew. Even foreign rivals, who might have been expected to make capital of our plight, admitted that the Connie would one day prove itself, as it did.

It is only fair to point out that transports from other factories also had troubles when they were adopted by the air lines. The superb DC-6, which went into service about nine months after the Connie scare, also had a brush with the authorities. This plane, already tested in thousands of miles of noncommercial operation, had a few "bugs" in it when it first became standard equipment on the air routes. It, too, had to be grounded, but like the Connie, it eventually proved itself. The point is that the American operator has never been content to ride along on time-tested equipment. He knows the risk of trying new things, but he calculates the risk and believes the end justifies the means.

This aggressiveness forced other nations to repudiate the complacency of operators willing to jog along in equipment long since written off the books. Immediately after the war the United States had the cards stacked in its favor, as far as air transport was concerned. Only America was ready to produce the super transports at once. We had the men and we had an excess of equipment. That gave us enormous bargaining power in our international negotiations. If the other nations hoped to start world air routes, they had to use American equipment. Until 1948 every foreign operator depended upon U.S. aircraft to haul its own air traffic. There was no room for smugness in this advantage, however. Indeed, there was great danger that foreign nations might some day run away with the transport business *just because America was committed to large-scale production of equipment developed during the war.*

All U.S. transports built and designed after the war were for the most part modifications of orthodox types. Some, like the Consolidated-Vultee Model 37, had been carried to extreme size. Others, such as the Douglas Mixmaster, or Lockheed Constitution, had novel power-plant arrangements. Even so, the new aircraft were merely modifications of existing craft. The transport plane of the future was likely to be as different from the postwar plane as the *Queen Elizabeth* was different from the *Flying Cloud*. For the revolution in propulsion might very well change our whole policy regarding air commerce. Foreign countries, with small inventories in war-type aircraft engines, might be able to turn to jet propulsion long before the United States could abandon emphasis on the reciprocating engine. It is significant, indeed, to note that leadership in jet propulsion began in Italy, Germany, and England, not in the United States.

There is nothing new in jet propulsion. Anyone who has seen a skyrocket launched has seen jet power in action. The rocket bomb and the "bazooka" gun are adaptations of the jet principle to weapons, but the principle is not even new to aviation. One C. J. Lake applied in France for a patent on a jet plane as far back as 1909.[2] A. A. Griffith and H. A. Constant described "reactive propulsion" to the Royal Aeronautical Society in 1926. In 1939 jet flight was first demonstrated when the Italians began testing a Caproni-Campini aircraft.* There was nothing complicated about the plane. It looked very much like any other aircraft, except that it had no propeller. There was a big hole in the nose, through which air was sucked. The air was superheated and then expelled at the stern. The Nazis improved on jet aircraft during the war. They concentrated on rocket intercepters capable of fantastic speeds. The rocket planes could stay aloft only a short time, however, and were not important from the transport standpoint.

Jet propulsion made the transport industry stop, look, and listen when the British began to achieve success with the gas turbine, or "turbo-jet." Father of the turbo-jet was Frank Whittle, who began his experiments while he was a Royal Air Force cadet. That was in 1928. Cadet Whittle was only twenty-one when he drew his first jet design on the back of some classroom notes. Some day those notes may take their places alongside the original Wright plane as significant contributions to

*The first successful flight was made by the Italians in August, 1940—an event that is of considerable importance in aeronautical history.

aviation, for the turbo-jet broke down barriers that were beginning to confine the transport designer.

Already the aeronautical engineers had encountered what they called "compressibility burble" at the tips of high-speed propellers. The phenomenon was characterized by the rapid falling off of efficiency. When a surface moves rapidly through the atmosphere, the air trends to be disturbed out ahead. A comparable action takes place when wet snow banks up in front of a sidewalk scraper. This disturbance prevents the air from flowing evenly over the surface resulting in loss of propeller thrust, or the equivalent wing lift. The phenomenon occurs when surfaces move through the air at about the speed of sound. Burble would appear at propeller tips when engines reached a certain power output. One way to expend this power is to use a longer propeller, but the wider the arc, the greater the speed. Speed can be reduced by turning the engine more slowly and adding more blades with greater pitch, but sooner or later the time must come when props can be driven no faster without reaching the burble point. Jet propulsion may be the answer.

That was what Pilot Whittle was after when he took out his first patent in 1930. The depression-ridden Air Ministry, then in control of all British aviation, offered no encouragement, and venture capital was scarce in those drab days, so it looked as though a great engineer would be lost to aviation. At the last moment, however, the Air Ministry decided it might be worth while to keep an eye on young Whittle. The Ministry sent him to Cambridge to study under one of Britain's greatest aerodynamicists, Professor Bennett Melvill Jones.

Cambridge changed Pilot Whittle from a tinkerer to a scientist. He won first honors in the mechanical science "tripos" of 1936. Teachers began to regard him with great respect. But he kept his hands greasy and his attitude realistic. The combination of practice and theory resulted in the organization of a small research company while Pilot Whittle was still a college student. The company was known as Power Jets, Limited, and its main function was to provide demonstrations for hypotheses worked out in the class room.

Frank Whittle went up in the world, literally and figuratively. He was an RAF squadron leader when he attracted the attention of Roxbee Cox, director of scientific research for the Ministry of Air Production. It was Cox who sponsored the construction of the first Whittle jet turbine. Under contract from little Power Jets, Limited, the British Thomson Houston Company turned out the first gas turbine in 1937. As a power plant the engine was a great success, but it took four more years for the engineers to learn how to install it in an airplane. By that time the war was on.

The British launched their first turbo-jet plane on May 14, 1941. It was a Gloster monoplane of otherwise conventional design, but it may well have begun a new era in aviation. Not much notice was taken at the time, however, because the British were preoccupied with other matters. It was during the week of May 14 that the Luftwaffe hit the Houses of Parliament. Westminster Abbey and the British Museum also were bombed. Rudolf Hess landed in the north with his fantastic offer of peace at a price. Yet nothing in that week was as important as the flight of the little Gloster.

So far, Europe had led in the development of jet propulsion, but the United States had also seen beginnings in this new field. Twenty years earlier Sanford A. Moss of General Electric had perfected the turbo-supercharger for standard aircraft motors. Its purpose was to pump more air into cylinders, but actually the device was a miniature jet turbine. Unfortunately, no one had developed it as a power plant. The skill and knowledge required to produce the supercharger were put to good use when the Whittle motor was sent to the United States late in 1941 as a not inconsiderable reverse of lend-lease. Within six months General Electric had turned out an efficient gas turbine. Westinghouse and Allis-Chalmers followed with what they believed were improved versions of the British model.

Soon planes were whiffling through American skies without benefit of propeller. Jet planes began to set speed records far beyond anything ever dreamed of by the designers of the conventional, Otto-cycle motors. An experimental jet fighter traveled more than 600 miles an hour before awed crowds at the Cleveland Air Races in August, 1946 — and this at low altitudes, where the jet operates least efficiently. Moreover, the jet had proved to be not only fast, but capable of sustained flight. The Lockheed P-80, one of the earliest operational jets, had crossed the continent several times. This was the feat that most impressed the designers of future transports.

The designer had begun to wonder if the delicate, highly-engineered gasoline engine was not getting near the limit of its possibilities. When the war started, 1,800 horsepower was about the limit for mass-produced aircraft motors. When the war ended there were engines of 3,300 horse power operating at the unbelievable ratio of one horsepower for every 14 ounces. That weight-horsepower ratio was achieved as the supreme effort of engineers who had been working with reciprocating engines for years. It did not look as if they could get much more out of such a power plant.* On the other hand, the gas turbine, which had reached about the same stage of development as had the reciprocating engine in 1914, gave promise of spectacular performance without sacrifice to weight. There were other good points about it. It had few moving parts, for one thing. It could also operate at full throttle. The conventional aircraft engine operates at full power only at take-off. From then on it will run safely at only about 60 per cent of full power, although it still has to carry the same weight around. The gas turbine engine operates best at 85 per cent of full power in even its crude stage, and the faster the plane travels, the better it runs. Again, only by developing expensive super fuels have reciprocating engines been brought to highest efficiency. Such fuels are not only costly, but dangerous. The turbo-jet will run on simple fuels that are much less a fire hazard. "The goddam thing'll run on peanut butter, if necessary," one enthusiastic pilot was heard to cry out gleefully.

---

*A 36-cylinder American engine rated at 5,000 h.p. was announced at the end of the war, and the French were said to have a similar power plant. Whether such engines would ever be useful commercially was still a matter of debate when this book was written.

There appears to be little doubt that the turbo-jet, or a modification of it, is the power plant of the future. America, however, is geared to the reciprocating engine. U.S. commercial
aviation, with fleets of conventional planes, and with stores of
engine parts, could not readily shift over. The British, starting from scratch in the development of air transports, might
one day turn the tables on the Americans who had everything
their own way at the end of the war. They have led in the development of jet propulsion, and they are determined to keep
that lead, regardless of the cost. S. G. Hooker, assistant chief
engineer of the Rolls Royce jet division, used almost these
words in telling members of the Royal Aeronautical Society
in April, 1946, what was in store for British aviation.[3]

The past record of the United States indicates that when the
time comes that the gas turbine seriously threatens the existence
of the conventional power plant, operators will scrap obsolete
equipment, regardless of waste and cost. No such drastic action
will take place, in all probability. America will simply edge
into the turbo-jet era. Our own jet program is well along.
Most likely there will be an intermediate stage, in which jets
and propellers are used together for shorter, lower altitude
flights. There will be, in all probability, a need for gasoline
engines long after the jet has been accepted. But when the
noonday of jet propulsion does come, the United States should
have little to fear from present rivals.

REFERENCES

1. For more on such planes see "The New Transport Planes: I and II,"
   Fortune, June, 1945, pp. 131 ff.; and July, 1945, pp. 141 ff.
2. B. T. Koleroff, "Possibility of Reactive Propulsion in the Air," *Aviation,*
   May 16, 1921, p. 624.
3. S. G. Hooker, "The Gas Turbine and Civil Aviation," *Flight,* April 10,
   1946, p. 2.

A NOTE ON SOURCES

For data on aircraft development see *CAB Docket No.* 855, the original volumes, particularly the exhibits of TWA and Pan American Airways. A discussion of postwar technical advances is given in "The New Transport Planes," *Fortune,* June, 1945, p. 131 and July, 1945, p. 141. See also Sidney E. Veale, *Tomorrow's Airliners, Airways and Airports,* London, 1945. Information on jet propulsion is discussed in a series of articles beginning with one by S. G. Hooker, "The Gas Turbine and Civil Aviation," *Flight,* April 10, 1946, p. 2; the reports of the Royal Aeronautical Society; and the annual reports of the National Advisory Committee for Aeronautics.

REPORT ON WINDS ALOFT

THE LAST chapter in the story of
the international air routes is difficult to write. In fact, there
can be no last chapter, since every month brings new developments. One thing is certain: the high frontier has been conquered, and today it remains only for the pioneers to consolidate
their empires. The industry, in short, has ceased to be an adventure. That is as it should be, for air commerce can never
be successful as a business until it ceases to have the glamor of
danger about it. Within a decade of the first commercial
flights across the Atlantic in 1939, international air transportation had become big business. But the end of the decade found
it suffering from postwar readjustment just as other important
enterprises suffered. The industry had to face many problems,
among them the attempt by a determined group to revise the
air transportation policy of the United States.

In the spring of 1947 the same forces that had fought for the
community company and chosen instrument made one more
attempt to sell Congress on monopoly for international air transportation. Senator McCarran's bill, S.987, was a retread of his
old All-American Flag Line measure, which had rolled so many
miles in previous years. A similar bill in the House was sponsored by Chairman Charles A. Wolverton of the Interstate and
Foreign Commerce Committee. Both bills called for "merger
and consolidation of international air carriers for the United
States," but there was a new wrinkle this time. The proposed
legislation called for participation in air commerce not only

by the domestic air lines, but by the U.S. railroads and steamship companies as well. Appropriately, then, Senator McCarran
called his latest plan the "United Front." [1]

On the whole, the factions lining up along the United Front
were about the same as in the days of the community company
and chosen instrument. Trippe appeared again to give an
impressive and charming discourse on the dangers of the competitive system. This time he was particularly alarmed about
subsidies necessary to nourish the struggling industry. His
advice was recalled ruefully by some of his erstwhile opponents
when the weather began closing in on the air lines in 1946–48.
Some of the labor groups, including the railroad brotherhoods,
always jealous of foreign wage standards, continued to argue for
Trippe's plan. So did several prominent Congressmen, including, of course, Senator Brewster.

A new foe appeared against the United Front allies. This
was the Air-Coordinating Committee (ACC), which took the
place of the old Seventeen Airlines Committee as spokesman
for the competitive school. The ACC was actually merely a
continuation of the Interdepartmental Committee appointed
by President Roosevelt, but it became an official body by an
executive order issued by President Truman in the summer of
1946. Soon it was recognized as the policy-steering organization for U.S. civil aviation. Because it cut through so many
agencies and departments, the ACC was recognized as an
important force.

It was significant, therefore, when the ACC voted unanimously to oppose the chosen instrument, regardless of its current
title. The President's five-man air policy commission, which
conducted long hearings on both civil and military aviation
issues, also denounced the single company. Its report of December 30, 1947, not only favored limited competition, but
also advised against letting surface carriers have anything to do
with international air commerce. [2] Assistant Secretary of State
Garrison Norton, former chief of his department's transportation division, told the House committee that the proposed
bills would only convince other nations that the United States

was turning civil aviation into a weapon of economic warfare. The proposals just did not harmonize with U.S. over-all policy regarding foreign relations, he explained.

Much of the pressure for the McCarran-Wolverton bills was applied by the steamship interests. They had learned a lesson from history. A century earlier the stagecoach and canal people had ridiculed the railroad companies because the steam engine was flimsy, unreliable, and capable of hauling only light cargoes at exorbitant rates. They had lived to see the railroad take over the transportation of the bulk freight that had appeared to be the insurmountable defense of the bargeman and drayman. This time, the older transportation systems did not mean to be left behind. They insisted upon taking part in the development of world air routes. They had been prevented heretofore by the interpretation of the Civil Aeronautics Act of 1938. According to the "Sea-Air" claque, the Civil Aeronautics Board was the villain.

It will be recalled that the CAB had no objections to an integrated sea-air service back in 1942, when the American Export Case was being decided. The Board went so far as to grant Amex, a subsidiary of a steamship line, a temporary certificate for an ocean air route. Pan American Airways had fought that decision, and had carried an appeal to the courts. Pan American had argued that the sea and air systems must be separate under the 1938 Act. That was the way they hoped to keep Amex out of the Pan American sphere. The court handed the case back to the CAB to decide, and the Board interpreted this as a dictum in favor of the Pan American argument. This assumption has always been disputed by the steamship interests, but in any case, the CAB had long since reversed its earlier policy and was unanimously opposed to sea-air integration by the time the steamship group was ready to do battle.

One of the most powerful lobbies in Washington is sustained by the steamship interests. That was one reason why proponents of the chosen-instrument bills desired to get the marine companies into the controversy. On the other hand, the steamship interests could put up good arguments for their inclusion in the aviation development plans. It was held that the U.S. policy of separating surface and air carriers was unfair to American shipping interests. U.S. steamship companies had strong competition from foreign rivals, all of whom had the backing of their respective governments. In most cases foreign surface and air carriers were integrated services under national control. Foreign steamship companies could thus offer tourists choices in transportation. Under this plan travelers could make a restful ocean voyage to Europe one way and return quickly by air, or vice versa. American companies were thus put at a disadvantage in selling travel, it was argued. The American public, said the sea-air spokesmen, "is not interested in travel by rail, water, highway, or air *as such,* but rather wants the best possible *service* at reasonable cost, whether that is rendered by one type of transportation, or by a combination of services." [3] Many aviation writers and newspaper editors agreed with this argument.* On the other hand, opponents charged that the railroad and surface carriers, with their powerful friends in Congress, would dominate any sea-air partnership. In that case, air lines might suffer whenever surface carriers were threatened by serious competition.

Another way of getting the surface carriers into the transportation picture was suggested by Representative Clarence F. Lea, chairman of the National Transport Inquiry Board, and coauthor (with Senator McCarran) of the excellent Civil Aeronautics Act of 1938. Representative Lea proposed a transportation department or agency to consolidate regulation of all carriers. The steamship group favored the plan, but it was overwhelmingly opposed by other transportation interests. The CAB, once sympathetic to the pleas of the surface carriers for a share in air commerce, had long since reversed itself by declaring for "regulated competition" by air lines free from the pressures of the older transportation systems. The air lines themselves had no use for the Lea proposal. Admiral Emory S.

*For a representative list of editorial comments, see the source notes at the end of the chapter.

Land of the Air Transport Association, former head of the Maritime Commission, had once advocated sea-air integration, but now that he represented air-line management he had come to the conclusion that aviation development could best be accomplished when operators were unfettered by the traditions of the older services. These views were verified by an elaborate report prepared by Lewis C. Sorrell of the University of Chicago.

At any rate, the community company forces were decisively defeated in 1947. There was talk during the following months of merging certain international routes, but that was a different issue, dependent more upon economic expedience than upon U.S. aviation policy. One reason for lack of interest in the chosen instrument after the 1947 attempted *putsch* was that the threat of foreign skulduggery on world routes was lessened by a series of conferences that materially improved relations between international rivals.

For a brief period after the signing of the Bermuda document early in 1946 the United States and Great Britain enjoyed peace in the air. Before long, however, the two rivals began to lodge complaints against each other. Each charged the other with sabotage of air commerce. The fact is, both nations had allowed operators to "stray from the reservation," as the new CAB chairman put it. Although the Bermuda Agreement remained a milestone in aviation progress, its application was carelessly enforced by both governments.

Americans had returned from Bermuda with the understanding that the document they had just signed was to be the model for all future agreements between the contracting parties and other nations. That, in effect, would have achieved the multilateral adherence to principles long held by the U.S. policymakers. The British did not see it this way at all. The Bermuda pact was strictly a contract between the U.S. and Great Britain, it was held, and they went right on making contracts with other governments without regard to the Bermuda model. This policy was clearly seen in the British negotiations with the governments of Argentina, Brazil, and Mexico. The resulting contracts were resented by Americans seeking privileges in these countries. The British, for example, were willing to grant Argentine operators an equal share of traffic between that country and the United Kingdom. When the United States started negotiations with Argentina, the British contract was cited as an example of what Argentina would demand of the United States. This was not the type of agreement our aviation leaders had in mind. They were willing to grant cooperative nations landing privileges for designated air lines, but if every country in South America insisted on fifty-fifty traffic rights to and from the United States, Americans saw themselves overwhelmed by competition. The British negotiations with Argentina therefore caused consternation in the State Department, for it was clear that negotiations in Mexico and Brazil were to be fruitless as long as British concessions could be used against us.

The new head of the CAB set about to repair the damage. He was James McCauley Landis, a distinguished public servant appointed to succeed Pogue in June, 1946. A former law dean at Harvard, and a protégé of the late Justice Louis Brandeis, Landis had held important positions under President Roosevelt. Later, there were aviation critics who accused him of failure to understand the problems of the industry and he was eventually dropped by President Truman from the CAB, but in the meantime he performed many valuable services for our expanding air commerce.

In August Landis flew down to Rio to see if he could soften the demands of the Brazilians. They were told that they had much more to gain by accepting limited privileges than by holding out for impossible concessions. Landis let the Brazilian representatives make their own suggestions for improving relations. In the end, they came around to his point of view. Both parties agreed to sign a bilateral document based on the Bermuda model.

In September Landis performed just as skillfully in London. He asked for "reaffirmation" of the Bermuda document and a promise that all future agreements by both governments would follow the Bermuda pattern. It was expected that Landis would have to dicker with the British for weeks before arriving at some kind of dubious compromise. Instead, the conference lasted only two days. Both countries had committed breaches of faith, and the representatives were willing to admit the abuses. They promised to cease sabotaging each other's operations. Each country sent out directives to that effect. Almost immediately relations between the rivals improved along the world's air routes. A further development was the collapse of opposition to U.S. offers of negotiation. Governments using British agreements as levers for prying concessions from the United States hastened to revise demands. All over the world long-established obstacles to aviation expansion crumbled. India, which had held out against U.S. routes into Asia, signed an agreement of the Bermuda type in November, 1946. Two weeks later China, Australia, and New Zealand hopped on the band wagon. These were important developments. The Chinese agreement, signed November 30, made it possible for Pan American, TWA, and Northwest Airlines to close the last gaps in their proposed round-the-world services. Bilateral agreements concluded with Australia and New Zealand ended months of seemingly hopeless bickering. Landis had indeed given a good account of himself in his six months as chief of the Civil Aeronautics Board.

After 1946 the problems of the air lines were internal, rather than national or international in scope. Commercial aviation, like any other big business, was faced with labor demands, as peace returned to the world. This was labor's chance to win concessions. High wages, shortage of manpower, pressure of business, and aggressive leadership combined to give organized labor the power that it needed in the struggle to raise wage standards. Aviation was particularly vulnerable, because its expansion period occurred long after most other industries had begun to retrench following wartime growth.

Almost all air-line pilots belong to a small but effective organization called the Air Line Pilots Association (ALPA), affiliated with the American Federation of Labor. It had been founded in the dark days of the depression, when air-line pilots were being offered starvation wages by some operators. President and father of the ALPA is David L. Behncke, a former airline pilot once discharged from one of the largest companies for his labor activities. Under Behncke are the elite of the labor world. Many pilots earn more than the captains of crack ocean liners. They and their employers often belong to the same clubs. A large percentage are college alumni. On the whole, they are anything but radical in their attitudes on social questions. Perhaps this explains why they resent having the ALPA referred to as a union. Nevertheless, that is what it is, and these "laborers" can fight for union principles as well as can any of their brothers in overalls.

From 1934 until World War II pilots were paid according to a wage formula established by the National Labor Relations Board under the famous Decision 83. The ruling survived the invalidation of the industrial recovery program by its inclusion in the air-mail laws. Under the terms of the decision pilots received a kind of retainer fee, or base pay, of $1,600 a year. This increased $200 a year to a maximum of $3,000. In addition, pilots received $4 an hour for flying planes with cruising speeds up to 125 miles an hour. For operating faster aircraft they received extra pay on a graduated scale.* Another provision limited pilots to 85 hours of flying a month.

The code worked well enough until the war. A fairly happy relationship existed between pilots and employers until big, fast airliners began to supersede the prewar equipment. All the new ships cruised at speeds well above the maximum prescribed in Decision 83. Furthermore, pilots had had a taste of big wages while the air lines were working under contract for the armed forces. During the war pilots on international routes received a flat rate of about $1,000 a month.† The operators held that wartime wages were no criterion for peacetime services. War wages were compensation for combat risks, they declared. Seamen, for example, had also been given fat bonuses

*Roughly, 20 cents an hour whenever cruising speed was increased 15 miles an hour, *up to a maximum of 201 m.p.h.*

†Highest wartime scale was under the Northeast Airlines contract. It provided for maximum wages of $1,150 a month.

because of the wartime hazards, but those extras were never meant to be offered in peacetime.

The pilots insisted that the war wages should be continued. They argued that the higher pay was not a risk bonus, as in the case of the seamen, but was remuneration for the greater skill required in flying four-engine equipment. Furthermore, nothing had been said in the contracts about reverting to pre-war scales. The pilots were right about that. As one air-line labor relations expert admitted ruefully, continuation of wartime wages was the result of "hasty and reckless" agreements with the ALPA. He confessed that the operators had been stupid not to add riders to the contracts stipulating a return to the old scales upon cessation of hostilities. As he explained it, the operators had been forced into their embarrassing position by the Army and Navy. The military chiefs were more interested in getting supplies and men delivered than they were in bargaining over wages. The operators were therefore told to give the pilots their demands. Wages could be put on the government bill, to be taken care of by the contract. In the heat of war, no one thought of the consequences, according to this spokesman. Behncke denies that there was any such misunderstanding. In a letter to the author he said: "You indicate that the air carriers apparently try to make light of certain agreements that were negotiated during the war. I am glad to be able to tell you that they never agreed to anything so easily. What they now choose to place in the category of 'acting hastily' and without due consideration was actually one of the toughest bargaining sessions the ALPA ever went through with the air carriers. It lasted for months." [4]

In any case, the pilots repudiated the formula as a method of determining pay scale. They demanded a different wage pattern, based upon plane design. Since big ships earned more for operators and required more skill of the pilot, wages should be higher in such cases, it was argued. The operators complained that such a pattern would entail lengthy negotiations every time a new model left the factory. Frequent negotiation was just what the ALPA liked, of course, but the operators saw it as an unnecessary and expensive annoyance. The pilots appeared to have some justification for this system, however. Under the formula plan of Decision 83 there were certain to be injustices, even if the terms were modified to conform to modern conditions. Mammoth flying boats of the Hercules type would require pilots of the utmost skill. But because the Hercules was designed to cruise at a speed only one bracket above that of the old DC-3's, a pilot under the old plan would receive much less than the pilot of a small, fast, easily handled aircraft, such as the proposed Republic Rainbow.

Pilots also insisted upon wage negotiations "company by company," whereas the operators demanded the right to meet the ALPA as an industry. If the pilots could organize, why could not the employers, they asked? They had formed what they called the Airlines Negotiating Committee, and they asked that this be recognized as the bargaining agency of the operators. The pilots of course resented this suggestion. Their plan was to hoist wages as they might lift up a table. Forcing one company to raise wages was like raising one corner. The union could run around to the other three corners and insist that equilibrium could be achieved only by raising each of the legs. This was the situation when the first air-line strike was called.*

TWA had been selected by the ALPA as the test, not because the company was particularly antilabor, but because renewal of its contract was about to come up and because the company was the first to use postwar equipment on a large scale. The company turned over negotiating powers to the airlines committee, headed by President Ralph S. Damon of American Airlines. As expected, the ALPA refused to meet with the committee, and eventually the dispute was heard by a mediation board. Hearings were called in New York, Washington, and Chicago, but they accomplished nothing because the operators insisted on industry-wide bargaining, and the

*Some students of aviation, including the author, have written of a "strike" against motor tycoon E. L. Cord's air line in 1934. Behncke holds that the Cord trouble must be defined as a "lockout," rather than a "strike." If he is correct, then the TWA strike was indeed the first in commercial aviation history.

union would not talk with the negotiating committee. On May 7, 1946, President Truman created an emergency board to investigate the charges.

Reporting at the end of sixty days, the board recommended return to the formula method of computing wages. On the other hand, it held that the ALPA should conduct negotiations on a company basis. The joker to this was that the Airlines Negotiating Committee was to be permitted to act as agent for the individual company contracts. On the whole, the report was a victory for the operators. On August 8, 1946, they notified the President through their committee that they would abide by the recommendations of the emergency board. The ALPA, however, would make no such compromise. Behncke says that the interpretations of the board were ambiguous, and that when he asked for clarification, he received no answer.[5]

Accordingly, TWA pilots gave notice that they would strike. At 4:59 A.M. on October 21, all TWA planes were grounded by the first organized strike in air-line history.[6] More than one hundred TWA ships between San Francisco and Cairo failed to meet schedules that day. A few passengers were left stranded at isolated way stations, but both the company and the union were concerned about public opinion and every attempt was made to take care of traffic.

The strike lasted twenty-five days. It cost TWA about seven million dollars in gross revenue. Public opinion, generally speaking, was apparently on the side of the operator.[*] The trouble ended when both sides agreed to arbitrate. The arbitration board was to consist of a company representative, a union man, and a neutral member acceptable to both. There was so much delay in selecting the third member that the mediation board was finally called upon to make the choice. In January of 1947 the board announced its decision. Both pilots and co-pilots were granted wages slightly higher than the

*Philip Murray of the rival CIO union called the strike a "row between capitalists." The Washington *Post*, liberal in its labor policy, called it an "irresponsible strike" in its editorial of October 23. See also the New York papers of this period and Eric Bramley, "An Unnecessary Strike," *American Aviation,* November 15, 1946, p. 1.

emergency board had recommended.* The air line resumed operation, but the more complicated issues of the dispute were not satisfactorily settled.

Coming at the end of a disastrous year, the strike almost ruined a great air line. TWA had gone into debt to buy new Constellation equipment. When these planes were grounded by the Civil Aeronautics Authority order of July 11, 1946, the company not only had to spend additional thousands of dollars modifying them, but lost the revenue while they were in the shops. There was also a serious loss in "customer acceptance" while the Connies were in the news, and during the months when the company suffered for lack of planes. A strike, added to these calamities, was almost enough to administer the *coup de grâce*. There was rumor that the international divisions of TWA might be sold to Pan American Airways. Within the company an internecine war raged over the management policies. But by the summer of 1947 the groggy company was sailing under more peaceful skies again, and the danger appeared to be over.

This was not to be the last of the labor troubles between pilots and operators. A strike against National Airlines lasted 295 days. Another against American Overseas Airlines was continued for 18 days. The TWA incident is cited merely as a case history of air-line labor trouble. Actually, aviation suffered no more than any other business from labor unrest. It was all part of the postwar readjustment. The only difference was that the air lines were not then as able to stand the strain as other, more established, enterprises. Most other industries had paid off expansion costs during the war. Aviation expansion came while others were retrenching. All the air lines were losing money in the process. Because of political strife in various parts of the world, air routes could not be laid out according to plan. Revenue had failed to meet expectation.

*Wages for first pilots on international routes were based on a flat scale ranging from $925 to $1,100 monthly, depending on years of service, with overtime at $13.50 an hour. Co-pilots received material wage increases. They had been the "forgotten men" in past negotiations, and the new wage scales benefited them more than it did the first pilots.

Even the domestic operators, untroubled by such problems, were losing twenty million dollars a year. A wave of accidents further depressed the market, for the one great asset of an air line is public confidence, and when this wanes, so do profits.

The financial difficulties of the international air lines resulted in various plans for reorganization. In the spring of 1947 TWA offered its stockholders a new management. Jack Frye and Paul Richter, president and vice-president respectively, and two of the oldest operators in the business, resigned from the company. There was something sad about their departure from the air line they had parlayed into one of the great air transportation systems of the world. From the days when they had been stunt flyers and operators of a one-plane air service between Los Angeles and Arizona resorts, Jack Frye and Paul Richter had been cronies. They had run into difficulties with the company after the war, when they were accused of reckless expansion and over-ambition. Howard Hughes, the wealthy sportsman and flyer, headed the opposing faction. As the main backer of TWA, Hughes demanded a more realistic approach to air transportation. On the other hand, some of the government agencies distrusted Hughes, and TWA had trouble getting an RFC loan that would have tided it over its current difficulties. Hughes was hauled on to the Congressional carpet to explain, among other things, the squandering of government millions on his mammoth flying boat. This was the beginning of the feud with Senator Brewster that made newspaper headlines across the nation — a feud from which the Senator had to retire with great discomfiture. In the long run the Frye-Richter forces were overcome. In April, 1947, La Motte T. Cohu, long identified with aviation promotion, was named temporary president. Hughes remained as chairman of the board.

American Overseas Airlines (AOA), the old American Export company taken over as the international division of American Airlines (AA), also ran into a front of reorganizational and financial turbulence. For years AA had spearheaded the attacks on the chosen instrument and community company programs. But by the end of 1948 the air line began to make up to its old rival, Pan American Airways. It looked as though AA international policy had been reversed by the series of misfortunes that had befallen world air commerce. Rumors began to spread that AOA was going to be taken over by Pan American. Late in 1948 these rumors were openly discussed in the trade publications. There was a storm of protest. AOA employees appealed to the CAB for permission to request an option in the event that sale of the company was approved. Top executives in American Airlines were also split apart by the pending negotiations to merge AOA and Pan American. Ralph S. Damon, president of American Airlines and long a spokesman for regulated competition on international routes, resigned to take over the presidency of TWA. It is true that Howard Hughes had been after Damon for five years to take over the controls of TWA, but the best explanation for his resignation from the company he had so long served appeared in a statement he issued on January 19, 1949, in which he declared: "Because I find myself increasingly out of sympathy with management programs and policies of American Airlines, including the proposed sale of American Overseas Airlines, I am today submitting my resignation." [7] Late in 1949 a CAB examiner's report approved the Pan American–AOA merger. Although approval by the Board and by the President was required for consummation of the merger, the report was very significant.

Other mergers were rumored from time to time. When the CAB proposed breaking up National Airlines, operating down the Atlantic coast and across to Cuba, Pan American Airways and Panagra were reported as ready to pick up the pieces. The fact is, the international operators were beginning to feel the headaches predicted for them by such "I-told-you-so" experts as Juan Trippe. All the uncertainty and fear of the postwar years appeared to be exactly as the monopolists had outlined for the future back in 1945. Trippe had indicated that sooner or later the United States would have to adopt some form of the chosen instrument or community company. It looked as though Pan American had only to wait in order to win the

North Atlantic either by a shift in CAB policy, or by default.

Others retained their optimism regarding the future of regulated competition on world routes. Top executives such as Ralph Damon and Tom Braniff were still active, and there appeared to be no immediate prospect of change in official U.S. policy. Any student of air commerce could have predicted serious economic problems during the critical postwar period of adjustment. The high frontier had always exacted a toll of adventurers. But the proposed air-line mergers, occurring only three years after the granting of seven-year franchises on some of the routes, showed that the U.S. international air-transport system was in need of tuning up. A shilly-shally CAB was partly to blame. But mostly the times were at fault. And there were some bright spots. Even the AOA merger talk, discouraging as it was, brought out some good news about international aviation.

Despite heavy financial drains for new equipment and a revised air-line map (forced upon it by Soviet refusal to cooperate in European service), American Overseas had an enviable reputation as an air line. At the very time when it was threatened with dissolution it was earning an annual profit of a million dollars. It stood near the top of the list in terms of passengers carried. It was one of the safest lines in the industry. Surely, its backers argued, it was too soon to sell out such a gallant organization. True, foreign competitors were draining away more and more passengers. Substitutes must be developed to replace military traffic, up to now the backlog of revenue. New capital for costly purchase of needed equipment must be found. But if the air lines could get over the hump of 1949, many believed the U.S. operators could begin to prosper. There were already signs of this.

One was the restoration of public confidence, following the series of fatal crashes during the initial period of peacetime operations. The casual passenger had often lumped together all air accidents, whether they occurred on domestic, foreign, or military routes. Actually, the international operations were remarkably safe. At the height of the accident scare TWA was reporting the safest period in seven years. Air travel was as safe as rail travel, measured by one standard, and in the postwar years the railroads suffered from accidents, too. Indeed, the improvement in safety was more marked in the air than on the rails. In 1936 Class I (the top-notch) railroads of the United States operated 25,292,000 miles for every passenger fatality. That year the airlines were responsible for one fatality every 1,449,000 miles. But ten years later, in 1946, which the public thought of as a bad year for flying, there was only one fatality for each 2,877,000 miles of air travel, while the railroads had dropped to one death in every 3,647,000 miles. The last three years of the decade showed the air lines in an even more favorable light. From 1943 through 1945 there was one air fatality per 3,515,000 miles. That exceeded the railroad record of 2,459,000 miles per fatality by more than a million miles.* These figures included both domestic and international operations, but in miles flown, the international routes were as safe as the domestic. After 1946, as the months rolled by, with schedule after schedule of ocean flying safely completed, public confidence was reflected in the traffic figures. In 1947 there was a 64 per cent increase in revenue passenger miles; 112 per cent increase in air mail; and 110 per cent increase in express. In 1948, 50 per cent more passengers entered the United States by air than by sea, and in 1949 U.S. international air lines operated without a single fatality.

What the future holds for international air transportation remains to be seen. Very likely some of the present U.S. oper-

*The figures are from the annual reports of the Civil Aeronautics Administration, and the Interstate Commerce Commission. The railroads appear in a much better light when safety is put upon a time rather than upon a miles basis. Passengers travel farther in planes than in trains. They spend less time in the air than in coaches. But the traveler is much more interested in how *long* he can ride on any given means of transportation before he can expect trouble. How *far* he goes before an accident is much less important to him. On the time basis, the railroads are still safer than the air lines. Nevertheless the above figures do help to measure the improvement in safety, and for that reason they are used. They do show that the air lines have narrowed the margin of safety long enjoyed by the much older transportation system.

ators will drop out or be merged. There is a remote possibility
that the nation may reverse its policy regarding competition
on world routes. One thing is certain; the United States is
irrevocably committed to internationalism. It can never be
isolationist, as it was at the beginning of the decade. In 1939
private companies negotiated for landing rights and trade
privileges, largely because the United States did not care to
become embroiled internationally. In 1949 the U.S. was the
leader in one of the great experiments in internationalism.

On June 11, 1946, President Truman had sent a special
message to the Senate requesting early ratification of the treaty
written at the Chicago aviation meeting in 1944. This treaty
was concerned with the so-called "Convention" providing for a
permanent international aviation body for the settlement of
civil air problems. The Convention had to be accepted by
twenty-six nations before it could be effective, and the United
States, as a leader in civil aviation, was expected to ratify early
as an example to others. Meantime, international aviation was
to hinge upon a Provisional International Civil Aviation Organization, better known as PICAO.

The United States was slow in reaching a decision on this
important issue. There was a powerful bloc, led by Senators
McCarran, Brewster, and Walter F. George, opposing ratification. Others asked postponement of action until the new Congress had convened. Not until after the President's message,
did the Senate move. Senator George called the Foreign Relations Committee together on June 19. Sentiment appeared to
be in favor of the treaty, but there was hesitancy. Certain
members were ready to delay the treaty in retaliation for the
executive agreement action taken by the State Department.
There had never been much enthusiasm for the transport
document written at Chicago, which provided for multilateral
adherence to fifth-freedom privileges. The transport document
was being discussed as an executive agreement. The Senate preferred treaties to executive agreements, and it held that bilateral documents gave the United States a chance to bargain
with foreign countries, whereas the blanket commitments of

multilateral agreements put us at a disadvantage when it came to forcing compromises.

Nevertheless, the Senate committee reported the treaty favorably to the Senate at large, as requested by the President. It might have fared badly here, because there were opponents of the fifth-freedom agreement who were prepared to make an issue over the treaty in the hope of delaying U.S. international participation indefinitely. At this point the State Department stepped into the picture. On July 25 the department issued a press release stating that it was giving the required notice for U.S. withdrawal from the Transport (Fifth Freedom) Agreement, already signed by fifteen nations. The department declared that henceforth it would exchange fifth-freedom privileges only through bilateral agreements.

The State Department notice was hailed as a victory for those who had opposed multilateral agreements. In reality, the State Department was making a very strategic retreat. Admittedly it had failed to sell Congress on the Transport Agreement. It could also have been accused of letting down the fifteen signers of the document, most of whom had followed the advice of U.S. diplomats. But there was good reason for the State Department reversal. It was giving up its fight for recognition of multilateral fifth-freedom agreements in favor of legislative support of the Convention treaty. The maneuver was successful. Senator McCarran at once withdrew opposition to the treaty — not without misgiving — and without his leadership, enemies of the treaty were routed.[8]

On March 17, 1947, President Truman proclaimed the ratification of the Convention.[9] It was to become effective April 4, just a month before the opening of the international aviation organization in Montreal. The United States was the tenth nation to ratify the Convention. Other governments watching to see what the United States would do, fell into line. By the time the representatives met in Montreal on May 6, forty-one nations had deposited documents of ratification. On that day, therefore, the international organization lost the "Provisional" part of its title and henceforth was known as ICAO (International Civil Aviation Organization). This was an event of great significance. It was notice to the world that aviation had reached maturity. It also showed that the United States was ready to assume its responsibility in world commerce.

Thus ended a decade of aviation progress such as the world had never seen before, nor would likely see again. Many of the key figures in this period have been mentioned in these pages. Others, who had just as important roles, may never receive credit that is due. Countless unimportant people — employees, airmen, and government workers — were the backbone of the industry during this glorious decade. The air lines that they built must be their monuments. And there were all those who failed — but whose failures taught valuable lessons. All of these were essential characters in the drama. They made U.S. air transportation what it is today. They are the ones "who at best know in the end the triumph of achievement, and who at the worst, if they fail, at least fail while daring greatly, so that their place shall never be with those cold and tired souls who know neither victory nor defeat."

REFERENCES

1. Senator Pat McCarran, "McCarran Offers Defense of Chosen Instrument Plan," *American Aviation,* May 1, 1947, p. 14.
2. A résumé of this report is given in the *Aircraft Yearbook for 1948,* Aircraft Industries Association, Washington, 1948, pp. 74 ff. (The *Aircraft Yearbook* from this date on became less a history of aviation for the preceding year than a compendium of important documents. It was also published under different auspices than it had been in the past.)
3. "Integration of Sea And Air Service," *Committee On Interstate And Foreign Commerce,* brief submitted in support of a request for the removal of administrative restraints by the Sea-Air Committee of the National Federation of American Shipping, Inc., a brochure put out by this committee March 10, 1946.
4. Letter from D. L. Behncke, dated December 3, 1946.
5. *Ibid.*
6. See footnote p. 315. There had been a pilot's strike in July, 1919, but air transportation was then under the Post Office Department, and therefore not, strictly speaking, a commercial enterprise.
7. "Damon Quits American, Becomes President of TWA," *American Avia-*

tion, February 1, 1949, p. 11.

8. See speech of Senator McCarran, *Congressional Record,* 79th Congress, 2d Session, July 25, 1946, p. 3 of reprint edition.

9. See *International Civil Aviation,* "Convention between the United States and Other Governments," *Treaties and Other International Acts,* Series 1591, Department of State Publication No. 2816, Washington, 1947.

A NOTE ON SOURCES

For a discussion of the "united-front" arguments on the chosen-instrument issue, see the hearings on H.R. 2827 and S. 987, Eightieth Congress, First Session, 1947. The Sea-Air controversy is covered in "Brief in Support of Request for the Removal of Administrative Restraints on the Integration of Sea and Air Service," submitted to the subcommittee on transportation, Committee on Interstate and Foreign Commerce, U. S. House of Representatives, March, 1946. The arguments of the aviation interests are given in *Reply of the Air Transport Association of America,* (to the National Transportation Inquiry), a brochure published by the ATA, Washington, 1946. See also the original copies of the *CAB Dockets,* Nos. 525, 855, and 1171 for statements of steamship officials. The issue is also discussed in *Transoceanic Aircraft and the Merchant Marine,* Executive Hearings before the Committee on the Merchant Marine and Fisheries, House of Representatives, Seventy-eighth Congress, Second Session, H. Res. 52, Washington, 1944. See particularly the statement of Admiral Emory S. Land. Typical editorial comment can be seen in the San Francisco *Chronicle* of December 18, 1943; San Francisco *Examiner,* January 3, 1944; San Francisco *Call-Bulletin,* January 10, 1944; Los Angeles *Times,* January 11, 1944; *Aero Digest,* May, 1947; and *American Aviation,* February 1, 1947. A concise history of events leading up to the TWA strike is given in *Report to the President by the Emergency Board,* created May 7, 1946, pursuant to Section 10 of the Railway Labor Act, Washington, July 8, 1946, (Emergency Board Report No. 36). The provisions of the important "Decision 83" may be found in *National Labor Relations Board Decisions,* Decision No. 83, "In the Matter of Air Line Pilots' Wage Dispute, May 10, 1934," (Washington, 1934). See also the report of two labor relations experts, Theodore W. Kheel and Donald B. Straus, of Management-Employee Relations, Inc., in *Air Transport,* May, 1946, pp. 29 ff. Material for this section was also supplied privately by the Airlines Negotiating Committee and the Air Line Pilots Association. David L. Behncke, president of the ALPA, added pertinent data in a long letter dated December 3, 1946. Information for this chapter was also obtained from interviews with L. Welch Pogue, former chairman of the CAB; James M. Landis, who succeeded Pogue until December of 1948; Senator Owen Brewster, chairman of the Senate subcommittee on aviation, Committee on Commerce; Jack Woods, labor specialist for American Airlines; C. A. Hodgins, executive director of the Airlines Negotiating Committee; John Dickerman, Washington representative of the Air Line Pilots Association; and Blaine Stubblefield, Washington representative of McGraw-Hill publications (*Aviation, Air Transport, Aviation News, etc.*).

Chronology and Index

CHRONOLOGY

Before 1920

1604   Freedom of the Seas concept first discussed by Hugo Grotius, Dutch barrister.

1817   Decision of Lord Stowell commits Great Britain to Freedom of the Seas.

1917   May 22: Civil Aerial Transport Committee establishes British air-transport policy for the next 30 years.

1918   November-December: British pioneer the Egypt–India air route.

1919   Dr. Peter Paul von Bauer organizes SCADTA in Colombia as one of the earliest air lines in the world.

         The Paris Convention on international aviation establishes the closed-sky policy.

         March 3: Edward Hubbard and W. E. Boeing carry first U.S. foreign air mail under private contract, between Seattle and Victoria.

         August 25: Aircraft Transport & Travel, Ltd., begins first British international civil air service.

         September 19: French establish air service to Morocco. Extended to Dakar in 1925. South American operations inaugurated in 1927. South Atlantic service started in 1934 after survey flights by Jean Mermoz.

         November-December: Captain Ross Smith and Lieutenant Keith Smith complete first flight over Kangaroo Route from England to Australia.

1920-1925

1920   October 15: Florida West Indies Airways, Inc., awarded a mail contract for Key West–Havana route.

1921   Appropriation Act provides $100,000 for foreign air-mail service, giving the Postmaster General the authority for the first time to establish an international service.

RAF inaugurates regular service from Cairo to Bagdad.

1924   Germans establish Kondor Sindikat as an attempt to develop an air-line system in South America.

April 1: Organization of Imperial Airways, Ltd.

September 28: U.S. Army Air Service completes round-the-world flight in three Douglas Cruisers.

1925-1930

1925   February 2: Passage of the Kelly Bill (Air Mail Act of 1925), turning over domestic air-mail transportation to private enterprise.

September 17: President's Aircraft (Morrow) Board investigates U.S. aviation and paves way for further development of the private air lines.

1926   May 20: Passage of the Bingham-Merritt-Parker Bill as the Air Commerce Act of 1926 — the charter of foreign and domestic civil aviation for the next twelve years.

December 27: British begin regular service, Egypt to India.

1927   May 20-21: Lindbergh flies from New York to Paris, thus publicizing the Great Awakening in U.S. aviation.

July 19: Pan American Airways wins its first air-mail contract for service from Key West to Havana.

October 19: Pan American Airways begins international service on the Key West–Havana run.

1928   Negotiations between Imperial Airways and Pan American Airways for the development of Atlantic services.

March 4: Postmaster General Walter Folger Brown becomes virtual czar of U.S. civil aviation in the Hoover Administration.

March 8: Foreign Air Mail Act provides stimulus for greater international air-transportation system.

April 12-13: Captain Herman Koehl, Baron Ehrenfried Guenther Von Huenfeld of Germany and Commandant James Fitzmaurice of Ireland complete the first nonstop eastbound crossing of the Atlantic in a Junkers monoplane.

May 31-June 10: Captain Charles E. Kingsford-Smith, Captain C. T. P. Ulm, Lieutenant Commander Harry Lyon, and James Warner fly from Oakland to Brisbane in Fokker tri-motor monoplane, *Southern Cross.*

1929 February 23: Letter from Frank B. Kellogg, secretary of state, to Dr. Enrique Olaya, minister from Colombia, agreeing to the Kellogg-Olaya Pact, the first U.S. reciprocal aviation agreement.

1930-1935

1930 February 18: NYRBA inaugurates mail service from Miami to Santiago, Chile.

August 19: NYRBA purchased by Pan American Airways interests.

September 15: Panair do Brasil, a Pan American Airways affiliate, organized.

1931 February 28: London–Capetown service inaugurated by Imperial Airways. (Regular schedules started January, 1932; first passenger service, April, 1932.)

April 1: Organization of the Air Line Pilots Association.

1932 February: First labor disputes between pilots and employers. (The Air Line Pilots Association refers to this as a "lockout," not a strike, but it was considered as a strike by the Post Office Department in subsequent references.)

1934 January 1: French spur the United States to activity in South America by making survey flights for a South Atlantic route connecting European and South American air-line systems.

January 18: Qantas Empire Airways organized for service between Singapore and Brisbane (later a link for British Overseas Airways Corporation).

February 19: Cancellation of all U.S. air-mail contracts, except those held by Pan American Airways, following a Senate investigation of transportation.

May 10: Decision Number 83 of the National Labor Relations Board becomes basis for future labor legislation affecting civil aviation.

December: Announcement of the Empire Mail Scheme (the "All Up" air-mail policy) in the House of Commons.

December 22: The Royal Dutch Airlines (KLM) Fokker monoplane, *Snip,* completes survey flight from Amsterdam to Curaçao in preparation for an Atlantic service.

1935-1940

1935   January 19: KLM begins West Indies air-transportation service.

January 22: Federal Aviation Commission offers 102 recommendations for the benefit of domestic and international air carriers.

March 28 and April 5: Reciprocal agreement for landing rights signed by Cordell Hull, secretary of state, and Sir R. C. Lindsay, British ambassador to the United States.

April 13: First passenger flight London–Brisbane completed over the British Commonwealth system.

July 2: First Interdepartmental Committee appointed by President Roosevelt to study international aviation problems.

November 22-29: Pan American Airways inaugurates trans-Pacific air-mail service from Alameda, California, to Manila, Philippine Islands.

December 4: U.S. extends invitation to a meeting at which world routes are topic of discussion. Pan American Airways is only U.S. operator to appear.

1936   Colonel Edgar S. Gorrell of the Air Transport Association of America works out a mobilization plan with military authorities for the emergency operation of air lines in time of war.

February: Inauguration of the trans-African route by Imperial Airways (Lagos to Cairo via Kano and Khartoum).

April: Railway Labor Act extended to include air carriers.

April 17: Captain Edwin C. Musick wins Harmon Trophy for his pioneering in the Pacific.

October 7-24: Pan American Airways begins passenger service across the Pacific (first pay load October 21).

1937 American Export Airlines organized as a subsidiary of American Export (Steamship) Lines.

February 22: Negotiations started in 1928 finally result in a reciprocal agreement between British and American air lines for simultaneous inauguration of Atlantic service.

April 27: Pan American Airways and Portugal sign a unilateral agreement for an ocean air route via the Azores.

May 25: Survey flights started by Pan American Airways and Imperial Airways preliminary to the inauguration of air service between the United States and Bermuda.

June 16: Pan American Airways and Imperial Airways begin commercial flights from Port Washington, Long Island, to Bermuda.

July 5: Pan American Airways and Imperial Airways planes pass each other over the Atlantic on survey flight preliminary to the inauguration of Atlantic service.

August 6: Juan T. Trippe, president of Pan American Airways, wins Collier Trophy for his development of Pacific air routes.

1938 Cadman Report results in the reorganization of Imperial Airways.

June 23: Civil Aeronautics Act becomes the charter of the U.S. air-transport industry upon approval of President Roosevelt.

July 20-21: *Mercury*, the upper element of the Mayo Composite makes nonstop flight from Foynes to Montreal with first British commercial cargo.

October: Pan American Airways and American Export Airlines (Amex) sign an agreement to avoid "wasteful competition." Agreement is repudiated by Civil Aeronautics Authority.

1939 May 18: *Lieutenant de Vaisseau Paris*, six-engined French flying boat, arrives at Port Washington on survey flight preliminary to the inauguration of a proposed French Atlantic service.

May 19: Civil Aeronautics Authority issues certificate signed by President permitting Pan American Airways to begin trans-Atlantic air service.

May 20: Pan American Airways inaugurates commercial flights (mail only) from New York to Southampton.

July 8: Pan American begins complete trans-Atlantic service (passengers, mail, and cargo).

July 15: Reciprocal aviation agreement signed by William C. Bullitt, American ambassador to France, and Georges Bonnet, French minister of foreign affairs.

Pan American wins concession from France for the inauguration of bi-weekly service.

August: Treaty with Canada for reciprocal air-transport privileges.

August 4: British Overseas Airways Bill signed, reorganizing Imperial Airways as British Overseas Airways Corporation (BOAC). Incorporated November 24 and begins service April 1, 1940.

August 11: Imperial Airways flying boat, *Caribou,* completes round trip commercial crossing of the Atlantic in preparation for regular service.

September 1: Colonel Gorrell of the Air Transport Association of America returns from Canadian hunting trip to complete plans for mobilization of air lines, as war breaks out in Europe.

October 31: Beginning of hearings on the application of American Export Airlines for an Atlantic route certificate (the so-called American Export Case).

November 4: President's Proclamation following the passage of the Neutrality Act bars U. S. carriers from "combat zone" around France and the United Kingdom.

Since 1940

1940 April 30: Tasman Empire Airways begins New Zealand–Australian service.

June 10: President's Proclamation putting Neutrality Act into effect bars air carriers from Mediterranean "combat zone" as a result of Italy's declaration of war.

June 11: Civil Aeronautics Authority becomes Civil Aeronautics Board, following President's Reorganization Plans, Nos. 3 and 4.

July 12: American Export Airlines wins temporary certificate for the inauguration of Atlantic services.

August: British organize Atlantic Ferry Service. First 21 bombers flown across November 11, 1940.

August: Italians produce first practical jet-propelled plane, the Caproni-Campini.

1941 National Aeronautic Association awards Collier Trophy to the air lines of the United States and the Army Air Forces for "pioneering in world-wide air transportation."

May 7: American Export Airlines denied mail appropriations by Congressional committee after winning an Atlantic route certificate.

May 14: A British Gloster monoplane flies successfully powered by a turbo-jet engine developed by Frank Whittle.

August 18: White House announcement names Pan American Airways as agency to build vast airway across Africa to supply British with lend-lease material for the decisive African campaign.

August 22: Beginning of the Latin American Rate Case, decided July 7, 1942.

December 12: Naval Air Transport Service (NATS) authorized by the Secretary of the Navy.

December 17: The Pan American Airways–W. R. Grace feud over control of the jointly owned Pan American–Grace (Panagra) Air Line flares up when Grace asks for a Panagra route extension to the U. S. in opposition to Pan American Airways wishes.

December 19: Civil Aeronautics Board permits American Export Airlines to operate via Foynes because of the war emergency.

December 24: Chief executives of the air lines sign government contracts to aid in supplying U. S. military forces throughout the world.

1942 April 18: American Airlines becomes first domestic operator to take over an international route when it is awarded a temporary certificate for service to Mexico City after President Roosevelt reverses a previous CAB decision.

April 18: First U. S. transport plane (a TWA Boeing Stratoliner) lands at Prestwick Field to start the Atlantic wartime transport service.

July: Air Transport Command organized on the framework of the old Ferry Command.

July 7: Civil Aeronautics Board announces decision on the Latin American Rate Case.

July 20: Brigadier General Harold George assigns air lines routes but announces that the Army will leave details of actual operation to the private companies.

July 30: Civil Aeronautics Board authorizes American Airlines to acquire control of American Export Airlines.

September: Organization of the British Lamplugh Committee, an unofficial group that had great influence in working out a U. S.–British understanding.

October 8: First scheduled flight of American Airlines Atlantic service.

November 14: Sindicato Condor reorganized as Services Aereos Cruzeiro do Sul (Southern Cross), following the denazification of South American air lines. Cruzeiro removed from the Allied Proclaimed List on November 21.

1943 Series of great debates in Parliament result in a definite aviation policy announced in the Swinton White Paper of October, 1944, just prior to the Chicago Conference.

January 25: Final decision of the Civil Aeronautics Board requiring American Export Airlines to divest itself of control by the steamship parent on or before October, 1943.

February 9: Speech by Representative Clare Booth Luce helps to clarify U. S. international aviation policy.

March 17: Northeast Airlines files application with the Civil Aeronautics Board for a certificate to operate from Boston to Moscow via London, Paris, or Stockholm, thereby becoming the first domestic operator to request a postwar world air route. The beginning of the celebrated North Atlantic Case.

May 5: Civil Aeronautics Board sends out questionnaire to "qualified persons" as a means of determining the interest in international air routes after the war.

July 15: Domestic air-line operators (United Air Lines excepted) announce they will demand a share of the postwar international air routes.

August 25: American Airlines applies for a certificate to operate from New York to London.

October: U. S. interests, headed by TWA, buy controlling stock in TACA air lines.

October 11-13: British Empire Air Conference at London fails to achieve Commonwealth agreement on international aviation policy.

October 26: Pan American Airways announcement first brings up the question of the "community company," later sponsored by Senator Pat McCarran as the All-American Flag Line Bill.

November 17: Pan American Airways completes its 5,000th ocean crossing.

1944   March: Curtiss-Wright report on future estimates of international air traffic exerts influence on the plans of air-line operators.

April: U. S.–British "preliminary conversations."

May 4: Permanent Conference of International Air Traffic Operators organized by the air-line representatives of 14 nations at London.

June 14: Civil Aeronautics Board announces it is ready to receive applications for certificates on world routes, and indicates competition is to be the official policy of the Board.

July 17: Civil Aeronautics Board announces Latin American Rate Case decision.

July 31: Termination of NATS contract operations on the Pacific–Alaska divisions.

September: Domestic operators announce through the Seventeen Airlines Committee that they will oppose the "community company," or any form of monopoly in the allocation of U. S. international route certificates.

October: Viscount Swinton appointed first minister of British civil aviation.

November 1: Representatives of 52 nations gather at Chicago for the International Civil Aviation Conference, the most important aviation meeting up to that time.

December 2: Reciprocal aviation agreement signed with Spain.

December 7: Chicago Conference adjourned after 37 days of debate and negotiation.

December 15: Selection of representatives from 20 nations (Russia later turns down its place) to serve as the Interim Council under the Provisional International Civil Aviation Organization (PICAO) established at the Chicago Conference.

December 16: Reciprocal aviation agreements signed with Sweden and Denmark.

December 30: TWA completes 6,000th ocean crossing.

December 31: Termination of NATS contracts with private operators for service on the Atlantic division.

1945 January 1: Pan American Airways resumes commercial operations following termination of wartime contracts.

January 16: Newfoundland signs the Two Freedoms document, thereby giving U. S. operators the essential transit rights for service to Europe.

January 27: Aviation agreement signed with Iceland.

February-March: Senate Foreign Relations Committee conducts hearings as to the validity of Executive Agreements following the Chicago Conference.

February 3: Bilateral agreement with Eire gives U. S. operators a foothold in Europe, despite attempts of the British to force us into restrictive agreements by withholding traffic privileges.

February 9: Chairman Bailey of the Senate Committee on Commerce withdraws his request for delay on the consideration of international route certificates.

March: Pan American Airways files application for transcontinental routes in answer to the demands of the domestic operators for international services.

March 13: Second Swinton White Paper announces that Great Britain will maintain the policy outlined at the Chicago Conference.

April 4: Aerovías Braniff begins Mexican service.

April 19: International Air Traffic Association is organized by 41 air carriers at Havana and is soon absorbed by the older International Air Transport Association, usually referred to as IATA.

July 5: Civil Aeronautics Board announces decision on the North Atlantic Case, awarding routes to Pan American Airways, American Export Airlines, and Trans-World Airlines (TWA).

July 6: Senator McCarran's All-American Flag Line Bill (S. 326) defeated after long hearing.

August 15: PICAO begins to function, with E. P. Warner, former vice-chairman of the Civil Aeronautics Board, as first president of the Interim Council.

November: Lord Winster, the new head of the civil aviation ministry, following the victory of the Labor Party, announces the policy of the British Government in a third White Paper on aviation problems.

December: Australian High Court rules that the Australian Air Lines Act of August 16, 1945, providing for the nationalization of all interstate air carriers, is illegal.

1946 TWA in the course of the year obtains a 40 per cent controlling interest in Italian air-line system over British protest. Later modified by State Department pressure.

January 15: Reciprocal agreements signed with France, Czechoslovakia, and Greece.

February 1: Repicrocal agreement signed with Belgium.

February 6: Swedish Air Line (SILA) wins first postwar permit to serve the United States on the basis of peacetime reciprocal agreements.

February 11: United States and Great Britain work out the Bermuda Agreement, one of the most important aviation documents in the history of international air transportation.

February 21: Civil Aeronautics Board approves the rate-making *machinery* (not necessarily the rates) of IATA.

February 25: North Atlantic Traffic Conference meets at Dublin.

March: Turkish bilateral agreement closes a gap in the proposed Pan American Airways trans-world route.

March: Second Assistant Postmaster General Gael Sullivan proposes 5-cent air-mail postage for domestic routes.

March 6: IATA sets temporary fares for Atlantic routes.

April: British Labor Government introduces legislation to implement the Winster White Paper by creating a monopoly of civil aviation under three Government corporations to be known as British Overseas Airways (BOAC), British South American Airways (BSAA), and British European Airways (BEA).

May 7: President's Emergency Board created to attempt a settlement of the disputes between the air-line pilots and TWA.

May 8: Civil Aeronautics Board disapproves of rates and fares set by IATA at first North Atlantic conference.

May 17: Civil Aeronautics Board announces its decision on the Latin American Route Case (Docket No. 525).

June 1: James M. Landis succeeds Lloyd Welch Pogue as chairman of the Civil Aeronautics Board.

June 11: President Truman sends special message to the Senate urging passage of the Convention on the International Civil Aviation Organization at Montreal.

June 20: Civil Aeronautics Board reaches decision on the Pacific Route Case (Docket No. 547) granting Northwest Airlines a certificate for service to the Orient. Approved by the President August 1.

July 8: President's Emergency Board offers recommendations for the settlement of the pilot's disputes.

July 11: Civil Aeronautics Administrator T. P. Wright grounds all Constellation planes for 30 days until changes can be made to improve public confidence following a series of accidents. Critics accuse CAA of being unfair to one of the great transport aircraft of the day.

July 25: State Department announces withdrawal from the controversial Transport (Fifth Freedom) Agreement signed at the Chicago Conference.

August: Pan American Airways and W. R. Grace declare an armistice in their feud over the control of Panagra.

August 13: Civil Aeronautics Board reaches decision on the South Atlantic Case. Approved by the President August 16.

August 15: Chairman Landis of the Civil Aeronautics Board goes to Rio to negotiate an important bilateral agreement on the Bermuda pattern with the Brazilians.

September: Bermuda Document reaffirmed after Chairman Landis of the Civil Aeronautics Board confers with British aviation leaders in London.

September: U. S. and Brazil conclude bilateral agreement negotiated by Landis late in August.

October: Air Coordinating Committee made official Government policy agent by executive order of President Truman.

October 21: First strike in U. S. air-line history; pilots of TWA walk out after fruitless negotiations.

November: Bilateral agreement on the Bermuda pattern signed with India.

November 30: U. S.–China bilateral agreement signed.

1947   January: Arbitration of 25-day pilot strike against TWA completed.

January: Bills proposed for putting all transportation in one department and for U. S. adoption of the chosen-instrument policy.

February 27: President awards Juan T. Trippe of Pan American Airways the Harmon Trophy for his direction of wartime services of the air line.

March: Jack Frye of TWA resigns as president.

March 17: President Truman proclaims treaty accepting the Convention written at the Chicago Conference for a permanent International Civil Aviation Organization (ICAO), to become effective April 4, 1947.

April 17: Air Coordinating Committee unanimously votes disapproval of the chosen-instrument bills then pending.

April 22: Hearings before the House Interstate and Foreign Commerce Committee on the issue of regulated competition versus monopoly.

April 24: Reorganization of TWA, with Lamotte T. Cohu succeeding Jack Frye as president.

May 6: The Provisional International Civil Aviation Organization (PICAO) drops the "Provisional" in its title and becomes a permanent body (ICAO) when 41 nations present documents of formal ratification of the Chicago "convention draft." The meeting in Montreal for the first time saw air commerce supervised by a permanent world body.

June 27: Pan American World Airways inaugurates round-the-world service.

July 15: Northwest Airlines begins service to the Orient by way of Alaska and Japan.

September 30: Pilots of American Overseas Airlines begin a strike against the company that lasts 18 days.

IATA meets at Rio for a successful attempt to standardize air commerce procedures. Representatives from 69 air lines of 42 countries attend.

James M. Landis leaves CAB as chairman, after President Truman fails to reappoint him. After two unsuccessful attempts to find a successor, Joseph O'Connell, Jr., is approved as CAB chairman.

December 30: Important report of President's five-member Air Policy Commission opposes sea-air integration and chosen instrument. Supports executive agreement type of documents for international air commerce.

1948   February 3: Strike against National Airlines begins. Lasts 295 days.

November 20: Strike of National Airlines ends.

December: Pan American Airways reported in trade journals as negotiating for purchase of American Overseas Airlines, subject to CAB approval.

1949   Ralph S. Damon resigns as president of American Airlines to become head of TWA, because of policy differences with AA directors, particularly over the proposed sale of AOA by American Airlines to Pan American Airways.

INDEX

Acheson, Dean, and executive agreements, 198-201

Aeromarine West Indies Airways, 8-9

Aeroplane, 195

Aerovías Braniff, 270

Aerovías Nacionales de Colombia, 68

Air-Coordinating Committee (ACC), 307

Air Line Mechanics Association, 220

Air Line Pilots Association (ALPA), opposes McCarran flag line bill, 220; opposes executive agreements, 267; formed, 312; postwar wage negotiations, 314-16

Air line strikes, 315-17

Air Mail Act (1925), 7

Air mail contracts, granted, 7; importance to Pan American Airways, 12-13; competitive bidding, 13, 21-22; canceled, 25

Air mail rates, early, 15, 23; investigated, 44-45

Air mail scandals, 25, 26

Air policy, Great Britain, development of, 95-96; "chosen instrument" adopted, 97, 107-8; "cabotage," 113; Lamplugh Reports, 114-15; Dominions disagree on, 116; Five Freedoms, 117-18; quota system, 119, 172; London Conference, 155-58; White Paper, 159; Chicago Conference platform, 169; Lord Swinton on, 171; and IATA, 250-54; Bermuda agreements with U.S., 256-63;

—United States, "chosen instrument" adopted, 13; Post Office Department and, 13, 21-24; regulated competition on world routes, 48-57, 205 ff; American Export Case, 56-58; imperialism, 134-35; internationalism, 137; merchant airman and, 138-39, 142-43; influence of plane design, 290-94; "United Front" proposal, 306-10; sea-air monopoly, 308-10

Air sovereignty, 126; arguments for, 126-28; international modifications of, 142, 150, 183 *passim*

Air surveys, Atlantic routes, 42; on postwar international transportation, 216-19

Air Transport Association, 74

Air Transport Command (ATC), record of, 73, 79; General Harold George and, 74, 218-19; made separate unit, 78-79; volume of air traffic, 219

Air Transport and Travel, Limited, 96

Airlines Committee For United States Air Policy, 208

Airlines Negotiating Committee, 315, 316

Airplane, costs, 42, 53; influence on air policy, 290-94; increase in size, 296-97

Airplanes, NC-4, 8; Stout all-metal transports, 11-12; Ford-Stout tri-motors, 12; Fokker tri-motors, 14; Consolidated Commodores, 18; Consolidated Catalinas, 18, 48; Consolidated Speedster, 19; Sikorsky S-42,